Digitally Enabled Social Change

Acting with Technology
Bonnie A. Nardi, Victor Kaptelinin, and Kirsten A. Foot, editors

Digitally Enabled Social Change

Activism in the Internet Age

Jennifer Earl and Katrina Kimport

The MIT Press
Cambridge, Massachusetts
London, England

For information about special quantity discounts, please email <special_sales @mitpress.mit.edu>

This book was set in Stone Sans and Stone Serif by Toppan Best-set Premedia Limited. Printed and bound in the United States of America.

Library of Congress Cataloging-in-Publication Data

Earl, Jennifer, 1974–
Digitally enabled social change : activism in the Internet age / Jennifer Earl and Katrina Kimport.
    p.   cm. — (Acting with technology)
Includes bibliographical references and index.
ISBN 978-0-262-01510-3 (hbk. : alk. paper) 1. Internet—Political aspects.
2. Online social networks—Political aspects. 3. Social action. 4. Social movements. 5. Social change. I. Kimport, Katrina, 1978– II. Title.
HM851.E23   2011
303.48′40285—dc22

                                                                2010021113

10 9 8 7 6 5 4 3 2 1

Contents

Acknowledgments

We are fortunate to have more people to thank than there are pages. Nonetheless, some people deserve special notice and appreciation. We both want to thank the academic editors of the Acting with Technology series, Bonnie A. Nardi, Victor Kaptelinin, and Kirsten A. Foot, and our MIT editor, Marguerite Avery. Foot and Avery were pivotal in our connection to MIT, and we are grateful for their support and feedback. We also thank the anonymous reviewers who helped us see ways to improve our work, and we especially appreciate Steven Schneider for his extensive comments. We also thank Jayson Hunt, Deana Rohlinger, Rachel Einwohner, Bruce Bimber, and others who read and commented on early drafts of our work. In addition, we want to acknowledge the financial support for this research provided by the Academic Senate and the Institute for Social, Behavioral, and Economic Research at University of California, Santa Barbara through their small grants programs.

Katrina would first like to thank her coauthor, Jennifer, for her mentorship and the opportunities that she has provided, not the least of which was the opportunity to build the collaborative writing partnership that produced this book. She would also like to acknowledge her family, David, Barbara, Rebecca, and Susie Kimport, for their continuous support of her pursuits, academic and otherwise, and offer gratitude, too, to Helen and Bob Buggert for their wisdom and perspective on the scholarly career path. Lastly, Katrina thanks Matthew Villeneuve, whose intangible and unquantifiable support helped make this project possible.

Jennifer would like to express her gratitude to Alan Schussman, who was her earliest collaborator on online activism, and whose shared work, conversations, and programs put her on the path to this book. She would also like to thank Carroll Seron, Sarah Soule, and Mayer Zald for their mentoring and friendship across the years. More personal thanks go to her mother, Marlene Dancer Adams, for her steadfast support and positive attitude, and for financing an expensive education and the sacrifices that entailed. Finally, Jennifer would like to offer her appreciation to her wife, Mary-Frances O'Connor, who is both an inspiringly accomplished scholar in her own right as well as a wonderfully supportive and patient partner.

With all of these thanks in mind, the responsibility for any remaining errors or omissions falls solely on us as authors.

I

1 Introduction

E-mobilizations

On January 27, 2007, four hundred thousand people gathered on the National Mall in Washington, DC, for a rally and march organized by United for Peace and Justice (UFPJ) against the war in Iraq.[1] People carried signs and banners, and some wore clothing emblazoned with protest slogans. Over the course of the daylong event, public figures such as Jesse Jackson, celebrities including Jane Fonda and Susan Sarandon, and political figures such as Ohio representative and 2008 presidential candidate Dennis J. Kucinich and California representative Maxine Waters lent their names to the cause and addressed the crowd. All echoed the event's antiwar message.

To the average person, this protest might have looked similar to the March on Washington in 1963 for civil rights where Martin Luther King Jr. delivered his famous "I have a dream" speech. That march included more than a quarter-million demonstrators, and represented the collaborative effort of major civil rights, labor, and other progressive organizations. The two events had much in common. Both had hundreds of thousands of attendees, both hosted speakers and political figures, and both were centrally about taking their message—against war in Iraq or for civil rights, respectively—to decision makers in Washington. These superficial similarities, however, belie vast differences in how these two events were produced. The 1963 march relied on local networks, printed flyers, and word of mouth to coordinate and produce the gathering. The 2007 rally and march made use of the Web.[2]

Starting just over two months before the January 2007 rally and march, UFPJ devoted a significant section of its Web site to the protest.[3] The UFPJ Web site served as a centralized location for a variety of activities for both the organizers and participants. UFPJ reported over 5 million hits on its site for January 2007, with 650,000 on January 24 alone (United for Peace and Justice 2007), suggesting that the site was a popular and effective source of protest information and coordination. For the organizers, the Web site was a quick, less costly, and easy way to coordinate the event. The site contained logistical details about the planned rally and march, including the start time, the march route, directions, and a list of the scheduled speakers. Days before the event, UFPJ took advantage of the ease and speed of Web communication, posting the weather forecast and warning protesters that the Mall might be muddy. Perhaps most important for the event organizers, through a secure link from the home page, visitors could make an immediate credit card donation to UFPJ.

UFPJ's Web site also facilitated and coordinated participation. It hosted a ride board where activists could coordinate travel plans to and from the event and provided tips on organizing bus transportation for large groups, complete with budgeting and scheduling recommendations. Similar to the ride board, UFPJ's Web site hosted a housing board where activists could request or offer housing in Washington, DC. For those who wanted to take on leadership roles, the site allowed activists to sign up to be local coordinators devoted to mobilizing people from their area, or volunteer for UFPJ in the weeks leading up to the protest either in its New York office or in Washington. In this way, UFPJ utilized its Web site to make efficient use of supporters' resources.

Beyond informational materials and event logistics, the UFPJ site served as a jumping-off point for the protest itself, with motivational calls to action posted at the top of the home page, and on- and off-site opportunities for activists to endorse the action. The site hosted a "call to action" that visitors could endorse by adding their names, either on their own behalf or as representatives of organizations. Elsewhere on the site, visitors could purchase official "J27" T-shirts, download flyers in four languages (English, Spanish, Arabic, and Persian), forward an email about the protest to friends, and learn how to post a button in support of the event on their Facebook or MySpace page.

This was not a unique use of the Web by UFPJ. It often uses its Web site to coordinate protests, with informational pages on the organization itself and its activist campaigns along with an events calendar listing protest actions throughout the United States. The site also functions as a coalition builder, spotlighting individual activists and organizations whose work resonates with UFPJ's mission. In fact, UFPJ is not a single organization but rather a coalition of over thirteen hundred groups.

In the end, UFPJ's March on Washington was coordinated in just over two months, thanks largely to the Web, and at a relatively low cost. The expenses for the organizers included the literal costs for things such as event supplies (signs, banners, stages, audio equipment, etc.), permits, and personnel time as well as the nonpecuniary costs such as volunteer time that could have been devoted to other organizational activities. The civil rights march in 1963, on the other hand, took longer to plan and was comparatively more costly to produce because none of the logistics could benefit from the cost- and time-savings tools that online coordination makes possible. In essence, having a Web presence allowed UFPJ to conduct collective action at a lower cost, on a larger scale, and more quickly than it could have done without the Web.

UFPJ's use of the Web—which boiled down to using online tools to facilitate an offline protest march and rally—is a common vision of Web activism; we call this kind of Web activism an "e-mobilization" because it uses online tools to bring people into the streets for face-to-face protests. Yet we argue that this is not the only way the Web is being used to organize or engage in activism, or more broadly to effect change on issues that people care about. We turn now to two more examples of the very different ways that protest can occur on the Web and then discuss how all three of our examples illustrate the larger trends in Web activism that this book will address.

E-movements

Two years before UFPJ formed as a coalition, the presidential election of 2000 was heating up in the United States. The two major party candidates, Al Gore for the Democrats and George W. Bush for the Republicans, were both facing third-party challengers: Ralph Nader on the Left and Patrick Buchanan on the Right. The election was shaping up to be one of the tightest and most contested in history, and one of only a few "electoral inversions," which is the term political scientists use to describe situations in which a popular vote winner for the presidency isn't elected because the candidate loses in the Electoral College. The third-party challenge by Nader was of great concern to many liberal and leftist voters who felt torn between supporting Nader and his Green candidacy and supporting Gore, who had a shot of beating Bush. Some worried that "a vote for Nader is a vote for Bush" since votes not cast for Gore would relatively advantage Bush. Others argued that Democrats had become too mainstream; they reasoned that only a Green Party candidate could deliver leftist policies, even if it cost Democrats the election.

In the midst of this political debate, a set of Web sites emerged that Jennifer Earl and Alan Schussman (2003, 2004; Schussman and Earl 2004) describe as the strategic voting movement. The basic premise of all of these sites was that if voters worked together—if voters thought of voting as a collective act—they could realize their conditional preferences. For instance, if two voters both were undecided in 2000 about whether they would vote for Gore or Nader, a strategic voting Web site could "match" them together if one lived in a "safe state," where Bush or Gore was predicted to win by a large majority, and one lived in a "toss-up state," where the contest between Bush and Gore was too close to call. The safe-state voter would agree to vote for Nader because a vote for Nader in this situation would support his chances of getting 5 percent of the popular vote, and hence better election funding the next time around, and would not affect the likely outcome of the election between Bush and Gore. The voter in the toss-up state would agree to vote for Gore, secure in the knowledge that in another state, Nader was being supported but that a vote here would help to defeat Bush.

Other arrangements were also possible: a Buchanan voter and a Nader voter from the same state could agree to vote their third-party preferences, which wouldn't affect the Gore versus Bush vote tallies. Or a safe-state conservative could have agreed to vote for Buchanan while a conservative in a toss-up state agreed to vote for Bush. No matter the match, the overall idea was the same: gaming the Electoral College to achieve one's total electoral preferences, not just to support a single, most-preferred candidate.

While there were potential policy solutions to the dilemmas that voters faced (e.g., abolishing the Electoral College or adopting "instant runoff" elections where people cast conditional preferences as part of their ballot), none seemed likely to break through at the national scale. In that policy gap, a small set of innovators—who did not know one another but all saw creative ways to use the Web to address a major dilemma—created practical solutions on the Web only weeks or sometimes days before the election.

The movement was almost exclusively run through the Web. Web sites ranged from information sites that educated voters about what strategic voting would mean, to portal sites that linked to other strategic voting sites, to "pledging" sites where voters from safe and toss-up states pledged to vote in a certain way but without actually being paired with a voter from another state, to actual pairing sites where the Web site matched pairs of voters based on each person's candidate preferences and the state in which each voter was registered. No matter the format of the Web site, it was important that strategic voting happened online; it would have been hard, maybe even impossible, to raise awareness among and coordinate thousands of people who did not know one another without the Web.

And as Earl and Schussman (2003, 159–160) report, these Web-based efforts took off:

Figures from only 11 strategic voting websites indicate that 36,025 on-line traders were mobilized and the websites were visited by 508,000 viewers who logged 2.9 million hits. While some strategic voting was carried out by friends and acquaintances living in different states, the larger strategic voting effort was carried out almost entirely on-line, facilitated by several websites that linked voters through various means.

The quick action taken by several secretaries of state and state election officials, who threatened legal action against some sites if they did not shut down, shows the potential of these sites to actually influence the election. Four years later, in 2004, the idea of strategic voting was back, this time most often referred to as "vote pairing," and again Web sites were the driving force in this movement.

But who was behind these sites and this innovative form of collective action? Given the existing research on social movements, it would be reasonable to guess that the innovations were created and run by longtime activists who shared extensive political backgrounds and formed organizations to forward strategic voting. This was not the case, though: in 2000, innovators who started these Web sites were as likely to have shared a background in computer science or engineering as they were to have shared any political experience, and most of the sites were created and managed by one to two people. Far from the image of social movement organizations (SMOs) and experienced political operatives running the show, these were large-impact sites run by individuals or very small groups with, generally, only occasional political experience.

Earl and Schussman (2003) demonstrate how decision making was affected by the structure of the movement and the lack of SMOs, how leadership dynamics were impacted (Schussman and Earl 2004), and how innovators dealt with legal controversy and threats (Earl and Schussman 2004). Across all of these topics, the trends were the same: this innovative use of the Web offered new, inexpensive opportunities for organizers and participants that could not have come to fruition as quickly, easily, or cheaply without the Web. For instance, because any kind of strategic

voting Web site was inexpensive to create (assuming one either had technical expertise or access to technical expertise) and inexpensive to run, sites
could pop up quickly in 2000 and reemerge easily in 2004. Since sites were
cheap, there was no real pressure to fundraise or create organizational
vehicles such as SMOs to manage that fundraising. And, the more the site
used "back-end" software functionality (i.e., server side applications, which
are applications on the Web site's server that run features of Web sites)
like databasing to match potential pairs of voters, the less work was required
by the organizer of the site.

Comparing the costs that strategic voting organizers faced to those that
UFPJ organizers faced makes it obvious that strategic voting was much less
expensive to organize. For example, there were no real supplies to buy; the
Web-related charges for bandwidth were reportedly quite low, and there
were no paid staffs (except for one site). Volunteering their time was the
largest cost that most strategic voting organizers had to pay.

For voters who wanted to use these sites, participation was fast and
simple: you did not need to know someone in another state and reach out
to them to coordinate your vote pairing, you just needed to enter your
contact information into an online database and wait to receive an email
about your match. In this way, participation was relatively costless. Assuming you were already going to vote, the additional time it took to find a
match online was only minutes. There were no expenses associated with
traveling to a common location, as protesters at the UFPJ march would
have incurred; the relative time one had to spend was probably orders of
magnitude lower for strategic voting participants when compared to UFPJ
marchers.

All of this helps to explain why strategic voting, as a practice and a
movement, was unique to the Web. Although the concept of vote matching is not inherently dependent on the Web, the challenges of scale as well
as the constraints of costs and time meant that strategic voting was prohibitively expensive and inefficient without the Web, and markedly
cheaper and efficient with the Web. We refer to this form of Web activism—where almost the entire movement unfolds online—as an "e-
movement." Earl and Schussman (2003) defined the term similarly, arguing
that e-movements were movements that emerged and thrived online.

E-tactics

In both e-mobilizations and e-movements, the Web facilitates protest—
offline actions in the first case, and an entirely online movement in the

second. Between these two poles lie numerous instances of collective action with varying degrees of off- and online components and varying degrees of affiliation with social movements and SMOs. We term these actions "e-tactics." For example, one of the more common ways that people are using the Web to organize collectively is online petitioning, and no site better encapsulates this trend than PetitionOnline.com. PetitionOnline was started in 1999 by Kevin Matthews and Artifice, Inc. Artifice is not a political consulting firm but rather a firm that designs architectural software and runs *Architecture Week*, the leading online weekly magazine on architecture. Matthews, the CEO and president of Artifice, developed PetitionOnline out of his belief in grassroots democracy and his desire to facilitate people's activism on whatever issues they are concerned about.

PetitionOnline allows petition creators to post their petition on the PetitionOnline Web site by entering the text, answering a few background questions, and setting a selection of preferences for the petition (including how signatures are shown on the petition). The entire process can take less than five minutes. PetitionOnline manages the signatures, while petition creators are responsible for marketing their petition in whatever manner they see fit. Although not all petitions get a large number of signatures, plenty do: from its founding to mid-2010, PetitionOnline has gathered over eighty-seven million signatures, and many of its petitions have surpassed one hundred thousand signatures. On any given day, thousands of active petitions are collecting signatures on the Web site.

It is easy to see why so many signatures can be gathered: participating in an online petition is even easier than creating it. Signers enter just a small amount of information online to register their signature. Participation can take less than a minute. Some people are tempted to think that actions that require so little from participants must culminate into ineffective campaigns. But to the contrary, PetitionOnline regularly features success stories from the petitions that the site hosts, including effective campaigns to change the corporate practices of leading firms such as Microsoft.

A free service to help anyone manage their petition would simply not be practical without the Web. While PetitionOnline still racks up expenses— it is supported through AdSense ads and donations—it operates close enough to the black that it can continue to be run by Artifice without being a drag on the company. In contrast, no well-intentioned company could afford to run a comparable physical operation; the duplicating costs alone for so many petitions would drive a company out of business, not to mention the costs of paying for signature gatherers to stand at large public venues in hopes of collecting signatures. Other e-tactics—such as boycotts that are run online, email campaigns, and online letter-writing campaigns—are like petitions in that they represent a form of Web activism that sits between e-mobilizations and e-movements. As we contend below, these features make e-tactics particularly fruitful to study.

Leveraging Affordances

An affordance is the type of action or a characteristic of actions that a technology enables through its design. According to our "leveraged affordances" approach (which we'll discuss in more depth in chapter 2), the Web has two primary affordances of relevance to a study of online protest: sharply reduced costs for creating, organizing, and participating in protest; and the ability to aggregate people's individual actions into broader collective actions without requiring participants to be copresent in time and space (and sometimes also allowing solo organizers to create and run movements). As different as e-mobilizations, e-movements, and e-tactics initially appear, they illustrate an important and strikingly similar story about protest and the Web: how the Web is used, and how affordances of the Web are leveraged, affects how substantially protest is transformed versus amplified by Web usage.

For organizers, the first affordance is fundamentally about start-up and scaling costs. The Web can allow communication, coordination, and information sharing at very low initial costs. The costs of scaling up communication, coordination, and information to larger and larger groups are also low, meaning that communication grows exponentially while expenses increase slowly. In the real world of action, this means that protest campaigns and even entire movements that leverage this affordance can fully emerge as well as thrive at low cost points. This affordance is as true of participation as of organization, such that organizers' costs are initially low and remain low despite scaling, and participants' costs are often also low and can scale at lower costs if the technology is fully leveraged. Of course, it is possible to poorly leverage this affordance such that organizers and participants gain few cost advantages from using the Web.

Since we have a long academic history of understanding how expensive organizing and participating in protest can be, the less leveraged uses of the Web are more familiar. For example, using the Web to schedule a meeting time does not make that meeting move faster or reach a conclusion more easily, it simply makes inviting people cheap and inviting more people cost the same as inviting a few. Similarly, downloading and printing a banner for a protest event, as in the case of the UFPJ march and rally, doesn't diminish the amount of time that the protest will consume or lower the risk of arrest while at the event but does make more consistent messaging possible at a low cost to the organizing unit. For its January 2007 march and rally, UFPJ capitalized on the low cost of Web communication to extend its messaging and marketing about the planned protest event, allowing it to save the printing and mailing costs that such actions entail in an offline setting. Such leveraging of the Web's cost affordance is minimal, but the benefit to UFPJ, from a cost-saving standpoint, is nonetheless clear.

Other instances of protest on the Web, as the PetitionOnline case demonstrates, leverage the cost affordance to a greater degree and, in the context of the academic history of protest, seem more novel. As noted above, for no cost aside from that of access to the Web, any person can create an online petition about an issue that they care about in less than five minutes. Free services, including but not limited to PetitionOnline, are happy to host that petition at no cost, no matter how many signers the petition garners, making scaling free to the organizer. Other sites host the back end of technology for letter- and email-writing campaigns, or allow protest organizers to post calls for boycotts for free. On the participation side, you can send a letter, fax, or email to your congressperson about the genocide in Darfur every day, if you like, at no cost and in only minutes using any number of Web sites currently engaged in Darfur activism.[4] This kind of protest—which is free (or mostly free) to create and participate in—is taking advantage of the low cost of creating and hosting Web content, and viewing and taking directed action online. We think of this as leveraging the cost affordance of the Web.

A second major affordance of the Web is that it allows coordinated action toward a common goal without copresence in physical time and space (and for organizers, may even go further by allowing for solo organizing). Signers of a petition need not stumble by the same signature gatherer in order to sign. More generally, the Web affords the opportunity to parlay small individual actions that are spread out across time and space into major collective, coordinated actions. Producers of a Web site not only don't need to work on their Web site from the same office—they can be spread out around the world, if they like. Moreover, many online efforts also can be run by a single individual, or by drastically small teams or groups. The strategic voting movement is an example of collective action that fully leverages this affordance. Organizers in both 2000 and 2004 were located throughout the United States, and in 2000 never met face-to-face for the purpose of movement coordination. Likewise, participants did not have to meet each other in order to engage in this action; even as their successful participation depended on pairing, such pairing did not depend on shared space and could happen during a continuous period leading up to the presidential election. The UFPJ march and rally coordination, too, leveraged this affordance of the Web, albeit to a much smaller degree. Using an asynchronous communication format, UFPJ communicated with interested parties without needing to be copresent. Conceivably, many participants had no direct contact with organizers or other participants before the event itself.

Affordances and the Dynamics of Protest

Rather than being three disparate instances of protest that have occurred on the Web, the three cases presented above illustrate a continuum of Web protest, differing from each other in the extent to which they leverage the cost and copresence affordances of the Web (table 1.1). The UFPJ march, an e-mobilization (first column, table 1.1), leveraged the two affordances we are focused on to the smallest degree: while the march did have some cost benefits in terms of coordinating logistics and getting consistent messaging at a low price through print-your-own banners, organizers still had to secure a permit for the march, negotiate with police, deal with audiovisual equipment and staging, find speakers, keep the program running on time, and so on. Similarly, while getting to the event was made easier by the UFPJ site, participation in the actual action took just as long for participants as it would have otherwise. By contrast, e-movements like

Table 1.1
The Continuum of Online Activism

E-mobilizations	E-tactics	E-movements
(e.g., UFPJ's march and rally in Washington)	(e.g., petitions on PetitionOnline)	(e.g., the strategic voting movement)
In e-mobilizations, the Web is used to facilitate the sharing of information in the service of an offline protest action	E-tactics may include both off- and online components, although largely are low cost, and do not rely on copresence for participants or organizers	In e-movements, organization of and participation in the movement occurs entirely online
Low leveraging of the affordances of the Web	Varying leveraging of the affordances of the Web	High leveraging of the affordances of the Web

strategic voting maximize the cost-based affordance for organizers: it was cheap and easy to set up and host a strategic voting Web site (last column, table 1.1). E-tactics, such as the petitions on PetitionOnline, can make the organizing of an action along with participation in it cheap and easy; they also clearly do a good job of aggregating individual efforts into collective campaigns. But some e-tactics leverage these affordances more successfully than others (middle column, table 1.1), which is a polite way of saying that some people design e-tactics that *don't* leverage key affordances well. How much a movement reaps the rewards of cost and copresence affordances overall will vary by how extensively it uses these e-tactics and the structure of the e-tactics themselves.

More generally, these examples map onto larger trends and help illuminate the impact, both transformative and augmentative, of the Web on protest. If one were to map the existing literature on Web activism, as we do in chapter 2, clusters of findings emerge: some scholars have studied cases where Web usage has critically reshaped activism (e.g., Earl and Schussman 2003, 2004; Schussman and Earl 2004), others have claimed that the Web is "business as usual" with only size, speed, and reach scale-related changes (e.g., Myers 1994), and still others have predicted no substantial long-term impacts of Web usage on social movements (e.g., Diani 2000; Tarrow 1998). One apparent explanation for these divergent claims lies in the question of what scholars mean when they discuss Web activism (see also Earl et al. forthcoming on this point). Some scholars understand activism as actually occurring online, while others see activism as limited to offline collective actions that may at most be facilitated through online organizing tools or only advertised online.

Digging slightly deeper than differences in whether the action is off- or online, one can quickly get to what we argue is a fundamentally important underlying organizing principle of this map of research findings: the more these two affordances are leveraged, the more transformative the changes are to organizing and participation processes leading to the need for what we dub "theory 2.0"; the less these affordances are leveraged, the more likely it is that researchers will find what we refer to as a "supersize" model where the Web leads to faster, wider, cheaper activism, but without fundamental changes to the dynamics of contention.

As we introduce in chapter 2, this is part of the leveraged affordances approach to understanding Web activism. Kirsten Foot and Steven Schneider (2002) refer to this difference in findings as that between scale changes (equivalent to what we term supersizing, where changes are only in extent or degree, or to what Sandor Vegh [2003] describes as

Internet-enhanced activism) and model changes (where the actual process of organizing or participation is altered, requiring a theory 2.0 approach; similar to what Vegh [2003] calls Internet-enabled activism). In model-changing/theory 2.0 explanations, well-understood relationships that have been used to explain social movement processes are disrupted or altered. One could think of these as game-changing dynamics. Supersize/scale changes are changes in degree, and do not culminate in changes to the underlying process.

A crucial point should not be missed in this fuss over naming: how people use technologies, through effectively or poorly leveraging a technology's affordances, makes a difference to social processes. Technologies don't change societies or social processes through their mere existence but rather impact social processes through their mundane or innovative *uses*, and the ways in which the affordances of the technology are leveraged by those mundane or innovative uses. Another way of saying this is that it is people's usage of technology—not technology itself—that can change social processes.

Understanding Leveraged Online Contention through E-tactics

An accurate map of existing research would also show that there has been far more research on less leveraged uses of the Web than more leveraged ones. (In chapter 2, we discuss some of the reasons why this is the case.) So in this book we focus our attention almost wholly on developing an understanding of more leveraged uses of the Web, and in so doing, demonstrate the theoretical value of attending to how and when affordances are leveraged. Because the most leveraged uses—such as strategic voting—have been empirically more rare, we concentrate on online tactics, or e-tactics as we named them above, such as online petitions, letter-writing campaigns, email campaigns, and boycotts to trace the contours of these more leveraged versions of Web activism as well as to understand what changes to the processes of organizing and participating might be taking place. Where relevant, we also reflect on other published research on well-leveraged uses of the Web for activist or cause-oriented action.

Our contributions are both empirical and theoretical. This book provides the first comprehensive empirical population-level view of e-tactics and their relationships to Web sites. Putting aside technical explanations for a moment, the book draws a picture of the "forest" of e-tactics by taking a random sample of Web sites offering online petitions, boycotts, letter-writing campaigns, and email campaigns.[5] We empirically trace what we argue are theoretically significant trends across these Web sites and e-tactics, particularly related to the two major affordances we discussed above.

For instance, in part II, which focuses on the cost-reducing affordance of the Web, we look at what it might mean to be a "five-minute activist"— someone who participates in various online actions such as online petitions—versus being a longtime activist—someone who organizes and/or participates in street protest over time. While some may deride five-minute activism, we consider its development to be important and explore its consequences, especially since cost reductions in participation are key to the creation of five-minute activism. Organizers have also been dramatically affected by the declining costs made possible with some uses of the Web. In chapter 5, we maintain that forms of action that strongly leverage the cost affordance will reduce the importance of SMOs as resource bundlers and, more generally, the importance of resources for starting a cause-oriented campaign.

We similarly trace the implications of leveraging the copresence affordance in part III. In chapter 6, we consider the implications of not having to be physically together in order to act collectively. We describe new opportunities and dilemmas that are created by this new vision of collective action as well. In chapter 7, we ratchet up that assertion to argue that collectivity at the level of organizers might not even be necessary with some smart uses of the Web. We discuss the rise of "lone-wolf organizers" who take the organizing on themselves or lead drastically small teams. We also contend that because start-up costs can be so low online, and these lone-wolf organizers are relatively less constrained by organizational histories and imperatives, organizing around issues rarely seen by social movement scholars before—such as movements to revive a canceled television show—can become somewhat common online.

The theoretical payoffs of examining e-tactics are high. In chapters 4–7, we detail our leveraged affordance approach by examining what supersize versus theory 2.0 effects would look like. In each chapter, we show that when affordances are heavily leveraged, theory 2.0 changes are likely, but when they are not, supersize changes prevail. We trace out theory 2.0 changes, such as the rise in five-minute activism, the declining necessity of organizations and even cooperative organizing, and the new kinds of causes that people choose to organize around. In many cases, these theory 2.0 changes aren't just interesting twists on existing scholarship but instead shine a light on ways that robust theories nonetheless require alteration when affordances are highly leveraged. For instance, in our discussion of costs, we question the utility of well-honed theories such as resource mobilization when the costs fall low enough; we claim that in some cases, what existing theories have always taken as constants may in fact vary. For social movement scholars, our analysis helps to deepen our understanding of existing major theories, and identify places where significant theoretical modifications or new developments are needed. For students of technology, our analysis makes clear how important studying both spectacular and mundane uses of technology is, and how much we might have to learn from thinking about leveraging affordances.

A Digital Repertoire of Contention?

In addition, we bring these different trends together to argue that a new "repertoire of contention" may be emerging, and describe what the aspects of that new repertoire are likely to be. As we discuss in chapter 8, the concept of a repertoire of contention was introduced by Charles Tilly (1978, 1979) to capture the set of tactical forms from which social movement actors can choose at any given historical moment as well as denote the common characteristics shared by the set of available tactical forms in a historical moment. That is, activists don't just make up new tactical forms every day, they choose from a limited set of available options (i.e., not from an infinite number of tactical options; Tilly 1995). Furthermore, the tactical forms in the set share a small number of fundamental characteristics.

Tilly's early research suggests that there was a single major shift in repertoires over time, from a "traditional" to a "modern" repertoire, which occurred in the West starting in the eighteenth century. While Tilly's work focused on identifying the differences between the traditional and modern repertoires, we are interested in what they share. We argue that both of these repertoires had unacknowledged similarities: both involved collective action that was understood to be collective because people gathered in time and space; both included tactical forms that were costly to organize and participate in, which in turn has a series of predictable consequences; and both strongly linked tactical forms, specific protest actions, and social movements together. We claim that the increasing availability of outlets for online participation, ranging from petitions to denial-of-service actions, may be leading to a shift in the overall repertoire of contention, or the emergence of a new repertoire that we label a "digital repertoire of contention."[6] In chapter 8, we describe the new digital repertoire and compare it to what was common across both prior historical repertoires of contention.

While it is too early to know conclusively whether this is a new pivot in history where new online protest forms and the online migration of traditional protest forms are ushering in a major shift to a new digital repertoire of contention, we argue that the data examined in this book and extant research on other online protests strongly suggest that scholars need to seriously examine this possibility. In chapter 8, we theoretically outline what such a new repertoire of contention would look like and mean for social movements.

A Bird's-eye View: Our Population-Level Study of E-tactics

Our data draw largely on the content coding of a quasirandom sample of sites gathered in 2004 that engage in one or more of four focal online protest forms (petitions, letter-writing campaigns, email campaigns, and boycotts) and that a user could find if not given the Web address (what we call "reachable sites"). We focus on these four tactical forms, or "e-tactical forms" as we call them throughout the book, because they are new, dynamic, and interesting, offering compelling examples of how protest occurs online and how tactical forms with offline progenitors operate in the online arena. They are also common online, and sit theoretically between e-mobilizations and e-movements in ways that help us better understand how affordances of the Web can be leveraged.

Our data set is unique in that it provides a population-level view of the use of these e-tactical forms on the Web. Charting the population of sites on the Web has been prohibitively difficult until now, largely due to the way that the Web is organized. Since Web pages aren't registered in a universal directory, nor are their addresses even patterned, it has been near impossible to produce a comprehensive list of existing Web sites, let alone a list of all Web pages. While prior technologies, such as phones, allowed sampling even when all the numbers were not known in advance (e.g., through random digit dialing), domain names lack any substantive patterning, thereby making such work-arounds infeasible. In the face of this challenge, scholars have turned to case studies of Web sites, or started from the online presence of a particular organization and mapped its network. While such studies have produced important findings about the workings of protest on the Web, their conclusions are limited: What if organizations aren't as central to online protest, as the example of strategic voting suggests? And what if online organizations aren't connected to each other in accessible networks?

We overcome these shortcomings by mimicking what a user would do to find information on the Web—namely, use search engines to find Web pages and follow links from those Web pages—to produce a population of sites that any user could reach (i.e., a population of *reachable* sites). For some sites and kinds of tactics we examine, we took the entire population, while for other kinds of sites and tactics, we took a representative sample, yielding a unique data set that gives us a population-level view of protest on the Web. Further details on how we technically operationalized this process and our sampling strategy are discussed briefly in chapter 3 and much more fully in the methodological appendix.

Sites fell into one of two general categories: warehouse sites and nonwarehouse sites. We elaborate on the distinctions between these two categories in chapter 3. As an initial introduction, the central difference between the two site types lies in their association with the content they host. Warehouse sites are generally hosting content that is submitted by users; they are really clearinghouses for protest. Nonwarehouse sites, on the other hand, are a diverse lot; we use the term nonwarehouse as a catchall because the category is so diverse, and the only singularly shared characteristic across such sites is that they do not warehouse other people's claims and actions. For our data set, we took a representative sample of nonwarehouse sites, examining 169 sites and all individual e-tactics housed on or hyperlinked from these sites, and the population of 15 warehouse sites. By "linked to," we mean e-tactics that were hosted on a different, external Web site but accessible from the sampled site via a hyperlink; "hosted" e-tactics were those actions housed on a page within the sampled Web site. Because of the volume of content on warehouse sites, we took a representative sample of warehouse site e-tactics to characterize these sites. Illustratively, at any given time, PetitionOnline, one of the warehouse sites that we look at, hosts tens of thousands of active petitions, necessitating the use of a sample of petitions from the site.

We explored the sites in our data set to investigate the number and kinds of claims they made (e.g., prolife or anti–discrimination against African Americans) as well as the forms of protest actions, both off- and online, they linked to or hosted. We also studied the relationship, if any, of these sites to social movements and SMOs. For individual e-tactics, we were interested in the number and kinds of claims they made along with their targets of action, including whether or not a target was governmental as well as the target level (i.e., local, national, etc.). In addition, we examined how the back end of sites facilitated the user's participation in protest: To what extent did the action take place online? How much work did the user need to do independently? A more detailed description of our quantitative content coding is available in the appendix. In all, we captured a broad range of information about the sites and e-tactics in our data set.

The expansive, population-level data we analyze here empirically detail the landscape of protest on the Web, offering evidence of the variety of ways that the two key affordances of the Web—its low cost and its elimination of the requirement of copresence—are leveraged while also supporting our contention that the Web can allow more than the simple augmentation of protest: innovative uses of the Web can transform protest. It is certainly true that popular Web sites change all the time, so a sample of Web sites drawn today would be different. For instance, in the few short years since we collected our data, Twitter was launched and Facebook has expanded beyond .edu addresses. We say little about either in this book (save some limited discussion in the conclusion) because they post-dated our data collection, but we think our arguments are enduring because they focus on how people use different technologies, not on particular popular Web sites.

Chapter Outline

After reviewing the existing research on Web activism in chapter 2, we provide a descriptive overview of the look and feel of Web sites that host or link to e-tactics in chapter 3. Our aim in this chapter is to sketch the *online* environment in which the protest actions we study take place; we also discuss the history of each tactic and review in slightly more detail some of our research methods. As the chapter will show, e-tactics are found on a variety of sites, produced by a range of different types of actors, and don't all look the same. We describe the four focal protest forms and the different ways they appear online, including: the appearance of the four focal e-tactical forms (What do these forms look like online? Do they always look the same?); where they are located, noting that individual e-tactics can be hosted or linked to as well as associated with either warehouse or nonwarehouse sites; how participation takes place, considering the degree of off- versus online involvement and any automation of the action; and when and how these online actions are combined with offline actions.

In part II, which focuses on leveraging the cost affordance, we first consider the rise of low-cost actions for participants in chapter 4. Specifically, we discuss the rise of "flash activism," and discuss how online tools can be used to drive down the time and energy required to participate collectively. Then, in chapter 5, we turn to the changing role of resources in online activism, arguing that by reducing organizing costs, the centrality of SMOs in producing protest has declined.

In part III, which concentrates on the leveraging of the copresence affordance, we start in chapter 6 with an examination of what collective action looks like when people don't have to come together physically in order to work together for social or political change. We also consider the implications of these changes, such as consequences for the formation of collective identity, a central component of sustained action (Taylor and Whittier 1992). In chapter 7, we take a look at the collective nature of organizing. We contend that while protest has generally been collectively organized, collective organizing is not entirely necessary with some innovative uses of the Web, and protest can, at the least, be organized differently.

In chapter 8, as introduced above, we discuss the major implications of our work and the possibility of a new repertoire of contention (Tilly 1978, 1979). We present the key contributions that our analysis makes to the study of social movements. Specifically, we highlight the importance of including e-tactics in particular and online activism more broadly in the study of social movements. We show online activism to be neither simply business as usual in the online environment, nor wholly distinct from the types of protest and collective action currently studied in the literature on social movements. Further, the conclusion emphasizes the analytic usefulness of beginning from the *uses* and *affordances* of the Web, noting that the e-tactics we study may be only the tip of the iceberg as people increasingly use the Web for protest, often in increasingly innovative ways. We also demonstrate how our findings impact not only the way that scholars study the Web but also how we think of offline protest. Indeed, we show that things that have historically been understood as constant—such as the costs of protest and the need for copresence—can actually vary, with implications for research on both off- and online protest. The implications of our findings are not limited to the field of social movements, and the conclusion will discuss the consequences of our findings for other fields such as Internet studies.

Of clear application to work on online activism, this book also offers scholars of protest more broadly important arguments about generalized understandings of collective action that have practical consequences outside the literature, affecting claims-making and mobilization not only in the streets but, we maintain, anyplace that people can go online.

2 Where We Have Been and Where We Are Headed

In this chapter, we discuss the existing research on the Web in general and Web activism in particular. In doing so, we point out key methodological and theoretical splits among researchers studying Web protest. Arguing that those splits have something to teach us, we introduce our use of affordances in more detail along with our leveraged affordances approach. We close by examining how the leveraged affordances approach seeks to expand, not cast out, prior social movement theorizing.

Prior Research on Web Activism

As Internet-enabled technologies emerged on the public stage in the late 1980s through electronic bulletin boards and then in the 1990s through the World Wide Web, scholars and social commentators were eager to study and debate the consequences of these new technologies on social life. Early research focused on who was going online, how fast Internet usage was spreading, and the potential inequality represented by the digital divide. As some of this research showed that younger, white men were the earliest adopters, worries of addiction began to capture the public's interest: Would these young men waste away, lonely and pale, in their basements, only talking to other isolates online? Research that suggested trade-offs between the time spent online and the time spent engaged in other more traditional activities fueled public concern (Nie and Erbring 2000).

Other skeptical commentators wondered about the oddity of a virtual environment that could offer potentially socially significant levels of anonymity and allow people to impersonate social identities different from their own: What could we make of a "world" where men could be women, women could be men, and anyone could choose their race? The fear of the unknown was exacerbated by work that warned of the sociopolitical dangers of Internet-enabled technologies: John Arquilla and David Ronfeldt's work on "netwars" (2001) suggested that a dangerous electronic world had indeed arrived. These dystopic views worried many social commentators, and spawned a good deal of research to track usage and social impacts.

On the other side of the spectrum, some commentators were bullish on information and communication technologies (ICTs), and what these new technologies might offer to social life and relationships. For instance, Howard Rheingold's work on virtual communities (1993) was an early manifesto that heralded the potential of bulletin board–based communities to offer substantial moral and practical social support as well as build thick communities of mutual concern and affect. Although his book could not anticipate the rich social communities that would develop online as so-called social media became more popular after the turn of century, Rheingold nonetheless evangelized about the potential of computer-mediated communication. Many shared his crusade and wrote prolifically about the good fortune that the electronic world could bring.

As time wore on and the research results began to separate the rhetoric from the empirical, it turned out that neither the gloomy fears of an electronic dystopia nor the wildly positive dreams of digital evangelists were coming to fruition; reality was far more complex and multidimensional (Rice and Katz 2004). With this shift, researchers moved away from the practical highs and lows predicted by social commentators, and began moving toward understanding how Internet-enabled technologies could fit into, expand, or question existing theoretical models about social life. For instance, Barry Wellman and his collaborators' prolific writings on computerized communications and social networks reveal how social dynamics might be shifting as people use these new technologies (Garton, Haythornthwaite, and Wellman 1997; Wellman and Gulia 1999; Wellman and Haythornthwaite 2002; Quan-Haase et al. 2002; Boase and Wellman 2006).

One can trace the same arc in academic and public commentary on the impacts of computer-mediated communications on institutional politics (read: politics through regular governmental means like voting) and contentious politics (read: protest and social movements; for a review, see Garrett 2006). Heralding the positive potential of Internet-enabled technologies as early as 1989, John Downing (1989) documented the effective use of email and conferencing systems through PeaceNet and EcoNet. He argued that grassroots activism could benefit from the low-cost communication structure offered by various Internet-enabled technologies. Yet others worried that Internet-enabled technologies, like other technologies before them, would become a tool of the powerful that could be wielded against the weak (McCullough 1991).

As activists and the politically engaged moved from bulletin boards and other electronic conferencing systems to the Web, the literature continued to be organized into forecasts of vast new possibilities, on the one hand, and danger, on the other. Stefan Wray's (1998) early discussion of electronic disobedience could be read in this way: electronic civil disobedience and hacktivism (i.e., politically motivated hacking) seemed to offer powerful new opportunities for subordinated groups that could muster the technological savvy to engage the Web, but hacktivism was also scary to many in its newness and potential disruptiveness.[1] Jeffrey Ayres (1999, 135) warned of a "global information riot," echoing outdated and negative views of crowd behavior and uncontrolled mobs (e.g., Le Bon [1895] 1960; as also described in Garner 1997).

Conversely, the speed with which political engagements could start and unfold, sometimes quite successfully from an activist point of view, suggested great potential for movements. Laura Gurak (1997) documented online campaigns against Lotus, Yahoo! and U.S. governmental regulations that were remarkable in their speed, and two of these campaigns were successful in gaining the desired concessions from power holders.

Just as the larger discourse on the relationship between Internet-enabled technologies and society moved toward moderation—identifying a much more complicated middle ground between salvation and an electronic apocalypse—so too did the literature on the political implications of ICT usage. For instance, Bruce Bimber (1998) and Benjamin Barber (1998) both argued against broad empirical generalizations, and suggested that future research should focus on how ICTs could impact the theoretical relationships in political and social life that scholars had already come to understand from decades of robust social science research.

This book shares more recent concerns about how to add nuance to the boom-or-bust stories of ICT usage. We want to know how little or how much theories and explanations built primarily around protest and social movements in the 1960s through 1980s need to change in order to explain Web activism. Most bluntly, are we as able to explain various online actions as we are to explain traditional protests in the streets? And if not, what needs to change in our theories?

Are Social Processes Accelerated or Altered?

While some work on social change and ICTs has been done by scholars primarily interested in ICTs and technology more generally (e.g., Downing

1989; Garrido and Halavais 2003; also see contributions to McCaughey and Ayers 2003), most of the existing scholarship has been produced by social movement scholars (for a more detailed review of early work in this field, see Garrett 2006). Researchers from this tradition usually orient themselves around the study of Internet activism, or to a lesser extent "cyberactivism," or "cyberprotest," without distinguishing clearly between the Internet and the Web. As mentioned in chapter 1, we are more precise in our language, using Web to refer to content located on the World Wide Web, and Internet to refer to the underlying protocols and processes that connect computers to one another globally. Nonetheless, we understand work on all ICTs and social change to inform our work, and thus present a broad review of the literature instead of one narrowly tailored to Web activism. Below, where authors were not actually discussing Web activism, we note the specific technology (email, listservs, etc.) that they studied.

From this broader literature, we identify two major schools of thought that have emerged. In the first, research studying protest and ICTs has found that ICT use—particularly Web usage—primarily increases the size, speed, and reach of activism, but has not had any definitive effect on the processes underlying activism. As we introduced in chapter 1, we refer to this as the supersize model of activism in that activism expands, but the processes enabling organizing and participation do not change. In the second camp, research has found that ICT (again, primarily Web) usage may change the actual processes of organizing and/or participating in activism, resulting in model changes to existing theories of activism, which we describe as theory 2.0 approaches.

Supersizing Activism: Scale-Related Changes

Scholars studying a range of ICTs recognized the impact of these new technologies on protest, finding that using the Web and other ICTs for activism adds new audience members, increases the reach and speed of messaging, and/or reduces messaging costs (van de Donk et al. 2004). Each of these outcomes, research argues, aids activists and SMOs in asserting claims, making ICTs especially useful tools for some kinds of activism. Significantly, this body of research does not find that ICT usage in any way changes the *processes* of activism, although it changes the scale on which activism takes place. Web usage may improve an organization's success at mobilizing a sympathetic audience, for example, but it doesn't upend our theoretical understanding of how movements encourage participation or the importance of that activity. In essence, this research contends that ICT usage augments—or supersizes—the processes of activism we already understand. The January 2007 rally and march coordinated by UFPJ discussed in chapter 1 is a prime case of how Web usage can supersize protest. The event itself looked much like the March on Washington in 1963 for civil rights, albeit one coordinated more rapidly and at a lower cost, exemplifying scale-related changes stemming from Web usage.

Findings that ICT usage changes the scale of activism are common and tend to focus on the Web's ability to directly disseminate information (e.g., Van Aelst and Walgrave 2002, 2004). The Web can be used to eliminate the traditional media as an intermediary and allow organizers to communicate directly with their target audiences. Dieter Rucht (2004), for example, argues that the Web, as a new media, can help SMOs reach their target audiences specifically by bypassing traditional media. And Victoria Carty (2002) describes the Web as allowing for the creation of micromedia by activists themselves. Loong Wong (2001, 387), too, highlights the ability of activists to independently transmit information without having to rely on traditional media channels, concluding that the Web is "a channel transmitting, augmenting and even magnifying political agency." Notably, the Web becomes a tool for contacting sympathetic audiences, but does not change the audience-generation process itself.

In addition to getting around the mainstream media, the ability of the Web to spread messages in hostile climates has been lauded by researchers (Danitz and Strobel 1999). In a study of political opposition groups in Saudi Arabia, Mamoun Fandy (1999) finds that the Web helped activists to circumvent government-imposed barriers to organizing, allowing them to spread their messages more quickly, in ways that were more difficult for the government to block. Pippa Norris (2002) raises the importance of online information access in authoritarian regimes such as China, where online information about the Falun Gong has been critical, even if difficult to consistently access (for more on online censorship, see Deibert et al. 2008).

The extensive literature on the Zapatista movement's use of the Web has also highlighted the way that the Web facilitates communication across borders, helping the Zapatistas to broadcast their message globally (Wray 1999; Garrido and Halavais 2003; Martinez-Torres 2001). In this set of research, the Zapatistas and other activist groups have used the Web to facilitate the formation of alliances with a speed and strength that alliances formed offline lack (Hasian 2001), but the underlying theoretical tools we have for understanding organizing, information sharing, and alliance formation are sufficient.

This increased ease of information dissemination comes with the added benefit of a low cost (Salter 2003). Tiffany Danitz and Warren Strobel (1999) maintain that not only did the listserv they studied enable prodemocracy activists in Burma to communicate directly with one another but it also did so cheaply. And Jacob Rosenkrands (2004) shows that the Web has allowed anticorporate groups to form global connections with one another specifically because online communication is easier, faster, and cheaper than traditional communication forms. The Web, research finds, can be used to disseminate information more directly to target audiences, and more broadly, quickly, and cheaply. But in this research, none of the cost reductions, accelerated speed, or broad distribution leads to qualitative changes in the processes underlying activism.

Researchers finding scale-related changes in activism online have looked beyond just messaging to how ICT (typically Web) usage impacts organizing. Carty (2002), for example, finds that the Web facilitated not only the distribution of information about Nike sweatshops but also the organization of a cross-country protest tour. And Peter Van Aelst and Stefaan Walgrave (2002) engage in a detailed analysis of how the Web facilitated demonstrations at the World Trade Organization meeting in Seattle in 1999 (see also Norris 2002). Other work has pointed to how Web usage impacts the organization of purely online protest actions, including how online communication can help coordinate organizers around the world (Klein 2001; Leizerov 2000). With the Web, organizers can asynchronously coordinate among themselves and also update participants at little to no cost, much like UFPJ's rally and march. The benefit of quick, direct, and low-cost communication among organizers as well as between organizers and participants is underscored in the literature, with most research concluding that the usage of Internet-enabled technologies benefits social movement organizing. According to this work, some ICTs allow organizing to happen quickly and less expensively, but the process of organizing is still understood according to the same processes detailed in the literature on organizing that takes place entirely offline.

Research finds that participation, too, can be supersized through ICT usage. In analyses of campaigns by privacy activists against Lotus and U.S. governmental regulation, Gurak (1999) finds that ICT usage meant not only that awareness of potential privacy threats was quickly spread but also that protest could be quickly registered in, for instance, emails and a forwarded online petition. In addition to email, the Web creates opportunities for new kinds of tactical forms such as hacktivism (Wray 1999; Cardoso and Neto 2004). Yet despite new tactical forms, in this research tradition Web usage is understood to improve participation—make it faster, easier, and more potent—but not to fundamentally change how it takes place.

Theory 2.0: Model Changes

Other research on the use of Internet-enabled technologies has generated far more dramatic findings. This work suggests that scholars may need to change their theoretical models of how organizing and participation take place to fully understand and describe Web activism. According to this theoretical approach, some innovative uses of the Web can lead to changes in the underlying theoretical processes that drive activism. Put differently, we expect that the engine driving protest would look and operate differently than it has before. We refer to these model-changing findings as theory 2.0 approaches to emphasize that we need a revised version of theoretical approaches to understand what is happening on the Web today. You could also think of this as a second-generation theory on Web activism, or theory 2G. We should note, however, that by using 2.0 we do not mean to focus on social software, as a comparison to the Web 2.0 moniker might suggest. Indeed, our data are drawn from the period just preceding the rise of many dominant social networking Web sites.

Work on e-movements, in particular, has pointed to the importance of a second generation of theory. As mentioned in chapter 1, e-movements such as the strategic voting movement often behave differently than theories of offline movement processes would predict. For instance, Earl and Schussman's study of the strategic voting movement (2003, 2004; Schussman and Earl 2004) illustrates multiple novel ways in which Web usage enables organizing. In contrast to what we might expect from the literature on social movements, SMOs played little part in the movement itself or the lives of the movement's leaders (Schussman and Earl 2004). Other research has argued that innovative uses of the Web reduce or perhaps even eliminate the need for central movement leadership (Castells 1997).

Daniel Bennett and Pam Fielding (1999) echo this emphasis on how Web usage changes the processes of organizing by investigating a novel type of activism facilitated by the online environment: flash activism. Organizers no longer need to cultivate the ongoing allegiance of participants to a movement or organization, and can instead mobilize rapidly, at a low cost, without a standing membership. Moreover, Bennett and Fielding contend that in the age of the Internet, anyone can become an activist—and they have. Using several case studies of individuals who made their cause into a movement thanks to the Web, the authors offer further examples of how Web usage has changed the dynamics of organizing and indeed the category of organizers itself.

Without calling it such, Clay Shirky (2008) implicitly argues for a theory 2.0 approach to organizing. He notes that the costs of managing collective endeavors have been high offline; even the efforts of a dozen people can require substantial management. Organizations have been an important adaptation in that they allow people to collectively produce everything from goods and services to social and political change while managing the expense of organizing social action. But Shirky (like others before him) maintains that some uses of the Web and related ICTs have dramatically reduced the costs of organizing collective action, making organizations less necessary.

The nature of activist participation has not been untouched by ICT usage either (Earl et al. forthcoming). Just as flash activism provides organizers with the ability to generate protest actions without cultivating an ongoing membership base, participation enabled by ICT usage more generally has been found to be less driven by a personal connection with a social movement (Brunsting and Postmes 2002; Bennett and Fielding 1999). While other researchers documented supersized uses of hacktivism, Mathew Eagleton-Pierce (2001) asserts that participants' role in actions such as hacktivism is different from previously studied tactical forms, and Richard Cloward and Frances Fox Piven (2001) claim that some forms of Web activism, such as hacktivism, are much harder for authorities and targets to control. These findings suggest that the processes underlying participation may be different; we need to adjust current theoretical approaches so that they can explain and account for innovative uses of the Web.

Bimber, Andrew Flanagin, and Cynthia Stohl (2005) detail one of the most significant challenges posed by Web usage to existing social movement theories of participation. Focusing on the low cost of participation online, the authors find that the primary barriers to participation such as its expense in time and money as well as the risk of stigmatization are much less considerable off- than online. This means that the processes by which individuals become participants are potentially quite different when Web usage comes into play; more specifically, the likelihood that sympathetic beneficiaries of contentious action will "free ride" on the actions of others is reduced. Free riding may not exist or may do so to a much lesser extent when it comes to online activism. This potential upsets a significant body of theory in sociology and political science that indicates that bystanders are not inclined to participate when they can experience the benefits of others' activism without its attendant costs (i.e., free riding on others). In other words, this work suggests that a latent variable of cost—a variable that has historically varied little and therefore hasn't been fully noticed—belongs in our 2.0 theoretical description of how participants are mobilized. It is not just models of organizing but also models of participation that are impacted by ICT usage. And scholars have wondered what other kinds of social movement theorizing might be impacted by ICT usage (McCaughey and Ayers 2003).

In theory 2.0 approaches, the use of Internet-enabled technologies changes the underlying processes of activism. Organization and participation, benefiting from the affordances of Internet-enabled technologies, are less expensive, quicker, and more convenient. As a consequence, who organizes and how organization takes place as well as who participates and their affiliation with a larger movement are not well accounted for by the existing theoretical models of activism. This set of research findings suggests that the use of Internet-enabled technologies doesn't just supersize activism; it can change how it takes place.

Sometimes You Find (Only) What You Look For

More than simply a question of scholars coming to different conclusions, we contend that the divergent findings showcased by a comparison between supersize and theory 2.0 scholarship mirror or perhaps are even produced by the cases that each camp tends to study. That is, they are not legitimately competing theories of protest on the Web but are instead the result of methodological choices (for a similar argument, see Earl et al. forthcoming). The first group, the supersize scholars, primarily study e-mobilizations, yielding uses that fall closely in line with existing theories of activism. The theory 2.0 scholars, on the other hand, have studied forms of Web protest that more substantially differ from offline forms—such as e-movements and e-tactics—and thus more frequently find that social movement theories of offline action are insufficient.

As illustrated in the examples discussed above, supersize scholars tend to study Internet activism through instances of offline activism facilitated by online messaging, or online efforts by groups that exist first offline and then later add a Web presence. In cases of the former, Web sites are used to broadcast information about offline protest actions and coordinate participation. While the UFPJ example from the first chapter makes it clear that these Web sites may employ technologically sophisticated software, such as UFPJ's online ride-share board, most of their use of the Web in particular and ICTs in general is in the service of offline action. To that end, the story of protest actions and activism is little changed. Certainly, a mass email can reach an organization's membership far more quickly than a newsletter sent by regular mail, but this online activity does not change the offline protest action and the theoretical processes that scholars use to explain it.

The second pattern among supersize research is its tendency to study organizations and movements with a long offline history that have migrated to the Web. Drawing on offline reputations, scholars select groups and causes for study in the online environment. The extent to which these cases are representative of Internet activism broadly, however, is dubious. As Paul DiMaggio and his colleagues (2001) argue, it is likely that organizations that emerged after the more pervasive use of the Web will use online tools in systematically different ways than those that predate it. By looking at organizations with a stable offline presence, supersize scholars are unwittingly selecting cases highly influenced by offline dynamics and therefore well accounted for in the existing theory. Confronted with these findings—that owe, we claim, largely to case selection—it makes sense that scholars would consider ICT usage to have a supersizing effect on activism, but not to require any changes to the existing theoretical models.

In contrast, theory 2.0 scholars—the second story of Internet activism—have found the existing theoretical models lacking in their studies of e-movements. Research arguing for a next generation of theory has studied activism where organization and/or participation take place exclusively online, rather than as a supplemental branch to offline organizing and/or participation. By looking at e-movements such as strategic voting, for example, theory 2.0 scholars begin from cases that are qualitatively different not only from offline organizing but also from the cases under consideration by their supersize peers. It is, in turn, not entirely unexpected that these fully online cases without offline progenitors might require new theoretical models for understanding.

Across all of this research on Web activism, e-mobilizations have been studied extensively and e-movements have received research attention as well, but e-tactics have not been the focus of much research. In part, this is due to simple oversight by these fields, and in part, we believe this is due to the way that scholars select online cases to study. As we discuss at greater length at the end of this chapter, this book concentrates on e-tactics because we view them as both an analytically and empirically privileged place for examining online protest dynamics. Most important, e-tactics are actions that have some characteristics in common with e-movements, but others in common with e-mobilizations: they're firmly online (like e-movements), yet also have clear histories as offline actions (like e-mobilizations). Since the former attribute has been associated with model changes and the latter with scale changes, the study of e-tactics offers an opportunity to study a set of cases that could substantially forward our understanding of the differences between supersize and theory 2.0 approaches along with the cases they represent. As we will explore shortly, they also provide fertile soil for investigating our own unique approach to this area of scholarship.

Further, as a common online phenomenon, e-tactics are part of the daily lives of many politically engaged individuals. In the United States, for instance, the Pew Internet and American Life Project reports that 19 percent of Internet users have signed a petition online and 25 percent of Internet users have contacted a government official about an issue important to them via email (Smith et al. 2009, 24). Two studies suggest that these trends are likely to be similar in Britain. Signing a petition (off- or online) was the next most common form of political engagement after registering to vote and voting in Britain; the same study showed that Internet users are more likely to have signed a petition than non-Internet users (British Office of Communication 2009). A second study (Dutton, Helsper, and Gerber 2009) reports that 15 percent of British Internet users signed an online petition in 2009, which is double the rate reported for 2007 (the study also shows that offline petition signing was declining across the same period). Understanding this new form of political engagement is key in its own right. Before engaging this question, we first take a step back and propose a higher-level distinction among the ways that people use the Web for social change.

It's All (or at Least Mostly) in How You Use It

Noticing that different uses of the Web have been associated with either supersize or theory 2.0 changes opens the door to an important science and technology studies (STS) observation that is at the core of this book: technologies don't inevitably lead to specific social or political changes. Instead, people's *uses* of technologies—sometimes mundane, and sometimes widely innovative—lead to (different kinds of) social and political changes. It isn't that e-mobilization researchers who found scale changes are wrong; for the ways of using the Web to facilitate social change that they study, they are probably quite right to focus on scale changes. Similarly, it isn't that the model changes found in studies of e-movements should be found everywhere. Rather, we are claiming that we should expect the social and technological effects of Web usage to vary because how people use the Web in social change efforts varies.

We go further, however, than simply saying "uses vary, so findings will, too." At the most basic level, we argue that when some of the most unique technological capacities of the Web (and other Internet-enabled technologies)—that is, the affordances of the Web— are leveraged, theory 2.0 effects result; but when these special technological capacities of the Web are barely leveraged, only supersize changes will follow. This section lays out this assertion in more theoretically precise language, and situates our approach within broader debates over how and when the physical, or "material," aspects of technologies should be considered in theoretical explanations.

Technological Affordances

To describe the special technological capacities of Internet-enabled technologies generally and the Web specifically, we use the term "technological affordance." Briefly put, this term refers to what actions or uses a technology makes easier (and therefore facilitates). At the most general level, this is how other scholars have used the term: a door affords opening; air affords breathing; a refrigerator affords cold storage. But we go a bit further: we think it is critical to stress what one technology facilitates versus the next most comparable technology. For example, a hallway with no doors affords passage, just as a door affords opening for passage. Yet applying the concept of affordances to think about what a door affords when compared to the next most comparable technology—an open hallway in this example—points to other socially relevant technological affordances of a door: it may be that the affordance of a door that has the most social meaning is not that it affords opening and passage but that it also affords closing and, with a lock, control over passage.

Thus, we more specifically define affordances as *the actions and uses that a technology makes qualitatively easier or possible when compared to prior like technologies*. This definition helps us be more precise in our analytic focus; to simply concentrate on the ability of the Web or ICTs more generally to facilitate communication isn't helpful—smoke signals and a whole plethora of other technologies can facilitate communication. What is helpful is thinking comparatively about, for instance, *how quickly* the Web can be used to communicate relative to other technologies. Using this comparative lens, we can distinguish between what a phone tree, say, affords in terms of the speed of information dissemination versus a listserv. There is, after all, a qualitative difference in the ability to quickly send messages to large groups through email (and even text messaging with the proper software). We hold that it is the harnessing or leveraging of such differences that can perturb previously well-understood social processes, and lead to changes in both processes and our understanding of them.

We also think it is crucial to take seriously the complexity of Internet-based technologies, which include the hardware, protocols, and software that allow one to publish and/or view a Web page. The Web is much more intricate than a door or refrigerator, and understanding its uses and the consequences of those uses can be quite involved, too. While more simple technologies help to illustrate the utility of the affordances concept—we don't have to discover that air affords breathing because we instinctively breathe air; even many small animals can comprehend the concept of a door—we maintain that the simplicity of these technologies and the obviousness of their technological affordances misses an important component of the theoretical story we are telling. With complex technologies, what a technology affords may be one of the hardest questions to definitively answer, since among other issues, not everyone notices all affordances, not everyone knows how to leverage all affordances, not everyone chooses to leverage all affordances, and not everyone succeeds in well leveraging all affordances of complex technologies.

Another critical component of our argument is hinted at above: it is not the latent affordances of a technology that really matter to social explanations; it is how people leverage technological affordances that counts. After all, your computer can't *do* anything without you turning it on and telling it to do something. That a technology such as a computer or the Web *can* offer an affordance doesn't really matter unless *people* leverage that affordance.

We call this the leveraged affordances approach, as mentioned earlier. We are claiming that social impacts of technologies depend on the extent to which people notice and then skillfully (or less skillfully) try to leverage key affordances. More generally, we expect wide variation in how the Web is used to engage in activism, and argue that at the aggregate level, the overall "impact" of a technology on a given process will represent the actual mix across users of, first, the desire to leverage (or not) key affordances, and second, skillful leveraging versus novice bumbling by people who notice and try to leverage key affordances.

Returning to the two camps of findings, the leveraged affordances approach contends that if organizers or protesters ignore affordances offered by the Web, or only marginally leverage them, we should expect supersize style changes. If uses of the Web strongly leverage its technological affordances, on the other hand, then we should expect theory 2.0 style model changes. In other words, in our approach the uses of technologies are key, but some elements of those uses—how much they leverage the key affordances of a technology—are especially significant to determining their theoretical importance and impact. To further illuminate our use of technological affordance as a term, the next section discusses how others have used it, and how our usage fits with or diverges from other applications.

Our Use of Technological Affordance versus Prior Uses of the Term
The concept of an affordance has been in use for thirty years, but hasn't always been used consistently. James Gibson (1979, 127) coined the term affordance, introducing it to perceptual psychology and noting that "the *affordances* of the environment are what it *offers* the animal, what it *provides* or *furnishes*, either for good or ill. The verb *to afford* is found in the dictionary, but the noun *affordance* is not. I have made it up." Affordances in Gibson's use of the term did not require perception (e.g., a hidden door nonetheless affords opening) yet did allow for misperception (e.g., as when someone bumps into a sliding glass door; for an excellent review of Gibson's perspective, see McGrenere and Ho 2000). The concept was soon imported into the study of human-computer interaction (HCI), which is broadly concerned with understanding how people use computerized tools and systems, and developing better interfaces. Donald Norman (1988) then adapted the definition somewhat to include perception (for a detailed discussion, see Gaver 1991), which was particularly helpful for students of HCI because it highlighted the importance of good design in facilitating users' understanding of how to use the action potential of an object or technology. For instance, door handles should be designed to suggest to the user whether the door affords pulling or pushing to open (for a lengthy look at this example, see Gaver 1991). At a broader level, well-designed technologies can seem intuitive to use or "natural" to users because the interface makes action possibilities—affordances—perceptually obvious.

Norman's importation and slight redefinition of affordance was followed by a further redefinition by other authors in HCI and related fields (for more on this point, see McGenere and Ho 2000; Gaver 1991). In each case, these riffs on the original definition were designed to enhance the utility of the concept for the specific field in which it was being used. To further augment the concept's utility to HCI and designers, for instance,

H. Rex Hartson (2003) has distinguished between cognitive, physical, sensory, and functional affordances in design.

Indeed, perhaps because of the potential power of the concept of an affordance, scholars from a variety of areas began using it with similar, but not entirely congruent, meanings. Scholars from STS, communication, education, management, and the sociology of technology, to name only a few, have used the term in ways that share a central concern for the material potentials embodied in a technology, but that differ in their specific twists on the definition. Just as Norman's redefinition of affordances to include perception helped to make it more useful to students of HCI, definitions in other fields have become tilted to each field's central concerns.[2]

We use the term in a way that is most consistent with its use within the sociology of science. Here, affordance is employed less to indicate good design goals (as it is in HCI) or to understand how people come to understand their world (as it is in perceptual psychology), but instead to provide a way to take the material aspects of a technology seriously without allowing those material aspects to determine human behavior or social outcomes. A debate in this area between one of the main proponents of affordances, Ian Hutchby, and a major detractor, Brian Rappert, is worth dwelling on for a moment since our use is quite similar to Hutchby's.

Hutchby (2001, 444) sees affordances this way:

I will argue that affordances are functional and relational aspects which frame, while not determining, the possibilities for agentic action in relation to an object. In this way, technologies can be understood as artefacts which may be both shaped by and shaping of practices humans use in interaction with, around, and through them. This "third way" between the (constructivist) emphasis on the shaping of power of human agency and the (realist) emphasis on the constraining power of technical capacities opens the way for new analyses of how technological artefacts become important elements in the patterns of ordinary human conduct.

And Rappert (2003, 566), in a comment on Hutchby's work, characterizes Hutchby's definition of affordances in this way: "[Affordances] are the perceived properties of an object that *suggest* (but do not determine) how it might be used. . . . These affordances are functional and relational properties of all physical objects; users must learn some and they can be designed in."

To readers new to the area of STS, Hutchby's comments about a "third way" are important but probably not immediately meaningful. If one thinks about the general theoretical question "How much does a material technology on its own directly impact social life," there are two, polar opposite camps ready to provide an answer. A "technological determinist" take, which Hutchby associates with "realists" in the quote above, would argue that material technologies can directly impact social life. For instance, a deterministic approach might claim that a technology has an inevitable use that will, without any human decision, affect social life.

Constructivists, the second camp, disagree, contending that both what a technology turns out to be and how a technology matters to social life are socially constituted, or socially constructed.[3] Constructivists are interested in how human agency and social processes shape technologies. For example, it turns out that the bicycle we know and love was not the only possible design but instead was the design that was sculpted by social processes and won wide recognition through those processes (Bijker 1995; Bijker and Pinch 2002; Pinch and Bijker 1984, 1987).

Constructivists also assert that material technologies underdetermine usage. Recall the urban legend about a disgruntled computer user who called customer service to complain that their desktop computer's coffee holder was defective. After extensive troubleshooting over the phone, it turned out that the customer believed their CD drive, in the eject position, was a cup holder—and was mad it had broken.

Hutchby is arguing that between the extreme of technologies affecting social life directly no matter what people do with them (a realist approach in his terms) and the other extreme of material technology not mattering on its own at all (a constructivist approach in his terms), there must be a middle way. His middle way, like ours, is to discuss technological affordances. Technological affordances have the benefit of simultaneously acknowledging the real material opportunities and constraints that technologies impose on users at a given moment while also acknowledging that without people using a technology in various ways, what it offers is meaningless.

Not everyone agrees with Hutchby, especially Rappert. Centrally, Rappert disputes the newness of this way of thinking about technology, even if the application of the term affordance is relatively new. Constructivists, according to Rappert, do not need a term like affordance because constructivist approaches are already sufficiently, but not too realistically, anchored in the material existence of objects. He further holds that affordances as a concept sidestep, or divert attention away from, important STS and sociology of technology questions about how a technology came to be in its current form (i.e., for STS readers, how technologies crystallized or reached closure).

We maintain that our leveraged affordances arguments address many of Rappert's concerns, while taking advantage of the promise of technological affordances as a "third way" (Hutchby 2001). First, far from diverting attention away from interesting theoretical questions, we believe that we substantially improve theorizing about the relationships between technology and people by specifying which specific characteristics of a technology may be leveraged in ways that alter social processes. In this book, we focus on two critical technological affordances of the Web: the reduced cost for organizing and participation, and the reduced need for copresence for collective action to take place. By honing in on changing cost structures and the changing requirement for copresence to coordinate actions made possible by the Web versus other pre-Internet communication technologies we identify exactly which affordances of the technology are important, thereby removing them from a theoretical black box for thorough inspection.

Of course, Rappert would want to know how the Web came to be as it was in 2004 when we collected our data. If we were using technological affordances to examine such questions, we would agree with Rappert's criticism of the affordances concept as sidestepping critical questions about human agency in shaping the development of the Web as a technology. Yet while we hope that he and many others focus on those questions (likely without using affordances in their work), our project here is different. We want to understand how people use a technology as it exists at a particular time and why that might matter.

To this end, acknowledging Rappert's (and constructivists') arguments, we note that we are not studying *the Web* but instead the Web as it existed at the time we collected the data discussed in this book. It is certainly true that what we identify as affordances of Internet-enabled technologies (including the Web)—low-cost collective action without copresence in time and space—are actually affordances of Internet-enabled technologies as we know them today (and for that matter, prior to our data collection), and the technology itself is the product of specific social, political, and technical decisions. And it is true that affordances may change. For instance, were the U.S. government to impose a postagelike tax on all Internet traffic, the low-cost affordance we look at might drastically change once the protocols driving communication automatically tracked and imposed such taxes. Our interest, however, is not in prior or current social, political, and technical decisions that together have literally built the Web but rather in how the Web as it exists now can be integrated into a causal relationship between technology and society.

Aside from positioning our own views in relation to the debate between Hutchby and Rappert, we also distinguish our approach from what some sociologists have termed "social affordances." For instance, Lucas Graves (2007) examines the social affordances of blogging. We are clearly focused on technological affordances, though, and do not regard blogging as a technology or material object but rather a social practice. Hence, our use of technological affordances would be misapplied in discussions of affordances related to blogging.[4]

In sum, our approach to affordances has much in common with the prior uses of the term in that we are interested in how people use and interact with technologies, and more important, believe that both technologies and behavior "matter" in social explanations. But we differ from the prior uses of affordances in acknowledging that affordances may sometimes be hard to identify (which Norman might disagree with), focusing on what a technology differentially enables versus its other nearest competitors (such as in our earlier example, where both smoke signals and the Internet afford communication opportunities, but critical relative advantages to the Internet include the message's reach and the speed of delivery) and on technological versus social affordances. Over the next several chapters, we outline our two focal technological affordances in much more detail as well as show how people variously leverage these affordances. In doing so, we hope to show that when these affordances are leveraged to their hilt, theory 2.0 changes occur, but when they are not, supersize changes dominate.

Throwing the Baby Out with the Bathwater?

By this point, many social movement researchers may have begun to sweat: reading the above discussion, they may believe we are suggesting that theory 2.0 requires complete restatements of existing theory, and that we might advocate discarding decades of rich and nuanced work by social movement scholars. This is not our argument, however. Social movement theory developed and tested over time is not rendered obsolete by emerging work on Web activism; indeed, even uses of the Web that strongly leverage affordances don't make existing social movement theory irrelevant.

Rather, we are contending that strongly leveraged affordances can lead us to see where existing social movement theory might require varying degrees of adjustment, which may even substantially enhance existing social movement approaches. For example, in research on offline activism and social movements, it is an accepted truism that organizing and participation are costly, and that resources, whether from external sources or those internal to challenging communities, can make or break social change efforts. As John McCarthy and Mayer Zald (1973, 1977) so bluntly put it, while troubles are ubiquitous, resources to address troubles and social movements are not so widespread. Their resource mobilization theory anticipates that the groups that are able to effectively gather and deploy resources will be more likely to thrive as social movements. Scholarship on offline activism has thoroughly confirmed the general importance of resource mobilization.

Yet, another way to see this situation would be to notice that costs were always high for the actions and movements historically studied. Sure, costs might have varied between really high and somewhat high, but organizing and action were never cheap, and thus social movement scholars have been able to think of the costs of action as a constant or even an assumption, instead of a variable. But as we will discuss at great length in chapters 4 and 5, the strong leveraging of the low-cost affordance of the Web can lead to low costs for participation and organizing. This evidence from the Web does not mean that costs no longer matter to organizing and participation anywhere and everywhere; quite the opposite. Through an analysis of how the cost affordance of the Web is leveraged, we see that the costs of organizing and participation can vary widely—not just between really high and somewhat high, but from really high to negligible. At a theoretical level, then, we should step back from resource mobilization and ask, "What happens to our theorizing when costs are thought of as variables, not constants?"

Our answer is that model changes result because theorizing has to account for cost variation, and hence variation in the significance of resource mobilization, or at least variation in how and when resource mobilization matters. Our arguments here are in some ways parallel to Earl and Schussman (2003) and Bimber, Flanagin, and Stohl (2005) in the specific sense of model changes due to costs. We diverge, though, in our broader claim that a central thread tying many model changes together is their recognition that something usually considered a constant or even an assumption in theoretical models can now vary, and that existing models must accommodate that variance.

Far from throwing out the baby with the bathwater, this insight actually calls for social movement scholars to revisit as well as extend their core theories by looking for assumptions and constants that could vary, and in turn, theorizing the consequences of that variation. This is not a brave, new world in theorizing where scholars are in the intellectual wilderness;

it's an exciting new day in theorizing where scholars get to tinker with parts of their theories that have never been seen as dynamic before.

Of course, there are likely to be many places in social movement theory where the affordances of the Web don't matter at all—places where even fully leveraged affordances don't affect social action. And there are also likely to be theoretical issues that pose the same difficult questions to scholars studying off- and online activism alike.

As an example, research on social movements has struggled to pin down the exact impact of social movements in general or specific mobilizations in particular on social change. It is not that researchers cannot document that social movements were organizing and acting, and that social change temporally followed, but rather it is hard to show with real social scientific veracity that social movements and not other things that were also occurring lead to the social changes of interest. (This is a topic we explore in more detail in chapter 4.) This is often referred to as a question of movement outcomes, successes, and/or consequences. As an illustration, did the women's movement lead to greater respect for women in the workplace, or did an expansion of women's labor market participation lead to that greater respect—or both? It is even harder to say whether particular tactics are more "effective" than others; does a letter-writing campaign or civil disobedience, for instance, more frequently lead to success?

In general, scholars of both off- and online protest have faced significant challenges in developing ways to study protest success, and what about a social movement, protest action, or tactical form makes it more likely to be successful. We will return to the issue of success in chapter 4, but for now we note that it is likely to be a place, much as it is for scholars studying offline protest, where hard-and-fast answers prove elusive, even though anecdotes about successes and failures abound.

Why Study E-tactics?

Research on Web activism has paid extensive attention to e-mobilization and therefore also to the supersize-style effects of Web usage. Critics of this research have wondered whether this style of Web activism was being studied so often that it was coming to stand-in for all Web activism (as a synecdoche). Other researchers have examined e-movements (albeit not at all to the degree to which e-mobilizations have been studied), revealing theory 2.0 changes. But critics have pointed out that fully engaged e-movements don't emerge every day, making the number of cases available to study somewhat limited and the likelihood of rampant theory 2.0 changes questionable. And few have studied e-tactics. This oversight in the literature is both empirically and analytically unfortunate for a range of reasons; this book is meant to address that gap in research.

First, e-tactics are prevalent online. From large sites like PetitionOnline hosting tens of thousands of petitions to personal blogs that ask regular readers to participate in email campaigns for change, e-tactics are far more common on the Web than their representation in the literature on online activism would suggest. Indeed, studies have shown that empirically speaking, understudied e-tactics are significantly more frequent online than relatively well-studied e-mobilizations (Earl et al. forthcoming). If we are to fully describe the lay of the land of Web activism, e-tactics most certainly merit attention.

What's more, the volume of e-tactics on the Web probably wouldn't surprise most Web users. E-tactics aren't a feature of the Web relegated to the far reaches of the digital universe, and familiar to only a select group of technologically savvy individuals or even activists. We come across e-tactics like online petitions all the time—and sometimes we even participate.

This study of e-tactics does more than just redress the gaps in literature on Web activism, however. As hinted at above, since e-tactics have elements in common with both e-mobilizations and e-movements, these cases may provide better purchase over the seemingly conflicting findings from studies of Web activism of both supersize and theory 2.0 changes. As we show in the opening pages of the next chapter, like e-mobilizations, e-tactics draw on histories of offline action. The four forms of e-tactics we study—petitions, boycotts, and letter-writing and email campaigns—have their roots in forms of action that take place entirely offline (email being a twenty-first-century adaptation of letter-writing campaigns). Yet, like e-movements, key components of e-tactics are online. While e-tactics may have offline ancestors, they're online now. In these ways, e-tactics are similar to and different from *both* e-mobilizations and e-movements. And so e-tactics represent cases between the two poles of e-mobilizations and e-movements, with clear ties to both.

Insofar as the cases of each of those poles have been associated with certain kinds of findings—of scale and model changes—e-tactic cases can better flesh out what about the cases is correlated with particular kinds of findings. That is, if work on e-mobilizations has generally found supersize effects of ICT usage while studies of e-movements argue for theory 2.0 effects, our analysis of e-tactics can navigate these differing camps using a set of cases that lie somewhere in between.

3   The Look and Feel of E-tactics and Their Web Sites

Before moving on to the Web, petitions, boycotts, and letter-writing campaigns had long histories of use by social movements. We begin this chapter with a discussion of these histories and then briefly review some of our research methods (interested readers should consult the methodological appendix for more details). Then we try to familiarize readers with the Web sites we studied, including outlining key distinctions between sites (especially warehouse and nonwarehouse sites) and reviewing various characteristics of sites. We repeat this for the e-tactics hosted or linked to from these Web sites, briefly surveying our research methods and then looking at key characteristics of the e-tactics we observed.

Petitions

Petitioning has an extensive history as a protest tactic, and played a role in several revolutions and many major social movements. Scholars have found that petitioning was important to the French and English revolutions (Zaret 1996, 1999) as well as some British social movements (Tilly 1998). Decades later, the tactical form was imported to the American colonies from Britain, ultimately playing an important role in the abolition movement in the United States (Zaeske 2003).

In recent times, petitions have continued to be significant to major social movements. For instance, petitions supporting the creation of the Martin Luther King Jr. holiday were critical to its federal adoption (King Center 2004), with one major petition for the holiday garnering 6 million signatures. Scholars have also discussed petitions as a key part of the struggle for civil rights in Mississippi (Andrews 2001), and petitions have played prominent roles in more localized protest campaigns, as Douglas Lober (1995) reports in his discussion of siting controversies (i.e., controversies over where to locate something like a toxic waste dump or a

Wal-Mart) in Not in My Backyard movements. Hanspeter Kriesi (1988, 1989) points out that petitions have been important parts of contemporary social movement history in other countries as well. For instance, the "people's petition" was a Dutch peace movement petition signed by 3.8 million people (Kriesi 1989).

Key works in social movement research also reveal the notable, if frequently overlooked, role of petitions in contemporary social movements. For example, Bert Klandermans and Dirk Oegema's classic work on micromobilization processes (1987, 524) finds that a distinguishing characteristic between individuals in their "mobilization potential" (i.e., those at risk of participating in the demonstrations that Klandermans and Oegema were studying) was their willingness to "sign a petition." Karl-Dieter Opp's influential study on grievances (1988) measured people's willingness to participate in petitions, among other legal protest actions, and Gregory Wiltfang and Doug McAdam's noted work on high-risk activism (1991) uses petitioning to distinguish between low-cost versus low-risk activism by observing that while signing a petition often is not as time-consuming as some alternative forms of engagement, it can be a risky way to participate in protest movements, depending on the petition and its context. More broadly, Anthony Oberschall (1993) discusses the role of petitions across movements generally, in addition to tracing out the role of petitions in specific movements.

On the Web, petitions are extremely popular. As we discussed in earlier chapters with PetitionOnline and we explore with other sites later, there are entire Web sites dedicated to the sponsorship of petitioning as a form of political engagement. Even outside these kinds of sites, petitions are among the most common forms of e-tactic that we examined. They are also part of the history of some important political organizations; MoveOn, for instance, was founded when a petition about censuring President Bill Clinton and then "moving on" caught fire online.

Boycotts

Boycotts, too, have played a critical role in social movements and social movement research. Illustratively, as many grade school history classes teach, the Montgomery, Alabama, bus boycott was an important campaign in the civil rights movement (Barkan 1984). Forced to sit in the back of the bus and give up their seats to white passengers, African Americans in the South were regularly reminded of their second-class citizenship. Nonetheless, they depended on the bus transit system to take them where they needed to go, including to and from work. On December 1, 1955, Rosa Parks, an African American woman, refused to give up her seat to a white man and was arrested for breaking the law. In response, the African American community of Montgomery coordinated a large-scale boycott of the bus service. People walked, carpooled, and took taxis, refusing to patronize the bus system until its segregation rules were revoked. The boycott garnered nationwide attention, including that of the courts, and eventually—381 days later, to be exact—the Montgomery buses were officially desegregated.

Beyond many notable examples of key boycotts, scholars who study these protest actions have found them to be rich opportunities for social movement research. J. Craig Jenkins and Charles Perrow (1977), for instance, studied the California grape boycott in support of farmworkers. The boycott itself was quite impressive since it brought middle-class and elite pressure to bear on farmworkers' issues. Jenkins and Perrow's article demonstrated how significant this elite support and brokerage was to the success of the boycott. One could easily identify other boycotts that have been featured in important and classic social movement research, such as Steven Barkan's analysis (1984) of civil rights boycotts and the influence of police response on boycott success.

Although boycotts were the least frequent e-tactical form in our data, they were nonetheless present in substantial numbers on the Web, demonstrating that the boycott form has successfully migrated to the online arena. As we discuss below, the boycotts we studied tend to target offline entities such as corporations that sell products in physical stores (versus boycotting Amazon.com, for example). Yet boycotts varied in how they tended to allow participants to express their support and participation in the boycotts (which is explored at greater length in chapter 6).

Letter-Writing and Email Campaigns

As with the other e-tactical forms we focus on, letter-writing campaigns have a rich social movement heritage. Among the most famous campaigns was one on behalf of a group that came to be known as the Scottsboro Boys in the early 1930s. In 1931, two weeks after being found on a train with two white women, eight African American boys were found guilty of rape and sentenced to death in Alabama. The fate of these boys sparked a wave of action in the United States and indeed around the world. Leaders and organizations in the civil rights movement protested the decision, generally through rallies, while members of the international Communist movement, unable to participate in actions requiring physical presence and not recognized as political constituents with access to traditional political channels, protested from nations far and wide in a coordinated letter-writing campaign (Miller, Pennybacker, and Rosenhaft 2001). In particular, Russian Communists entered the fray, sending letters and telegrams pressuring the Alabama Supreme Court to hear an appeal of the case. The case eventually reached the U.S. Supreme Court, where the convictions were overturned. Lest the impact of the letters and telegrams be underestimated, the mother of two of the boys was said to have credited the Russians with saving her sons (Miller, Pennybacker, and Rosenhaft 2001).

Of course, not all letter-writing campaigns have proven as successful, but they have nonetheless been used widely by social movement actors as a protest action. For instance, the prominence of letter writing as a way to effect social change is highlighted by Amnesty International's efforts to pressure and persuade human rights abusers to reform their policies and free specific individuals (Scoble and Wiseberg 1974). Similarly, Suzanne Staggenborg (1991, 1988), in her in-depth study of the history of the prochoice movement in the United States, argues that congressional letter-writing campaigns were one of the major tactics employed by prochoice organizations during the 1970s. We should further note that Staggenborg considers letter writing to be distinct from more conventional, nonprotest actions such as state and federal lobbying campaigns, as shown by her typology of tactical forms (see Staggenborg 1988, table 5).

With the anecdotal successes and familiarity of letter-writing campaigns, it is little wonder that they would proliferate on the Web, and we found a substantial quantity of letter-writing campaigns online. Some of these campaigns have shifted from standard paper letters to email campaigns, extending and changing letter writing's tradition as a form of protest. While we anticipated email campaigns, and they are among our four focal e-tactical forms, we did not anticipate the evolution of letter-writing campaigns into online fax campaigns. As we observe below, because we recorded data on all Web-based protest opportunities on a Web site, whether expected or not, this means that we can speak to online fax campaigns as well to some limited extent.[1]

With rich protest histories in tow, petitioning, boycotting, and letter writing have gone "mainstream." And as our research demonstrates, these forms have gone mainstream on the Web, too. In the next section, we describe how we went about collecting our data.

Studying E-tactics

As briefly touched on in chapter 2, much of the existing research on Web activism has located Web content for study in one of the following ways: by examining popular Web sites, such as MoveOn, in case studies; by examining Web sites associated with established SMOs, such the National Organization for Women's Web site; by examining Web sites connected— that is, hyperlinked—to key SMOs' Web sites, such as Web sites connected to important Zapatista Web sites; or by examining groups of Web sites that are densely connected to one another through hyperlinks, such as right-wing Web sites that share a high volume of links to one another. While any one of these approaches can be helpful in addressing specific questions about Web activism, none is designed to create a larger view of Web activism or a larger picture of its particular forms.

We approach the issue quite differently with the hope that our methodology will allow us access to empirical findings that existing studies cannot assess because of their design. Our project starts with a straightforward descriptive question: How are people using e-tactics, especially petitions, boycotts, and letter-writing and email campaigns? Or rephrased with a strong focus on available Web content, What are the range and characteristics of petitions, boycotts, and letter-writing and email campaigns on the Web? If we wanted to follow the path of prior research methods, we would have then tried to answer these questions by studying a single large site, like PetitionOnline, or how an existing SMO or set of organizations are using e-tactics. But these approaches would have produced limited answers to the more general question of how people are using these e-tactical forms and what e-tactics are available for use.

Instead, we opt for a population sampling approach. Even for readers less familiar with sampling, the idea and its benefits are quite clear-cut. Let's say you wanted to understand what Americans thought about a particular issue. An excellent approach would be to define the population of Americans that you want to understand (e.g., adults residing in the United States) and then find a way to draw a random sample of those individuals to interview (e.g., use a survey center to randomly call houses using random digit dialing and administer the survey). The advantage of defining a population and then randomly sampling from it is that the findings from the sample are usually generalizable to the population level with some defined margin of error. So if 35 percent of the sample said that they strongly approved of the sitting president, you could have some confidence that about 35 percent of Americans would strongly approve of the sitting president.

We wanted to be able to make the same kinds of statements about the characteristics of e-tactics on the Web. To do so, we had to acknowledge what many Web users already know: e-tactics don't exist in isolation; they are housed on larger Web sites. A complete picture therefore involves data on the Web sites that house e-tactics and data on e-tactics themselves. Drawing on this analogy between surveying people and surveying online content, we have designed and implemented a method to sample Web sites housing e-tactics and e-tactics themselves (technically, we draw on an analogy to the kind of sampling common in survey research, not to surveys themselves). The methodological appendix provides much greater detail on how we designed and conducted our data collection, but it is worth discussing here with broad brushstrokes so that the claims we can and cannot make using our data are more evident.

First, we had to decide on our population, which we defined as reachable Web sites hosting or hyperlinking to one of the four kinds of e-tactics we focus on. (It is worth repeating here that we did not start out with a focus on fax campaigns and so did not define our population to exhaustively include fax campaigns; fax campaigns found in the data co-occurred with at least one petition, boycott, letter-writing campaign, or email campaign.) To unpack that, we decided to study only what we define as reachable sites, meaning sites that users could reasonably find if they were not given a URL in advance. We made this decision because protest is an inherently public act, so we wanted to find e-tactics that were publicly accessible (i.e., this ruled out e-tactics on password-protected Web sites where a general user could not access them). We also restricted our population to sites that hosted or linked to e-tactics since our fundamental question is about the uses of e-tactics on the Web. The methodological appendix describes our definition of the population in more detail.

Second, we had to generate a list of Web sites in this population. We relied on multiple, automated queries to Google, each of which resulted in one thousand results that could be combined across queries to produce larger population lists of Web sites hosting or linking to petitions, boycotts, and letter-writing and email campaigns. As the methodological appendix reports, we completed a number of Google queries for each kind of e-tactic and then concatenated those results, eliminating duplicates that came up across several searches. This gave us something like a population list of reachable Web sites hosting or linking to instances of each e-tactical form. Significantly, these lists were far more extensive than other ways that

Google has been used by researchers; generally, researchers using Google have only studied the first ten, fifty, or one hundred results from a single Google query, which doesn't generate anything close to the population lists we generated (the exact numbers of queries and results can be found in the methodological appendix).

Next, we randomly sampled from each list. This step is critical because it allows us to generalize from our data on online content in much the same way that surveys are able to generalize about populations of people. The methodological appendix details how exactly we collected content from the sample sites and how we then analyzed that content. But before we move to a general discussion of those topics here, it is important to introduce a crucial distinction among the kinds of sites we found when we pretested our research methods.

The Geography of E-tactics: Warehouse versus Nonwarehouse Sites

As we began to pretest the method outlined above, we found that a number of sites appeared over and over again. Although the presentation and organization of the sites we collected varied widely, we did discover that when it comes to their basic relationship to e-tactics, there are really two major kinds of Web sites that hosted or linked to e-tactics. First, there are what we refer to as *warehouse sites*. As we described in chapter 1, Petition-Online, a warehouse site in our data set, is a site where any Web user can create a petition and have it hosted for free in a matter of minutes, just by filling out a Web-based form. The site hosts tens of thousands of petitions, and has handled the collection, for free, of millions and millions of signatures. The topics are not limited by the site; people can and do post petitions about international, national, and local politics, but people also create and post petitions about other concerns, ranging from environmental degradation to religious or entertainment-related issues. The creator of PetitionOnline, Kevin Matthews, didn't design the site to forward a specific issue but rather to forward petitioning as a form of political and social engagement.

All warehouse sites share this clearinghouse character with PetitionOnline in that they allow users to submit the petitions, boycotts, letter-writing campaigns, and/or email campaigns. (We did not find any warehouse sites that specialized in faxing, although fax campaigns were not an initial focus of our data collection, so it is possible that such a site did exist and we simply didn't find it.) For instance, KarmaBanque.com works much like PetitionOnline, but it serves as a clearinghouse for boycotts instead of petitions. While most of the warehouse sites we studied were not limited by a topic or cause, a few of them did restrict user submissions to a broad topic (e.g., conservative, leftist, or antiwar activism). We consider the sites to be warehouse sites nonetheless because they serve as clearinghouses for e-tactics designed by others.

Other sites in our pretest Google searches lacked this clearinghouse quality. Some sites were blogs that had a single letter-writing campaign on the site; other sites were set up by individuals or small groups, and had several protest actions focused on a specific issue, but didn't seem to be run by a formal organization; and still others were what social movement scholars are accustomed to studying: Web sites of traditional SMOs like Amnesty International. This eclectic group of sites hosting or linking to individual e-tactics seemed to only share one key characteristic: they were *not* clearinghouses. While the label lacks fanfare, we discuss these as *nonwarehouse sites*.

The distinction between warehouse and nonwarehouse sites will become more meaningful as the book progresses, but for now it is important to understand this difference because our data collection took this distinction into account. Quite simply, warehouse sites showed up in large numbers in our pretest Google searches because they host and link to a large number of e-tactics (as we will demonstrate later). In fact, they hosted and linked to so many e-tactics that we worried that e-tactics from warehouse sites might entirely overrun our samples. We thus created parallel processes for identifying warehouse and nonwarehouse populations, which we could randomly sample from if the population size warranted it. These processes are explained in far more detail in the methodological appendix.

To offer a basic outline of our process, we started by identifying the warehouse sites through our pretest runs, examining any domain that showed up more than forty times to determine if it was a warehouse site or not. Ultimately, we identified fifteen warehouse sites, which constituted the population of warehouse sites, and we archived and quantitatively content coded the main site pages for all of these sites. Then, as described above, for nonwarehouse sites, we ran a series of Google queries for each type of e-tactic in our study that excluded the domains for warehouse sites, concatenated the roughly one thousand results per query, and eliminated duplicate URLs. This created four populations from which to sample, respectively, petitions, boycotts, letter-writing campaigns, and email campaigns. We then randomly sampled sites from those populations, archived the sites, and quantitatively content coded those sites that were in fact found to host or link to at least one e-tactic (for more detail, see the methodological appendix). In the end, we coded 169 nonwarehouse sites.

The Look and Feel of Web Sites

While all the sites (both warehouse and nonwarehouse) hosted and/or linked to specific petitions, boycotts, letter-writing campaigns, or email campaigns, the sites did not necessarily look much alike beyond that. For instance, the style of the Web sites that we collected ranged widely. Some were authored by groups, including familiar SMOs, while others were the product of a single individual; some were neatly organized and well maintained, while others were less coherently structured and full of broken links. To offer a sense of the breadth of Web site styles, we describe in detail the appearance of two nonwarehouse sites in our data.

The first, Amnesty International USA's Web site, belongs to an SMO quite familiar to students of social movements.[2] This human rights organization has a long history and well-known offline presence. When we examined it, the Web site contained news, information about the organization and its activist campaigns, and ways that a site visitor could participate in protest actions. Amnesty International USA used multiple linked Web pages, such as a page with contact information, a page listing its campaigns, and individual pages with information on each campaign. On each page, there was a navigation bar containing a list of links to other pages, facilitating easy navigation around the site. From the page listing the campaigns, for example, the user could click a link to a page detailing a particular campaign. Once the user was done with the page for that campaign, using the navigation bar, they could return to the campaign overview page or move to other pages such as "contact us." The individual pages contained both text and photographs. Most of the pages were formatted with a wide center column of content and narrower side columns containing, for example, short teasers about other pages on the site along with links to those pages. Sites such as Amnesty International USA's were characterized by transparent navigation and clear site organization.

Other sites were less well organized, with internal pages that linked to one another, but with no available site map to cue visitors to the overall architecture. On a site run by the American Patriot Friends Network, there was no navigation bar facilitating movement among the Web pages on the site.[3] The content appeared to be entirely produced by the organization, which on further investigation of the site, listed only a single member: its founder. The site's main page was a single column of text, graphics, and links to other Web pages, both internal and external. The column ran long in a continuous stream with no obvious organization. Links from the site's home page to other pages on the site had little information about the linked page. For instance, a link titled "Take a moment to picture this" took visitors to a page about the U.S. government's use of force in Waco, Texas. Once there, a user could return to the home page only by clicking the browser's back button or retyping the home page's URL; there was no internal link from the page on Waco to the home page. Sites such as this one were characterized by a simple structure, sometimes consisting of only a single Web page, and unsophisticated organization.

The diversity of Web site styles was also apparent in how the sites connected users to particular e-tactics. Some sites hosted the actions themselves, others linked to actions, and still others did both. Figure 3.1 displays this by mapping the percentage of nonwarehouse and warehouse sites that host, versus link to, versus host *and* link to e-tactics.[4] Sites that *hosted* their own e-tactics were the most frequent in our sample, with 54 percent of

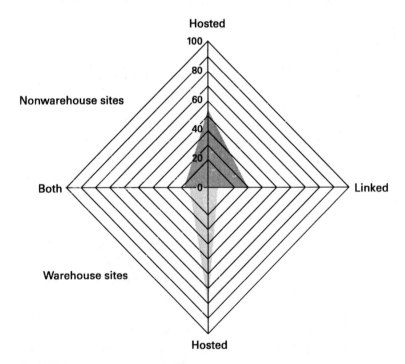

Figure 3.1
Hosting and/or linking on nonwarehouse and warehouse sites.

nonwarehouse sites and 80 percent of warehouse sites exclusively hosting their own e-tactics (see also Earl 2006b). They were also extremely diverse. Examples of this kind of site include: a site devoted to protesting the war in Iraq that contained a sample protest letter that visitors were encouraged to print, sign, and mail to the president; a personal Web site that included, along with musings on the site author's current social life, a call for participation in a boycott of Nike for its use of sweatshops; and PetitionOnline with the tens of thousands of petitions it hosts. All but one of the warehouse sites hosted e-tactics.

Other sites directed users to protest actions on other Web sites through links, as was true of 30 percent of nonwarehouse sites and a single warehouse site. Instead of including information about participating in an e-tactic on their own site, these sites referred visitors to other sites where they could participate in an e-tactic. We refer to these sites as ones that *linked* to e-tactics. Generally speaking, sites in this category made claims on their own site, but directed visitors to follow hyperlinks in order to participate in action for the cause. For example, a site that supported animal rights asked visitors to show their support by following a link to a petition on ThePetitionSite (a petition warehouse site) and signing that petition.[5] Although posting a hyperlink to another Web site is relatively easy, technically speaking, sites that linked to e-tactics were less common than those that hosted their own e-tactics. Save for the one warehouse site, all of the sites that linked to e-tactics were nonwarehouse sites.

Finally, some sites both hosted and linked to e-tactics (17 percent of nonwarehouse sites and 13 percent of warehouse sites). These sites might contain multiple e-tactics for the same cause (e.g., hosting an email campaign, complete with email addresses and sample text, on their site, but linking to a petition about the same issue on another site), or host and/or link to e-tactics with different claims.

If we examine the claims made on Web sites, we can see how diverse the sites are as well. As figure 3.2 shows, seventy-one unique issues were addressed on the main pages of the sites coded. Pressing a bit further to account for different positions that could be taken on the same issue (i.e., support for or opposition to a single issue), we find eighty-eight unique stances on the Web sites that we studied (see also Earl and Kimport 2009). Substantively, sites advocated for and against a diverse array of issues, from vegetarianism to the Iraq war, from taxes to civil rights, from abortion to globalization.

Moreover, although many claims emerged repeatedly across different sites, for the most part no claim dominated. As we can see from

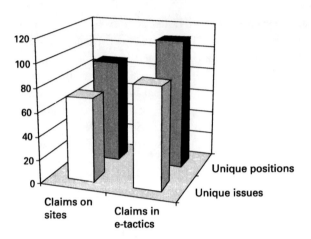

Figure 3.2
Unique claims on sites and e-tactics.

table 3.1, which reports the frequency of coded claims across nonwarehouse sites, there was a broad distribution of claims across the sites in our
data set with no claim found in more than 15 percent of the sample.

Sampling and Coding Specific E-tactics

In addition to coding a random sample of the nonwarehouse sites that we
collected through our Google searches, we coded the e-tactics hosted or
linked to from these sites, including petitions, boycotts, and letter-writing
and email campaigns, and also instances of other e-tactical forms that were
present, such as online fax campaigns (for the handful of coding exceptions, like e-tactics located in archives, see the methodological appendix).
Generally speaking, nonwarehouse sites tended to host or link to a lower
volume of protest actions. Some hosted only a single action, while others
perhaps hosted a handful, but sites that contained more than ten protest
actions were rare. In all, we coded 748 e-tactics identified through nonwarehouse sites (i.e., the sites hosted or linked to the actions): 153 petitions, 82 boycotts, 212 letter-writing campaigns, 152 email campaigns, and
to our surprise, 149 fax campaigns.[6]

As mentioned above, warehouse sites were another story: some of them
hosted tens of thousands of petitions, making it prohibitively time-
consuming to code every protest action on the fifteen warehouse sites.
Instead, we randomly sampled the e-tactics on warehouse sites at rates

Table 3.1

Distribution of Claims across Nonwarehouse Sites (in Percentage)*

Claim	Nonwarehouse sites
International human and civil rights, democratization	14.8%
2003 Iraq invasion	13.0
Government policy, not elsewhere classified	11.8
Environmental movement	11.2
Civil rights, other groups not elsewhere classified	10.7
Health	10.1
Labor	8.9
Political figure, party, or candidate	8.3
Freedom of speech/assembly	7.7
Israel/Palestine conflict	7.1
Other, not elsewhere classified	6.5
Animal rights movement	5.9
Peace movement, not elsewhere classified	5.9
Specific religion	5.3
Entertainment industry	4.7
Civil rights, gay, lesbian, and transgender	4.7
Civil liberties	4.7
Violence against women	4.1
Abortion/reproductive rights	4.1
Reducing noise pollution	3.6
Indigenous peoples' rights	3.0
Education	3.0
Globalization or free trade	3.0
Sweatshops	3.0
Feminist or women's movement, not elsewhere classified	2.4
Rights for foreign political prisoners	2.4
U.S. foreign policy	2.4
Death penalty	2.4
Same-sex marriage	2.4
Gun control	1.8
Poverty/hunger	1.8
Intellectual property	1.8
Corporate responsibility, anti–business corruption	1.8
Anti-Semitism	1.8
Nuclear power movement	1.2
Small or family farmers or organic movement	1.2
Human rights policy or foreign law	1.2
Restriction of pharmaceutical/chemicals	1.2
Government or "big government"	1.2

Table 3.1

(continued)

Claim	Nonwarehouse sites
Hate crimes	1.2%
Civil rights, African American	1.2
Civil rights, disabled	1.2
U.S. military intervention, not elsewhere classified	1.2
Anti-immigrant movement	0.6
Anti-"transnational union" movements	0.6
NAFTA	0.6
UN	0.6
NATO	0.6
Discrimination in employment for women	0.6
Atomic testing and weapons	0.6
Afghanistan war	0.6
Draft	0.6
Non-U.S. war (with no U.S. participation)	0.6
Rain forest preservation	0.6
Tax increases	0.6
Homelessness	0.6
Drug control	0.6
Child abuse, sexual crimes	0.6
Victims' rights	0.6
Pornography	0.6
DC representation	0.6
Police brutality/harassment against African Americans	0.6
Favorable media depictions of African Americans	0.6
Transgender rights	0.6
Increased funding for AIDS/HIV research	0.6
Favorable media depictions for Native Americans	0.6
Historical grievances by Native Americans	0.6
Favorable media depictions of Latinos	0.6
Water quality protection	0.6
Rights of domestic protesters	0.6
Conservative religious claims	0.6

*The percentages do not sum to 100 percent because more than one claim can be made per site.

tailored to the individual sites (as discussed in the methodological appendix, to correct for oversampling we report weighted percentages throughout the book). More details on this procedure are available in the appendix. We coded 362 warehouse e-tactics: 287 petitions, 49 boycotts, 12 letter-writing campaigns, 10 email campaigns, and 4 fax campaigns.[7] We should emphasize here that these fax campaigns were found on warehouse sites devoted to other e-tactical forms (e.g., petitioning) or a broad cause, and happened to co-occur with another e-tactic; we did not look for or find any warehouse sites that specialized in fax campaigns.

The individual e-tactics in our sample varied in their likeness to their offline counterparts. In the case of petitions, some hosted on the Web were nearly identical to traditional offline petitions, requiring a user to download and print the petition, and then have others add their signature. Others deviated quite noticeably from offline petitions. For example, in a PetitionOnline petition, signers called on Florida governor Jeb Bush to direct the Florida courts to try a sixteen-year-old accused of armed robbery as a juvenile rather than as an adult.[8] At the top of the page, the Web page names the target, with a stream-of-consciousness explanation of the e-tactic's claim below. Users could sign the petition by following a link to a page where they could enter their name, contact information, and any additional comments. After signing the petition and then authenticating their signature through an email confirmation, the signers were listed in the order of when they signed, along with their location and any comments they made. Unlike offline petitions, users could sign the petition anonymously. And unlike offline petitions that have generally been sponsored by SMOs, this petition appeared to be written by the sixteen-year-old's mother. When we archived the petition to study it, 693 people had signed.

Online boycott campaigns, too, diverged from standard offline boycotts, although not as frequently as online petitions from their offline counterparts. For example, participation in online boycotts was regularly tracked in ways that participation in offline boycotts is not—a topic that we return to at much greater length in chapter 6. How participation was tracked varied. On one individual's Web site mentioned briefly above, for instance, the author called for a boycott of Nike products because of the company's use of sweatshop labor.[9] Users could email the site owner about their participation. Other Web sites facilitated more sophisticated mechanisms for registering participation. On several warehouse Web sites that host boycotts, each boycott campaign, in addition to detailing a target and a claim, allowed users to create a user name, sign in to the site, and register their participation in the boycott. For example, on KarmaBanque, users could log in and add their name to the list of supporters of a boycott of McDonald's for its labor practices. Likewise, boycott organizers could track participation in the action.

Similarly, while some online letter-writing campaigns looked quite similar to their pen-and-paper predecessors, other online letter-writing campaigns were more sophisticated. They included, for instance, a sample letter that a user could edit, print, and mail. Or in some cases, Web sites even automated sending the letter through a Web interface in which the user could edit and electronically sign the letter, while the campaign host would take care of the back-end activities including printing and mailing the letters.

In one such sophisticated letter-writing campaign, the Rainforest Action Network Web site asked users to write to government agencies, including the U.S. Department of the Interior and the California Department of Fish and Game, demanding increased protection of endangered species in the Willow Creek forests of northern California.[10] The Web page provided a brief description of the campaign, the organizations and addresses targeted, and an editable sample letter laying out the campaign's claims. Participants could send the letter as written by simply entering their name and contact information into fields at the bottom of the page and clicking the "Send Letter Now" button. Or they could edit the letter—or even delete it and write an entirely new one—and then furnish their contact information and click "Send Letter Now."

As with letter-writing campaigns, the sophistication of email campaigns varied, with some e-tactics listing only the email addresses themselves, and others offering sample emails or even a mechanism to send the email from the Web page. The Web site for Global Response hosted several email campaigns, including one targeting an international oil company to protest the construction of an oil pipeline through land occupied by indigenous people.[11] Following a detailed write-up of the issue, Global Response provided the email addresses of key decision makers at the oil company, and asked visitors to compose and send emails to these targets. In this coordinated campaign, visitors were asked to collectively protest the company's actions using email in a format that directly echoes offline letter-writing campaigns.

Stepping back from particular examples, the petitions, boycotts, and letter-writing and email campaigns that we studied ran the gamut on claims and targets, as was true of the sites on which specific e-tactics were housed. By way of illustration, the claims found in the e-tactics that we studied were as diverse as those we saw for sites. As figure 3.2 shows, 86 different issues were the subject of specific e-tactics, representing 110 unique stances if we distinguish between different positions on the same issue.

Generally speaking, the e-tactics that we studied also addressed a diverse set of targets. Online protest actions were directed at both state and private actors. For example, we found a petition that targeted a local store, a boycott of an international company, and a letter-writing campaign directed at the French government (for a more detailed description of the targets coded, see the methodological appendix).

There were some general trends in the targeting practices of the e-tactics in our sample (for a more extensive discussion of e-tactic targeting and a fuller look at the figures reported here, see Earl and Kimport 2008). Boycotts, for instance, almost exclusively targeted businesses, not state actors; 89 percent of the boycotts on nonwarehouse sites and 99 percent of the boycotts on warehouse sites were directed at businesses. Petitions, letter-writing campaigns, and email campaigns, in contrast, tended to target the state in their claims making, regardless of whether they were housed on warehouse or nonwarehouse sites. But they didn't do so all of the time. Anywhere from 25 (of letter-writing campaigns on nonwarehouse sites) to 47 percent (of petitions on warehouse sites) of the protest actions that took these three forms were directed at nonstate targets.

If we consider state actors themselves as a diverse body of agencies, departments, councils, and officials rather than as a monolithic entity, the variety of targets named in online protest actions becomes even wider. The e-tactics that we studied were directed at legislative, judicial, law enforcement, and executive officials, everywhere from the local to the state to the national level. And some e-tactics were even aimed at foreign governments. Of the state actors targeted in petitions, letter-writing campaigns, and email campaigns on nonwarehouse sites, members of the legislative branch were most frequent, followed closely by the executive branch. For actions on warehouse sites, the executive and legislative branches were also common targets, as were government agencies. Interestingly, the judicial branch was an infrequent target of actions on either warehouse or non-warehouse sites.

One similarity between warehouse and nonwarehouse sites, though, was that their e-tactics tended to name only a single target, not multiple, different ones. The highest rate of combining targets on a nonwarehouse site belonged to petitions, and even then only 13 percent targeted two governmental entities simultaneously, and only 1 percent targeted three or more such entities at the same time. For warehouse sites, 21 percent of letter-writing campaigns and 23 percent of email campaigns named two distinct governmental actors. The sole exception to this trend was warehouse email campaigns that targeted three governmental entities at once, 46 percent of the time. For both warehouse and nonwarehouse sites, instances where actions combined a governmental target and a private one were exceedingly rare; only between 1 and 2 percent of all e-tactics combined any targets across such a border (for more detail, see Earl and Kimport 2008).

An additional axis of variation among e-tactics is also worth initial mention here (with more discussion in later chapters): e-tactics had varying levels of automation. Some protest actions required more work on the part of the participant than others. Thinking of the examples offered above, to participate in the boycott of Nike you must actively change your purchasing patterns. Similarly, for Global Response's email campaign, you would need to write up and send an email to the addresses it provided. At the opposite end of the spectrum, some Web sites automated much of the action required to participate. The Rainforest Action Network's letter, for example, was already written and formatted—all that was left for a participant to do was enter limited contact information—and the site promised to complete the mailing procedure on the participant's behalf. For the PetitionOnline petition, participation was also fully automated; one only needed to fill in a few fields with personal information and then click the submit button. We offer a much fuller discussion of automation and its effects in later chapters.

Three of the e-tactics in our data had an even higher degree of automation: they were what we describe as "one-click actions." By checking a box on a Web page hosting a one-click e-tactic, the participant could engage in more than one action. For instance, a user could enter personal information for a letter, say, to their senator supporting same-sex marriage, and by clicking a box, simultaneously send an email, sign a petition, or both.

Another scenario that we have observed online, but that is not present in our data, takes this even further. After entering personal information just once, a user could click a box causing this information to be populated into multiple different letters to different targets for different issues, all hosted on the same site. Conceivably, such a sign-up could apply to future tactics, automating participation without a user needing to even visit the site. We believe that one-click actions have become more common over time on nonwarehouse sites, although subsequent longitudinal research will have to empirically assess that hypothesis.

Table 3.2

Percentage of Sites Discussing Selected Offline Protest Forms*

	Nonwarehouse sites	Warehouse sites
Rally/demonstration	15%	7%
March	5	0
Strike/slow down/sick-ins	4	7
Vigil	4	0
Picket	2	0
Civil disobedience	1	0

*Rows are sorted by the frequency of observed offline protest. Sites can include more than one form of offline protest.

Of course, it would be a misrepresentation to suggest that the only actions that Web sites in our sample hosted and/or linked to were e-tactics. Indeed, there were some e-mobilizations on the Web sites that we studied. A number of the sites in our study, for instance, endorsed offline protest actions, either through language on their own site or by linking to other sites with more information. In fact, about 25 percent of nonwarehouse sites had or linked to information on rallies, demonstrations, marches, vigils, pickets, civil disobedience, and/or strikes. Yet only about 6 percent of warehouse sites hosted or linked to information on one of these classic offline protest forms.

Table 3.2 includes the percentages of sites we studied that discussed or linked to an instance of one of these classic protest forms. Since e-mobilizations are not the focus of this book, we do not include an in-depth analysis of these actions but nonetheless emphasize the complex nature of the sites under study as well as the extent to which e-tactics and e-mobilizations share the same (virtual) space.

Finally, in the analyses discussed in the following chapters, we draw on one additional data source. Subsequent to coding the Web sites and e-tactics, we conducted a small number of supplementary interviews with the owners, administrators, and operators of Web sites that hosted or linked to e-tactics, including operators of some of the sites in our sample (as well as interviews with the owners, administrators, and operators of Web sites identified through a subsequent sample of Web sites identified using the same sampling methods).

II Leveraging Low Costs Online

In this part of the book, we examine how e-tactics can be designed and used to leverage the low-cost affordance of the Web. A leveraged affordances approach to understanding e-tactics has us start from the key affordances of the Web. In the following two chapters, we focus on the cost affordance of the Web and trace how it has been leveraged in e-tactics. As one might expect, we find rich variation. In both chapters, as our leveraged affordances approach would predict, we observe a mix of supersize and theory 2.0 findings.

In chapter 4, we examine how the different ways that the cost affordance is leveraged impacts participation in protest. We also offer, in more absolute terms, a discussion of the overall potential of low costs to impact participation. By looking at variation across e-tactics as well as the apparent ceiling and floor for the costs of e-tactics (no e-tactic in our sample, for example, had high costs for participants), we articulate what this affordance can mean for both participation and social movement theorizing.

In chapter 5, we turn to the impacts of low costs on organizers. We argue that just as with participation, the cost affordance of the Web can have significant impacts on organizing protest. Specifically, we compare e-tactics organized by SMOs to those organized by non-SMOs in several ways, and discover that for some types of protest, SMOs don't have a clear advantage in organizing. We look at what this might mean to scholars' understanding of organizing.

4 Taking Action on the Cheap: Costs and Participation

For both activists and students of social movements alike, when we think of protest, we think of moments when people came together for a cause, sometimes risking a great deal to speak truth to power. The civil rights movement of the 1960s, for example, is often cited as the heyday of activism. From the March on Washington in 1963, to the boycott of segregated buses in Montgomery, to the lunch counter sit-ins, the civil rights movement drew people of all races and ages from around the country to challenge the treatment of African Americans in the United States. Reaching further back in time, we might think of the parade in New York City in 1912 by supporters of the women's suffrage movement. Wearing long skirts and hats, and waving American flags, women took to the streets to advocate for their right to vote. Over half a century later, other women took to the streets of Washington in support of women's right to an abortion.

Seminal examples of protest include not only actions on behalf of equal rights, be they for African Americans, women, gays and lesbians, or immigrants, but also those motivated by safety or labor concerns. For instance, the residents of Pennsylvania towns surrounding Three Mile Island, a nuclear power facility, rallied in opposition to the plant's operation after it suffered a partial core meltdown in 1979. Their concern over the safety of nuclear energy set off a wave of protests across the country against nuclear power. Advocacy over labor policies, too, has disrupted communities throughout the world, as with the miner's strike in the United Kingdom in 1984–1985. During this sixteen-month strike to protect miner jobs, over ten thousand people were arrested and eleven people died.

Across these cases—which traverse time, place, and the specific movement involved—at least two things were fixed: organizing and participating in protest was relatively socially expensive (i.e., it took time, risk, and sometimes also pecuniary costs), and people had to come together in time and place to protest, which is what we refer to as copresence. A more academic spin on these two constants is that they are both characteristics of all prior repertoires of contention—a subject that chapter 8 is dedicated to examining.

But for now it is enough to note that no matter the kind of action, almost all protest forms in history have required people to come together physically (with boycotts as a potential exception) to accomplish collective ends, and have required organizers and participants to bear the nonnegligible costs in doing so. Indeed, even though the "price" of protest has varied within a small range across time, the going rate or "average cost" has never been particularly low and has certainly never been almost costless. Even the offline tactics that we might consider of "lower" cost, like a petition drive coordinated in front of your local grocery store, still have clear and significant costs associated with them. Whether these costs come in the form of risk, stress, time, or actual money to travel or procure supplies, they have been relatively high throughout the history of protest.

Novel uses of the Web, however, may allow these two seeming constants to become variables: innovative uses of the Web for protest can substantially lower the costs associated with participation (we discuss reduced costs for organizing in the next chapter) and can allow for meaningful collective action without copresence (which we explore in part III). In this chapter, we focus on the role of costs in classic social movement theory and research; the emerging literature on Web activism that suggests that innovative uses of the Web can reduce costs, which is compatible with our leveraged affordances approach; what data in our sample of specific e-tactics can show about how innovative online actions look and how they reduce costs for participants; and the potential implications of these changes.

Costs in Social Movement Theory and Research on Participation

Early social movement theorizing centered on psychological dispositions (e.g., the importance of authoritarian personalities to participation) or the anomic qualities of social movement participants (Kornhauser 1959; Smelser 1965) to explain participation (for an excellent intellectual history of social movement scholarship, see Garner 1997). In the 1960s and 1970s, however, the costs of taking action started to be considered more seriously. Across time, costs have come to be central, especially given robust findings that costs are often a key predictor of individual participation in collective action and social movements. Also, when one aggregates the effects of expenses up to the level of entire movements, costs are a crucial predictor of the overall levels of movement activity.

The Development of Resource Mobilization

This shift toward paying attention to costs can be dated back to 1965, when Mancur Olson published *The Logic of Collective Action*. The book quickly began to radically change the debate about participation. Olson's work focuses on the production of "public goods" generally (not social movements particularly), and considers public goods to be physical goods like roads and national defense, but also less physical productions like equal rights legislation. Public goods differ from private goods in that they can be enjoyed by multiple people without lessening the benefit to any individual (more technically, public goods are "nonrival"; e.g., equal rights would be nonrival in that multiple people can benefit simultaneously while toothpaste, a private good of finite quantity, is a rival good), and once produced it is difficult to prevent nonproducers from enjoying a public good (more technically, public goods are "nonexcludable"; e.g., clean air is nonexcludable while toothpaste is excludable). These characteristics, Olson argues, mean that potential producers of public goods face substantial social obstacles to their production. Most important, even though producing a public good would be beneficial to individuals, they will not necessarily participate in its production:

But it is *not* in fact true that the idea that groups will act in their self-interest follows logically from the premise of rational and self-interested behavior. It does *not* follow, because all of the individuals in a group would gain if they achieved their group objective, that they would act to achieve that objective, even if they were all rational and self-interested. Indeed, unless the number of individuals in a group is quite small, or unless there is coercion or some other special device to make individuals act in their common interest, *rational, self-interested individuals will not act to achieve their common or group interests.* (Olson [1965] 1998, 2)

Olson labels this quandary the free-rider dilemma, and contends that when people are in a large enough group, they will realize that they can enjoy the public good even if they do not participate in its production. In such a scenario, Olson claims, people will free ride off of others' efforts, unless coerced to help produce the public good or provided with selective incentives, which are essentially personal rewards for participation. That is, because there are costs associated with taking action, but the rewards can be enjoyed whether or not one participates in the production of the collective good, Olson maintained that absent some sort of mandate to participate, other incentives would have to be supplied in order to encourage participation. To understand selective incentives, think of your local National Public Radio station's most recent pledge drive: in exchange for a donation (which is a contribution toward the public good of National Public Radio), donors can receive free tickets or free goods from the station. These freebies are selective incentives that give people a direct and personal reward for their contribution, and might motivate an otherwise-reluctant supporter.

Although Olson isn't addressing social movements specifically, McCarthy and Zald (1973, 1977) took his arguments seriously as they crafted the beginnings of resource mobilization, which would come to be one of the dominant theoretical paradigms for understanding social movements.[1] In the 1960s and early 1970s when resource mobilization was being formulated, one only needed to look around to readily observe how costly participation in a social movement could be. On the extreme end, physical and economic reprisals against African Americans working for civil rights in the South demonstrated the high price that might have to be paid for social movement participation. In less extreme scenarios, social movement participation still required a good deal of time (e.g., at least several hours participating as well as getting to and from a street protest like a rally), and could require personal expenses or take an emotional toll. While some of the costs—time, stress, and so on—are not pecuniary ones, they can still be quite important to understanding social movement participation. In this analysis, we don't distinguish between the pecuniary and nonpecuniary costs of participation since we regard both as significant.

McCarthy and Zald (1973, 1977) assert that resources are critical to social movements partially because they allow for the provision of selective incentives, which might be able to outweigh the costs associated with protest and reduce free riding. As we discuss in chapter 5, organizations became critical to social movements because they could facilitate the collection and strategic deployment of resources (and in doing so, fund selective incentives). In acknowledging how embedded costs are in resource mobilization, Jenkins's (1983, 528) review of the emerging approach argues that the first key tenet of resource mobilization is that "movement actions are rational, adaptive responses to the costs and rewards of different lines of action."

Beyond Resource Mobilization: Costs in Other Accounts of Collective Action

Later theoretical paradigms, such as the political process model, which is another dominant approach in social movement studies, largely agree that costs are important to explaining movements. Political process scholars take a different view from resource mobilization scholars in that, among other notions, they contend that resources are not the only necessary conditions for a movement to emerge and thrive, and that the needed resources can come from within disadvantaged communities so that social change need not be externally funded (McAdam 1982).

In addition to being important to several of the leading theoretical paradigms in social movement studies, costs are key to many other theoretical concepts and empirical findings. Starting at the individual level—the level that the free-rider dilemma was meant to speak to—it is clear that costs do impact participation decisions. For instance, a number of empirical studies have shown that people with more discretionary time—referred to as biographical availability—are more likely to participate in protest than those with less discretionary time (e.g., most significantly, Klandermans and Oegema 1987; see also McAdam 1986; Wiltfang and McAdam 1991; Hirsch 1990). Given that for participants (versus organizers), time has been one of the major known costs to movement participation, this finding can be interpreted as connected to costs: those who can afford to absorb the time costs of participation are more likely to participate.

Debates about the impacts of police or private action taken against protesters—often referred to as repression or protest control—also tend to center around how repression can raise the potential or real costs of participation. The motivating idea is that by making repression more likely, the state or other hostile actors may be able to discourage participation (see Davenport 2007; for more on this relationship, see Earl 2006a). Potential participants evaluate the risk of punishment, and then decide that they either cannot or do not want to bear the costs that punishment will bring (here, costs might be pecuniary like lost wages or nonpecuniary such as stress from police surveillance).

One can imagine that the impacts of costs on individual decision making about whether or not to participate in protest can also be aggregated up to the movement level. For instance, all other things being equal, one would expect that movements that are systematically associated with higher costs would either have lower participation rates, or would develop much stronger ways of offsetting or reducing those costs to ensure ample participation. As an example, the costs associated with being a Communist during the McCarthy years ensured that the Communist Party in the United States would wither. Similarly, substantial costs to African American civil rights participants (and some white participants as well) undoubtedly limited the overall rate of participation in the civil rights movement.

And there is little doubt that being associated with the Falun Gong in China, whether it is seen as a movement or a religion, is a taxing, and deterring, enterprise.

Even when costs are not associated with repression, they can affect movement trajectories. For instance, true adherence to animal rights principles is far more taxing than participation in many other movements, requiring large-scale changes to one's lifestyle in addition to participation in protests or other movement activities. The same could be said for many radical factions of larger mainstream movements.

Besides being useful for explaining overall movement trajectories, cost calculations can also be aggregated up to understand participation in large-scale protests or certain other kinds of tactics. For example, fewer people are willing and able to bear the costs to attend a march on Washington than are willing and able to assemble in their own towns. (But marches on Washington are still quite large because they pool the protesters from many towns who are able and willing to bear those costs.) It is likewise reasonable to believe that more people are willing to click to sign an online petition than are willing to go to a protest rally in their city because the cost structure is so relatively inexpensive for clicking. Survey data supports this assertion: while a relatively small percentage of Americans have attended a protest in the last year (4 percent), almost one in five Internet users have signed an online petition (Smith et al. 2009).

The costs associated with participation have also been used to explain the larger ebbs and flows of the overall levels of protest in a society, which is often referred to as a protest cycle. Sidney Tarrow (1994) is perhaps the scholar most associated with this concept. He argues that the United States and Western Europe were experiencing a peak in the protest cycle during the late 1960s and early 1970s, as evidenced by the large levels of overall protest activity at that time. In contrast, other historical moments are associated with low levels of protest activity, which represent valleys in the cycle. These trends in the level of protest activity, when plotted across time, look like a sine or cosine function that makes up the overall cycle of protest.

Costs are explicitly related to cycles of protest because they play an important role in explaining why protest may become increasingly frequent and help us understand the consequences of rampant protest for each new protester who might begin to participate. Tarrow (1994) contends that declines in costs associated with participation in protest can lead to an overall higher level of protest participation. Then, as more and more people protest, some of the nontime-related costs to protest decline even further. For instance, any potential stigma connected with being a protester is thought to decline as more and more people participate. Similarly, Tarrow maintains that the likelihood that any specific individual will personally experience repression also declines as protest becomes ever more frequent. As these costs decline, more and more people begin to participate, which in turn lowers the costs further, easing the obstacle to participation for even more people. This self-reinforcing positive relationship between participation and declining costs helps to fuel the development of peaks in cycles of protest.

Supersizing Participation

A supersized approach to participation argues that the fundamental dynamics of participation cannot be altered by innovative uses of the Web, but that the Web can be used to increase participation levels or diversify participation. Dana Fisher and her colleagues (2005), for instance, show that the Web and email, among other ICTs, can be used to help advertise and motivate participation. They see the Web as so clearly part and parcel of SMOs' standard outreach portfolio (albeit one that is cheap to use and broadly reaching) that they actually group people contacted through the Web by organizations with protesters informed through other organizational communications. Another way to think about it is that they lumped together what we would call e-mobilizations with entirely offline mobilizations. Dave Horton (2004) looks at the use of a range of ICTs among environmentalists. He doesn't find that ICT usage changes how people decide to participate in actions (usually of the form that we would call e-mobilizations) or that ICT usage changes the nature of their participation. Rather, he discovers that ICT use helps environmentalists to become more informed and connected, and assists them in managing multiple environmental commitments and forms of engagement at the same time.

Likewise, W. Lance Bennett (2003a, 2003b, 2004a, 2004b) discusses the Web in terms of what social movement scholars would call "mesomobilization," where SMOs are working to activate one another, and in doing so, are also working to activate the people associated with other SMOs. Bennett claims that this process is not fundamentally changed with the Web, and thus the groups are not fundamentally changed, but that they can use the Web and other ICTs to effectively create ephemeral coalitions that drive mobilization for a single, large event. In each of the above instances, ICT usage generally and Web usage specifically helps to foster participation. Yet the underlying processes are unaffected, and only e-mobilization cases are studied. In the next section, we investigate other kinds of Web activism that tell a different story about participation.

Theory 2.0 Participation

Although few social movement scholars have examined the relationship between costs and Web activism (save a few notable examples discussed below), there are a number of projects by Internet studies scholars that showcase the importance of costs to participation and hint at a theory 2.0 account of low-cost participation. For instance, Laura Gurak and John Logie (2003) describe resistance to a change in the Yahoo! policy governing content on GeoCities Web sites. Yahoo! altered its terms of use policy to imply that content hosted on GeoCities sites would, in effect, be Yahoo!'s to use as the company pleased. This roiled many longtime GeoCities users, who quickly organized collectively. Led by the blog entries of a particularly impassioned GeoCities user, GeoCities Web site operators who opposed the change began to gray out their pages in what they called "hauntings" to protest GeoCities. The goal was not to remove all content from GeoCities, which might have been effective in preserving the site operators' ownership of the posted content but would not have allowed potential visitors to learn about the dispute with the terms of usage. Instead, site owners made sites difficult to read but left readable notes explaining the haunting. Participating in the haunting was quite straight-forward and could be accomplished with small changes to the underlying HTML code of the Web sites. Since all of the site operators were already programming their own sites, modifying the HTML code did not represent a major burden. Faced with these hauntings, an online email campaign, and online petitions—all of which were relatively easy to participate in—Yahoo! quickly reversed course and modified its terms of use to resolve the dispute.

Gurak and Logie (2003; Gurak 1999) also look at similar battles against Lotus Marketplace, which was a product to be launched by Lotus in the 1990s that some privacy advocates felt went too far in compiling and selling personal data. Again, through relatively costless online actions such as emails and online petitions, a major product was halted before going to market. Yochai Benkler (2006) also explores the relatively low costs of some forms of online activism (although this is certainly not the focus of his work).

Perhaps the best-known organization engaged in online activism, MoveOn, is also one of the best examples of how quickly relatively costless participation can aggregate into truly effective collective action. After all,

MoveOn was born out of an online petition that its founders sent to friends, who sent it to their friends, who forwarded it on again until the petition to censure, but not impeach, President Clinton and then move on (hence, the name of the resulting organization) gathered over a half a million signatures. (It is worth noting that counterpetitions supporting the impeachment of President Clinton also took advantage of the relatively low cost of online petitioning as they gathered tens of thousands of signatures.)

Bennett and Fielding (1999) see a common trend in these kinds of examples, arguing that they are cases of five-minute activism. Drawing on the history of MoveOn, for instance, Bennett and Fielding contend that MoveOn represents a new model of mobilization in which small-time investments by participants allow scores more individuals to participate—and to do so quickly. Casting this model as flash activism, they make an analogy to flash floods where the power comes from the quick and massive level of water, which then quickly subsides. Here, Bennett and Fielding assert that the power of flash activism comes not from the expensiveness of the participation and people's willingness to bear great costs to partici-pate but rather from the massive influx of participation that is possible when the costs of participation are lowered enough that a much larger percentage of ideologically sympathetic individuals are willing to partici-pate. Importantly, in their—and our—use of the term five-minute activism there is no suggestion of a negative evaluation of this kind of protest as somehow less meaningful or impactful. Indeed, as we discuss later in this chapter, the efficacy of five-minute activism is an open question.

While most examples of relatively inexpensive activism online take the form of the e-tactics we examine in this book—online petitions, boycotts, and letter-writing and email campaigns—we do not want to suggest that other, more confrontational forms of activism online cannot also be used in five-minute activism campaigns. For instance, hacktivism involves the use of hacking-related techniques to disrupt an opponent's or target's Web site. Hacking, too, can be engineered to be quick and easy (although it can also be engineered to be time-consuming and difficult). Tim Jordan and Paul Taylor (2004), for instance, discuss the creation of FloodNet, which was a downloadable Web application designed to facilitate a distributed denial-of-service attack in a manner that diverges from standard denial-of-service attacks. Usually such attacks are undertaken by large, distributed botnets that are under the control of a much smaller number of program-mers. In those situations, attacks operate by having a large number of computers request that a targeted Web site refresh its Web page frequently.

When a large enough number of computers continue to make those frequent refresh requests, the target's server can be brought down. Because this can be done by a botnet that is controlled by a small number of individuals who are using infected computers, however, a standard distributed denial-of-service attack need not be a large collective effort.

FloodNet was designed to facilitate such a denial-of-service attack, but in contrast to standard denial-of-service attacks, it required users to download and launch the application as part of their participation. This was not a difficult requirement, but it did ensure that real people were behind each machine requesting repetitive refreshes, which was important to the software creators' vision of collective action and hacktivism. In fact, the creators wanted *people* to participate in the collective shutdown of targeted Web sites, not just their computers. While participation in such an attack could have negative legal implications for participants in the long run, in the short run and to those unaware of the potential legal implications, the action most likely seemed relatively costless, since it was easy to download the application and double click to launch it.

Five-minute activism obviously involves a different vision of social movement participation (as relatively costless) and collective mobilizations (as powerful but ephemeral) than the literature has historically embraced. But how can we explain it generally, or account for specific examples of flash activism? Gurak (1999) and Gurak and Logie (2003, 31) hold that there is an "instant-ethos" online that prizes speedy activity, and that standard hierarchies can be bypassed through the less intermediated design of the Web, also facilitating faster mobilization. Nevertheless, we think something else more fundamental than an ethos might be at work. We argue that when participation is relatively inexpensive, it is much easier to build high levels of mobilization in short periods of time. More pointedly, the instant-ethos that Gurak and Logie focus on might not exist without the ability to engage in relatively low-cost collective action.

Other research also supports our cost-based explanation. As noted in chapter 2, Bimber, Flanagin, and Stohl (2005) maintain that some kinds of collective action are so inexpensive that the free-rider dilemma may no longer apply. They actually go much further by asserting that the free-rider dilemma may be a "special case" that applies only when the production of public goods is expensive. In a related argument, Benkler (2006) posits that public goods are much easier to create online and are sometimes created without intention as searches transform people's private efforts into public goods. And certainly Bennett and Fielding (1999) were focused on the low-cost nature of online actions such as petition signing.

From this perspective, far from high-cost participation being the necessary theoretical and empirical norm, innovative uses of the Web can shift the balance of participation costs downward over time as more and more collective actions are conducted online. In turn, we would expect that more people would participate in these low-cost actions, and that like the cases discussed above, participation will tend to follow a flash flood model (although there are also reasons to believe that online participation will have a long tail, with small numbers of people still beginning to participate as they belatedly learn of the action).

If flash activism is here to stay, it is also crucial to understand the processes that might drive this kind of activism and, as scattered research suggests, the potential implications. First, Suzanne Brunsting and Tom Postmes (2002), who compare online and offline participation in activism, find that cognitive factors such as efficacy are more important predictors of online participation, whereas emotional returns might be important to offline participation but not online participation. Given that we are essentially arguing for a cost-benefit decision-making calculus where the costs of participation drop enough to make it affordable to the masses to participate, Brunsting and Postmes's emphasis on cognitive factors could be read as supporting our claims. We are not disputing that emotional motivators may matter at times and for some kinds of Web activism, but where five-minute activism is concerned we are contending that low participation costs are a large selling point and that lower amounts of efficacy may be required to agree to spend less than five minutes working on an issue you care about.

Others have asserted, though, that participation in collective endeavors (whether protest or not) might also be driven by the private passions of individuals who are physically and/or socially unknown to one another, but who can find common cause and engage in common action online. Shirky (2008), for instance, opens his book by discussing an online effort to secure the return of a lost cell phone that was in the possession of a purportedly new owner (under "finder's keepers" rules). To recover the phone, a Web-savvy friend of the original owner started a Web site. Through the involvement of hundreds of people, the original owner was able to gather substantial information about the new owner of the phone and gain insight into how to effectively pressure the New York Police Department to get involved in retrieving it. Shirky's argument more generally is that open online forums allow people who are passionate about an issue to contribute their time when they have time to do so. So people who were interested in this case and passionate about it for a variety of reasons (they too had lost a phone, were upset by the story, found the detective work interesting, etc.) came together out of those disparate as well as sometimes idiosyncratic motivations to work on a collective project. And as Shirky critically points out, there are many people who are passionate about many things, leading to a wide diversity of online collective efforts. We maintain that this is true, but stress that it is the lowered price point of some kinds of online engagement that facilitates the transition from private passion to public action.

In line with the research discussed in this section, we argue that participation is influenced by lower costs and that some uses of the Web can lower the costs of participation, pointing to two related questions, which we take up below. First we ask, In what ways can and do online actions leverage the cost affordance of the Web? Second, we consider the implications of these findings for supersize and theory 2.0 visions of protest on the Web.

It Doesn't All Cost the Same

A central premise of the leveraged affordances approach is that the Web affords the possibility of dramatically reduced costs of participation for certain kinds of collective actions. Further, even though many Web sites enjoy cheaper costs for information distribution and education, we are arguing that only some Web sites offer actions that take advantage of this cost structure for participation in collective actions. Our empirical analyses allow us to sketch the variety of these sites and examine the frequency with which sites actually design actions that leverage the participation-related cost affordance of the Web.

Among the costs most frequently associated with protest participation are those of time and money, both of which can be substantially reduced when an action takes place online. For example, a protest action that is completed entirely from one's computer such as signing an online petition requires absolutely no marginal monetary spending by the participant. The computer, Internet connection, and physical space where the computer is located are being paid for regardless of whether the user signs the online petition, so participation is effectively free. And there are no transportation or housing costs incurred specifically in relation to the petition.

The time costs of some online actions are also often incredibly low, particularly compared to the hours (or sometimes days) usually demanded for entirely offline protest actions and even e-mobilizations. With the online facilitation of participation, participating in an e-tactic can take just a few minutes. Moreover, the flexibility afforded by the asynchronous participation format of an online action means that the time cost to the participant can be reduced to even lower levels. Unlike most entirely offline tactics and e-mobilizations, the online petition that a user signs is available any time of day, any day of the week. Users can participate at the most convenient time for them, rather than be required to work around a specific schedule. This flexibility reduces the impact of the time spent participating in the action on the participant. In turn, this suggests that the volume of discretionary time that potential participants have available (i.e., biographical availability) may be less important for participation in online actions.

In the next two sections, we look at two aspects of the e-tactics in our data set to illustrate how protest actions leverage—to varying degrees—the low-cost affordance of the Web. First, we analyze the extent to which the actual participation in these protest actions (versus an initial introduction to the action) takes place online. Second, we explore how much work the participant must do to complete the action compared to how much the Web site facilitates through back-end or server-side programs.

Looking at these two characteristics of e-tactics together, we show first how each can dramatically reduce the costs of activism, supporting findings in the literature, and second, that e-tactics vary in how fully they take advantage of these means to lower the costs of activism. Significantly, while online actions hold the potential to reduce the costs of activism, we find that not all e-tactics take full advantage of this possibility and the reduction in costs for online actions turns out to vary markedly.

Virtual Participation

Although all online protest actions require a degree of online access, not all need an Internet connection for the duration of participation. While some actions, for example, require an Internet connection for the entirety of a user's participation, others are largely advertised online but the bulk of their participation takes place away from the Web. We think of where an individual action falls on this continuum as a measure of how "virtual" the participation is.

We argue that actions that are, in our terminology, "more virtual" better leverage the cost affordance for participants because these actions usually require the least time and effort to complete (unless your Internet connection goes down). An email can be dashed off in just minutes, and an entirely online petition can be signed in seconds. More important, participation in these sorts of highly virtual actions can be completed immediately after one learns of the action; the time spent learning about and participating in the e-tactic can be quite small, and thus of marginal cost to the participant. In contrast, actions that users learn about online that require some offline participation are likely to necessitate more time and effort, and thereby be more costly to the participant.

We measured how virtual participation in e-tactics in our data set was by assessing the extent to which an Internet connection was required for participation—that is, How much of one's actual participation could be completed even if the Internet connection went down? Individual e-tactics such as emails where an Internet connection was required for all of the participation were coded as entirely online. Similarly, a boycott of a Web business such as Amazon.com would be coded as fully virtual, and a petition that a user signs by emailing the petition author would likewise be considered an exclusively online action.

Actions where most of the participation, but not all, required an Internet connection were coded as mostly online. For example, a letter-writing campaign that formatted a letter online based on a user's entered contact information but still required the user to print, sign, and mail the letter would be considered as mostly online.[2]

Other e-tactics were coded as mostly offline. For example, a boycott of a business with physical stores may be advertised online (perhaps even exclusively online), but the bulk of participation in this action takes place offline in the form of not making purchases at the actual locations. There is still an undeniable online component even though most of the participation takes place offline: without the Web, participants would not know of this action. Unlike a rally or other offline actions, a potential participant cannot physically stumble into a boycott (the same could be said of all of the other e-tactics in our sample for that matter, which is why none of the e-tactics were coded as entirely offline).

From Emails to Boycotts: Strong to Weak Leveraging

Turning to the specifics of our data, we find two major trends in the virtual component of individual e-tactics. First, we find that e-tactical forms themselves have certain tendencies in the extent to which their participation takes place online. All of the email campaigns in our sample, for instance, required entirely online participation since the format of the communication itself was Internet dependent. In some cases, this meant that potential participants needed only to enter their personal information and click "send" to have the site email a prewritten message to the target, as with an email campaign to save the Arctic National Wildlife Refuge that had a prewritten message that users could sign and send by entering their contact information into fields on the Web page.[3] In other cases, users were asked to copy and paste a message into their own email provider and send it, as with an email campaign targeting the National Park Service's director with a request that a book offering a creationist history of the Grand Canyon be sold in National Park Service gift shops.[4] The site offered the text of the email and the target's email address; with a few clicks, participants could complete the action. Finally, some email campaigns explained their claim and published the target's email address, but asked users to compose their own message using their own email provider. An email campaign calling for the government of Bangladesh to release four prisoners of conscience, for example, provided extensive background on the issue and asked users to email a "personal appeal" to the target.[5] Nonetheless, participants could draft and send this personal appeal without straying from their computers, rendering even this slightly more involved action, along with all other email campaigns, low in terms of time costs.

At the opposite end of the spectrum, boycotts never took place entirely or even mostly online in our sample. Although we had anticipated boycotts of online stores such as Amazon.com, 100 percent of the boycotts we found targeted offline businesses or other offline organizations. It is worth noting, though, that some boycotts on warehouse sites occasionally included additional online participation, but it was usually described as optional. For instance, on boycott warehouse sites like KarmaBanque and BoycottCity, users could sign up online for a boycott, thereby registering their participation and support. On KarmaBanque's home page, users were welcomed with the statement that "you don't need guns or money to destroy American companies—and the environmental catastrophes they thrive on."[6] Instead, the site encouraged the use of boycotts to compel companies to change their business practices. As a warehouse site, Karma-Banque allowed activists to post their own boycotts, complete with detailed descriptions of why the particular company was being targeted. For example, one poster called for a boycott of Wal-Mart for its failure to meet human rights and labor standards.[7] In addition to reading an explanation for the boycott, site visitors could add their own reasons for the boycott in a forum posted below the original boycott text. Further, visitors could create an account with the site—in just ten seconds, promised the site— and officially "join" the boycott. While participation in the boycott, strictly speaking, only required individuals to refrain from shopping at Wal-Mart, they could register this participation online through KarmaBanque.

BoycottCity, too, allowed users to join boycotts, with the added feature of permitting registered users to also "drop" boycotts.[8] While KarmaBanque just listed the number of registered participants in any given boycott, BoycottCity allowed site visitors to search among registered accounts. One could see which boycotts a given user had authored and/or joined. Among the top 10 "most boycotting" registered site users, the number of authored and/or joined boycotts ranged from a high of 37 to a low of 13 of the approximately 575 available boycotts.

Of course, registration was not inherently required to participate in boycotts on either site, and judging from the levels of registration, was not a commonly used feature. On BoycottCity, the boycott with the highest number of registered participants boasted only 59 joiners, and most of the boycotts on the site could claim fewer than 5 registered participants. Similarly, on KarmaBanque most boycotts registered fewer than 10 participants, with two outliers listing over 100 participants. In contrast, among petitions in our sample, an e-tactical form in which registered participation (i.e., signatures) is integral to participation, we found only four instances where participation numbers were reported that had fewer than 10 signers while six listed over 100,000 signers, including one with 375,420 signatures.[9]

Because these online components of KarmaBanque and BoycottCity boycotts were supplementary rather than integral to participation, boycott registration processes increase the time that participants spend. This poorly leverages the cost affordance of Internet-enabled technologies by increasing the costs of participation, at least compared to other online boycotts. And significantly, this increased time is ephemeral to a participant's decision not to buy particular products or shop at specific stores. Therefore, we think it is possible that this form of online participation and these sorts of registered online boycotts themselves will become less common or even disappear over time.

Petitioning, faxing, and letter-writing campaigns, meanwhile, included individual instances of both entirely online participation and mostly offline participation (see figure 4.1). For example, we found a letter-writing campaign targeting the governor of Florida with an appeal to change the state's laws banning gays and lesbians from adopting children for which participation could be completed entirely online.[10] The site provided an editable letter that participants could populate with their personal information by completing a series of fields on the Web page. The site itself took care of delivering the letter, so a user could learn about and complete this action in just minutes, without leaving the computer.

Nonwarehouse petitions

Mostly offline
17%

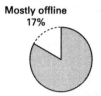

Entirely online
83%

Warehouse petitions

Mostly online
>1%

Entirely online
100%

Nonwarehouse letters

Entirely online
9%

Mostly online
1%

Mostly offline
90%

Warehouse letters

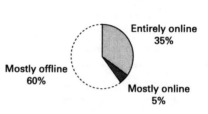

Entirely online
35%

Mostly offline
60%

Mostly online
5%

Nonwarehouse faxes

Entirely online
9%

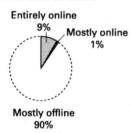

Mostly offline
91%

Warehouse faxes

Mostly offline
100%

Figure 4.1
Extent of online participation in three e-tactical forms.

Some faxes, too, enabled entirely online participation, as was the case for a fax campaign calling for the protection of overtime pay laws.[11] The site promised to fax an editable message to the U.S. president on behalf of participants after they entered their personal information, without requiring them to complete any part of the action offline. (Though here, as elsewhere, we caution readers to not put too much weight on fax-related findings since we did not collect and code an independent sample of faxes; for further discussion, see the appendix).

For petitions, the PetitionOnline examples we have already looked at are prime cases of entirely online petitions. That said, plenty of petitions found on nonwarehouse sites also enabled users to complete all of their participation immediately and entirely online. On a nonwarehouse site calling for the impeachment of the U.S. attorney general, for instance, interested users could simply populate a series of fields with their contact information and click the "Submit Petition" button to sign the petition, thereby completing all of their participation online.[12]

In contrast, participation in other instances of these three e-tactical forms took place mostly offline. This was true for a letter-writing campaign calling on the director of the U.S. Commission on International Religious Freedom to support Muslims' right to complete religious journeys to Jerusalem.[13] The Web page laid out its claim and listed the target's mailing address, but the remainder of the participation in this e-tactic could take place without an Internet connection. Participants had to compose, sign, and mail the letter on their own. Similarly, some petitions required participants to print and physically sign the petition, and most fax campaigns asked participants to print, sign, and fax the message themselves, all of which are offline activities. This was true of a fax campaign lobbying a governor to grant clemency to a prisoner on death row.[14]

Although petitions, faxes, and letter-writings campaigns all included individual e-tactics with different degrees of virtualness, figure 4.1 shows that there are nonetheless trends by e-tactical form in how much participation happens online. Specifically, most petitions facilitated entirely online participation (over 80 percent on both warehouse and nonwarehouse sites), while far fewer letter-writing and fax campaigns did so (less than 35 percent of letter-writing campaigns and under 10 percent of fax campaigns on both nonwarehouse and warehouse sites). In other words, the bulk of the petitions in our sample facilitated entirely online participation, just as the attorney general impeachment petition and PetitionOnline petitions described above did. The majority of letter-writing and fax campaigns, meanwhile, required users to complete large portions of their participation offline. For the most part, as with the letter-writing campaign in support of Muslims' ability to complete religious journeys to Jerusalem as well as the fax campaign urging clemency for a prisoner on death row, that offline participation included printing, signing, and delivering the protest messages. For letters, this meant putting the message in the mail; for faxes, it entailed sending the fax to the target.

These findings suggest that all e-tactical forms may not be equivalent in the practice of leveraging the cost affordance, and perhaps even in their ability to leverage this affordance. As our data show, all email campaigns highly leveraged the cost affordance in that email campaigns allowed users to complete their participation immediately and to do so entirely online. This makes sense given that emails have appeared in most of the case studies of flash activism that exist. In Bennett and Fielding's study of MoveOn (1999), for example, and their development of the flash activism model, emails figure prominently. Emails exemplify a means of participation where the costs are so low, in both time and money, that more of the individuals already sympathetic to a cause are willing to participate. In their structure, emails can easily leverage the cost affordance of Internet-enabled technologies, and the data prove that they do.

Petitions, too, have a high rate of leveraging the cost affordance of the Web by facilitating entirely online participation that, again, is consistent with findings from case studies. Research on campaigns against private companies has pointed to the speed with which petitions have been mounted and their success in garnering significant levels of participation rapidly (Gurak 1999; Gurak and Logie 2003). Our finding of the highly virtual nature of participation on the significant majority of nonwarehouse petitions and nearly all warehouse petitions offers further evidence of petitioning as an e-tactical form that can and does leverage the cost affordance. Letters and faxes, on the other hand, are a mixed bag, with some individual e-tactics leveraging the cost affordance through entirely online participation, but many more that did not.

Finally, boycotts were the least likely to leverage the cost affordance through online participation. Even with the rise of e-commerce, boycotts require the most offline participation and therefore benefit the least from the cost affordances of the Web for participants. In our data, no boycott facilitated entirely online participation, and even the online aspects of participation they did facilitate are dubious in their ability to lessen the costs of participation to potential participants, as we suggested above in our discussion of KarmaBanque and BoycottCity. Boycotts may still benefit from cost affordances for organizers, though, which is the subject of the next chapter.

The Warehouse Difference

Turning to the second trend in the data, we also found that warehouse petitions and letter-writing campaigns were more often completed entirely online than their nonwarehouse counterparts. Nonwarehouse petitions, for example, could be completed entirely online 83 percent of the time (see figure 4.1). The occasions where a nonwarehouse petition required some offline action usually asked participants to print out the petition and gather in-person signatures, as with a petition to be delivered to the government of China in support of Chinese citizens' right to practice Falun Gong.[15] Their warehouse counterparts, on the other hand, allowed for exclusively or mostly online participation an incredible 100 percent of the time. On warehouse sites, users could sign petitions to protest the death penalty in the United States, contest the implementation of certain local traffic laws, or make a claim about animal cruelty in India, all without leaving their computer.[16]

In a similar pattern, although letter-writing campaigns were less frequently structured to allow entirely online participation than not, warehouse letter-writing campaigns were entirely online over four times more often (at 35 percent of the time) than nonwarehouse letter-writing campaigns (at only 9.5 percent of the time). As in the campaign above in support of Muslims' right to make religious journeys to Jerusalem, over 90 percent of nonwarehouse letter-writing campaigns required participants to print, sign, and deliver—usually via an envelope and stamp—the letters themselves. Warehouse letter-writing campaigns, in contrast, offered entirely online participation 35 percent of the time, such as a letter requesting clemency for a prisoner on death row.[17] For this campaign, participants entered their contact information and any personal message entirely online, and the site took care of the letter's delivery.

We understand this increase in the portion of highly virtual actions on warehouse sites, compared to nonwarehouse ones, as an effect of warehouse sites' specialization in online protest. Warehouse sites, after all, are structured as clearinghouses for activism, often in the form of a particular kind of e-tactic, and are designed to facilitate participation in activism. As relative specialists in specific formats for action, it is understandable that warehouse sites would develop and implement, on average, more advanced ways to leverage a cost affordance.

But a notable exception to this suggests that specialization and innovation may nonetheless be bounded by costs. A slim 9 percent of faxes found on nonwarehouse sites could be completed entirely online, and none of the handful of fax campaigns we found on warehouse sites could, keeping in mind, though, that none of the warehouse sites in our data collection specialized in fax campaigns (i.e., the fax campaigns we found were on sites that otherwise did not specialize in fax campaigns). Thinking about the expense required in coordinating a fax campaign entirely online—as opposed to collecting signatures for a petition—makes this a less surprising finding. Fully online fax campaigns require a delivery system designed to reach a terminal fax machine over a phone line. While it is possible to circumvent the requirement for an originating fax machine through software that initiates a fax from the Web, sites that send faxes on behalf of participants still internalize the costs of the fax. This cost is sensitive to even marginal differences in participation levels, unlike back-end database software that drives online petitioning, for instance, which does not cost noticeably more to run and operate with each additional signature. It may simply be that few warehouses sites are interested in investing, or able to do so, in forms of action that are relatively more expensive to produce. Of course, given that we did not independently sample for faxes, it is possible that this trend is true only of faxes that co-occur with our other e-tactics and that the larger explanation we offer about faxes would not hold up in the face of better data on faxing.

Automating Protest

We also assessed whether the sites and e-tactics we studied further reduced the time cost to participants by facilitating participation through automation. At the most facilitated end, e-tactics required participants to simply fill in their contact information, and then the Web site populated and completed the action (e.g., sent the email); we coded these e-tactics as "automated" since the e-tactic hosts took care of key parts of participation, including ensuring that the petition reached its target. By using technology that took care of the back end of participation, including populating fields in a protest letter or adding electronic signatures to a petition, online actions further reduced the amount of time that participation takes. Participation really can take just five minutes, and sometimes even less, rendering biographical availability of minor importance to participation. We argue that actions that offer more automation better leverage the cost affordance for participants, principally by allowing the action to be completed more quickly.

E-tactics where most, but not all, of the participation was automated were also observed and were coded as semiautomated. In these cases, the tactic host took care of some elements of participation even though the remainder fell to the participant to complete. Included in this category would be a letter-writing campaign where the Web page formatted the letter with the user's submitted personal information, but still required the user to print, sign, and mail the letter.

We also observed e-tactics where nearly all of the action was completed by the participants themselves (e.g., composing, signing, and sending a fax), which we coded as not automated. These actions poorly leverage the cost affordance that we focus on.

From Petitions to Boycotts: Strong to Weak Leveraging

Variation in automation was present across the five different forms that we report on in figure 4.2. According to the data, participation was more frequently automated in some e-tactical forms (i.e., petitions) than in others (i.e., boycotts), illustrating variation in how thoroughly e-tactics take advantage of the automation facility of the Web. Petitions were the most frequently automated e-tactical form with over three-quarters of them on both warehouse and nonwarehouse sites automated. The e-tactic hosts made participation in these petitions easy. To sign on to a petition in support of affirmative action in Michigan, for example, participants needed only to type in and submit their name, city, and state.[18] The same held true for all of the petitions on the warehouse site ThePetitionSite; participation was fully automated such that interested individuals only had to enter their contact information and click a submit button in order to sign a petition.

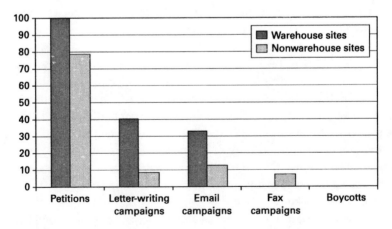

Figure 4.2
Percentage of e-tactics with some automation of participation.

Of course, server-side databases that are used to automate the petition signature and aggregation functions of Web sites are fairly well-known, with databases implemented on a wide variety of Web sites. In the next chapter we discuss how this may impact the costs of protest to organizers, but here we note that it is possible that the relative ease of database jobs such as petition signature handling increases the rate at which this e-tactical form is likely to be augmented by automation. The ease of participation through automation that signature-gathering sites like PetitionOnline afford helps to buoy engagement.

Boycotts, on the other hand, were never automated, on either warehouse or nonwarehouse sites. As an example, to protest Citibank's treatment of the rain forest, individuals were encouraged to boycott the financial institution.[19] Such a boycott meant that participants had to close any accounts with the bank and refrain from purchasing any of its services. Practically speaking, there is not a way to automate participation in such a boycott, and so like all other boycotts in our sample, the Citibank one was not at all automated. Given that boycott participation in our sample never required an Internet connection to complete because it involved withholding obligations to offline organizations, or avoiding a particular physical store, brand, or product, it is not surprising that ways of automating that participation would prove impossible. Importantly, though, this means that relative to other e-tactical forms, boycotts face a double disadvantage in terms of leveraging affordances to lower the costs of participation.

Email, letter-writing, and fax campaigns tended to fall in between these two poles, with at least some implementations that automated participation (see figure 4.2). For example, participation was entirely automated in an email campaign to protect the buffalo in Yellowstone National Park.[20] The Web page formatted the email to address the participant's senator and congressional representative, and supplied a prewritten message, requiring only the participant's personal information to complete the tactic. The site even delivered the email, meaning that the participant did not need to have an email provider in order to participate.

There were similar examples of fully automated participation among letter-writing campaigns. On the American Conservative Union's Web site, for instance, visitors could send a letter to their congressional representative in support of medical liability reform.[21] The target's address and the message itself were provided by the site, leaving interested participants able to entirely complete the e-tactic by simply typing in their names. Participation, in this case, was fully automated.

Fax campaigns, too, were sometimes fully automated. One could participate in a fax campaign in support of fair trade coffee that targeted Starbucks by entering contact information and clicking the submit button.[22] The site took care of all the other elements of the e-tactic, including presumably delivering the fax itself.

These cases, however, constituted a minority of the instances of these three e-tactical forms on both warehouse and nonwarehouse sites; as we can see in figure 4.2, most email, letter-writing, and fax campaigns were not automated. Email campaigns tended to follow the form of a campaign to free journalists in foreign jails where the claim was made and an email address listed, but participation was not further facilitated.[23] Similarly, most letter-writing and fax campaigns, as figure 4.2 shows, were not automated.

While these examples from our data chart differences in the degree to which an e-tactic is automated, there is an even more highly automated form of participation on the horizon: one-click actions. As we briefly mentioned in chapter 3, there were three e-tactics in our sample that through a simple click of the mouse, enabled the participant to engage in two distinct actions at one time. In actions such as these, by checking a box on the Web page, participants could elect to have the same message delivered to a target via two e-tactical forms (e.g., as an email and a letter), effectively completing two actions with the same amount of effort that it takes to complete just one. And with the additional possibility we floated in the previous chapter of Web sites enabling users to register for participation in *future* actions that have not yet been developed about a cause they sympathize with, we can see how Web sites have the potential to leverage the cost affordance even further. Imagine that you could sign up as an opponent of genetically modified food on a site, and then direct the site to send an email or sign a petition on your behalf for any campaign—now or in the future—protesting genetically modified food. For literally no added cost, you would be able to register your support for the claim repeatedly.

The Warehouse Difference Redux
As with the findings on the extent to which participation took place online, in looking at the frequency with which e-tactics were automated, we find variation between e-tactics on warehouse and nonwarehouse sites for each e-tactical form (save for boycotts, which were never automated). As we can see in figure 4.2, for all but fax campaigns, warehouse implementations were more often automated than their nonwarehouse versions.

Warehouse petitions, for example, were automated 99.8 percent of the time, while nonwarehouse petitions were automated a still-high 79 percent of the time. A similar 20 percent gap was found between the percentage of warehouse email campaigns that were automated (33 percent) and the percentage of nonwarehouse automated email campaigns (13 percent). The difference between automation rates for nonwarehouse and warehouse letter-writing campaigns was even more substantial, with just 8.5 percent of nonwarehouse letter-writing campaigns automated compared to 40 percent of warehouse letter-writing campaigns.

As with the higher degree of entirely virtual participation on warehouse sites than nonwarehouse sites, an explanation for this finding likely lies with the clearinghouse nature of warehouse sites: they are explicitly designed to make participation in protest easy. Insofar as automation decreases the costs of participation, as we've argued, it makes participation in protest easier and can help warehouse sites facilitate efficient participation in advocacy on a large scale. The volume of protest that warehouse sites usually support may also encourage them to automate participation.

Fax campaigns are again the exception to this trend (see figure 4.2), but likely also because of their technological complexity (or because all of the examples of warehouse fax campaigns occurred on warehouse sites devoted to other e-tactical forms, like petitioning, or a broad cause, since we did not generate an independent sample of faxes as with the other e-tactics that we study). While 7.5 percent of nonwarehouse faxes were fully automated, none of the faxes found on warehouse sites were at all automated. As noted above, there are many back-end elements of a fax campaign, including sending a fax over a phone line to a fax machine, and their automation is likely more complex than compiling a database. In contrast, a petition has relatively few back-end actions—a site only needs to be able to capture and store signatures—and as such is more easily automated. It therefore makes sense that fax campaigns would be the least commonly automated (aside from boycotts) and that petitions would be the most commonly automated. And further, it follows that warehouse sites would be less likely to invest in the automation of this e-tactical form thanks to fax campaigns' back-end complexity.

Connecting Costs to Online Participation and Automation

As this chapter has shown, there is substantial theoretical reason to believe that participation is driven higher by lower participation costs. We have contended that when participation can occur online, participation will generally be less costly and thus should spur flash-style mobilizations in which large numbers of people participate (and typically in short and episodic intervals, according to the existing research). There is also ample anecdotal evidence from the literature to support this at a general level, whether from strategic voting during the 2000 election (Earl and Schussman 2003), campaigns against major corporations (Gurak 1999; Gurak and Logie 2003), or the birth of major flash activism organizations like MoveOn (Bennett and Fielding 1999). In fact, Deana Rohlinger, Leslie Bunnage, and Jordan Brown's interviews with MoveOn members (2009) suggest that the ease of participation is critical to the participation of many. They also found that biographical availability seemed to matter less in the face of low-cost forms of participation, just as we predicted.

While we don't have interview data for participants in the actions we studied that would allow us to replicate Rohlinger, Bunnage, and Brown's findings (2009), we believe that their results would hold for the actions we studied, too. We can, however, take advantage of variation in the leveraging of the cost affordance and to a limited extent see whether it impacted participation. Specifically, since e-tactics that include a relatively larger share of online participation and more automation are better at reducing costs than those that require more offline participation and have less automation, we expect participation in these ultra-low-cost actions to be highest. Although, as we discuss in chapter 6, many sites (particularly nonwarehouse ones) do not report on participation values (meaning that we can only assess participation rates when they are reported), our data do show that greater virtualness and automation pay off in terms of participation. For nonwarehouse sites, the average number of participants for entirely online actions was 45,726.[24] Warehouse sites demonstrated more variation in participation: of entirely online warehouse e-tactics, participation ranged from a low of 3 to a high of 317,299, with a mean of 9,664 participants.[25] Participation values for the few e-tactics on either warehouse or nonwarehouse sites for which participation was not fully online were much lower.

For automation, there was no variation for warehouse sites because all warehouse sites that reported participation were also automated (for reasons that we speculate about in later chapters). That said, participation in these e-tactics was impressive: a mean of 9,628 participants. For nonwarehouse sites, acknowledging that there are only a few cases to compare, the 19 nonwarehouse e-tactics that reported participation and were fully automated had a mean participation of over 33,000, while the mean was only about 750 participants for the less than fully automated nonware-house e-tactics.[26]

We will have more to say about why participation may be so infrequently tracked and/or reported as well as the potential consequences of this phenomenon in chapter 6, but for now, and acknowledging the substantial limitations caused by the lack of participation reporting, our findings are consistent with our expectations and the anecdotal evidence available from case studies of flash activism. In short, facilitating greater online participation and greater automation appears to make a difference.

Indeed, we think that it makes a big difference, even though we have tried to acknowledge any major qualifications to our findings. Consider, for instance, our numbers compared to estimates of offline participation. While we do not have comparable figures for 2004, when our data was collected, Sarah Soule and Earl (2005) examined the participation rates in offline protest such as rallies and marches from 1960 to 1986 in the United States. Their data suggest that protests with fewer than 100 participants dominate offline collective action; in only three years did the percentage of protests with fewer than 100 people drop below 50 percent of all protests, and then only into the 40s (and it went as high as almost 90 percent of all recorded street protests in one year). Moderately sized protests (those with 100–9,999 participants in Soule and Earl's study) made up most of the rest of protests in each year, with only a few percent of these actions having mobilizations of 10,000 participants or greater. They do show that the mean size of mobilizations grew across time, to a mean of 4,350 participants per protest across all protests in the 1980–1986 period (the last period for which they report data), but they also find that there were fewer overall protests. This indicates that participation became concentrated in fewer actions. Our average participation is much higher, and we offer evidence of a prolific online protest sector in which participation is not concentrated into a few large mobilizations but instead spread over a range of mobilizations.

Revisiting Supersizing versus Theory 2.0 Explanations

We outlined some differences between supersize and theory 2.0 expectations earlier in the chapter. Having the benefit of digging into the e-tactic data more, we can go further in understanding the differences between supersize and theory 2.0 approaches to participation. Supersized activism would include the continued relevance of factors like biographical availability and, more fundamentally, the continuing relevance of higher costs to participation decisions. We have argued that some ways of designing e-tactics can powerfully leverage the cost-reducing affordance of Internet-enabled technologies, allowing for much lower costs to participation than ever seen before.

Where cost reductions were substantial, we anticipated flash-style activism that includes larger participation and would be unlikely to be affected by classic factors such as biographical availability. These are theory 2.0 changes. While our data do not contain participant surveys or interviews, we do have data on how much cost affordances were leveraged, and to a lesser extent on the participation that those lower costs garnered. Even with some data limitations, we think that the opposing theoretical claim to ours—that five-minute activism would be bound by things like biographical availability in the same way that attendance at a march might be—is a hard claim to make in light of our findings.

Our leveraged affordances approach suggests that this kind of powerful leveraging will not be ubiquitous, although we do believe that e-tactics as a category leverage these affordances better than e-mobilizations. Among e-tactics, we expected that the leveraging would vary, too, with some e-tactics powerfully leveraging cost-reducing potential and others poorly leveraging that potential. Our data confirm all of this, and to a limited degree (because of nonreporting on Web sites), we find a link between overall participation and leveraging of these affordances.

The Participant and the Activist

Another shift that we might expect to see in how people engage in protest is foreshadowed in the language we've used throughout this chapter. We have talked about the people who complete these e-tactics as participants, and sometimes as users or site visitors. This is in contrast to the term often used in relation to offline activism: activist. While we do not have data on how end users think of themselves as they engage in these online actions, we have noted significant differences in the process of completing an e-tactic compared to participating in an offline action. It is not a stretch to surmise that the experience of the individual who signs an online petition or participates in an email campaign might be different from that of an attendee at a rally or march. They may be more like users than like protesters, which Earl and Schussman (2003) first suggested in their study of an e-movement. With that in mind, we have opted not to migrate, whole scale, terminology from offline protest to describe those petition signers and email senders. Instead, we have used the dually more cautious and expansive term participant to describe them.

This looser sense of connection and commitment might also mean that participation can vary over time more readily. Rohlinger, Bunnage, and Brown (2009), for instance, found in their interviews with MoveOn participants that over time, people's level of activity varied quite substantially. Specifically, because respondents did not feel like they had to be all in or all out, their activity could rise and fall. Importantly, Rohlinger, Bunnage, and Brown (2009) actually found this to be a source of robustness for MoveOn: since people felt able to turn on and off their participation over time, they did not feel that they had to entirely exit the organization when they were unable to regularly participate. In our account, this kind of behavior, coupled with the organizing dynamics that we discuss in later chapters, can create sharp rises in participation, sporadic participation, and/or episodic participation.

It is, of course, an open question whether there is a meaningful difference between a participant and an activist on other levels. Some longtime activists might dispute characterizing online participants as activists, noting the ease of online participation, just as we have highlighted above. For some, activism might have to be difficult, by definition, and entail confrontation and hardship. Sending a letter by entering your name on a Web site and clicking a button might just be too easy to qualify as activism; it might be seen as, at best, lazy activism. And yet, others might view these differences as existing along a continuum of activist identity.

Whatever the case, the differences in the process of online activism and the likely differences in the experience of online activism, compared to offline activism, suggest that scholars' theories about who participates in activism of any kind and why might require revision. That is, the potential difference between a participant and an activist calls for theory 2.0.

Skeptics Corner: Do Low-Cost Actions "Matter"?

There are still several open questions that bear on the implications of our arguments and findings, though. First, and perhaps most important, a skeptical reader might say, "Even if I stipulate to the above arguments and findings, high levels of participation in low-cost actions do not influence protest targets and are not likely to be successful." Our skeptical reader would be getting at the heart of a common reaction that many social movement scholars and activists have to low-cost, online forms of engagement: even if people are engaging in them in large numbers and in larger numbers than they are engaging in offline protest, these actions still "don't matter" or "aren't important."

Ours is not a study on the effectiveness of e-tactics, and so although we are aware of many successful online campaigns, including efforts in our data set, we cannot empirically address this claim with any certainty beyond going toe-to-toe with cases that show a success for each of our skeptic's examples of failure. Given that, we take this open empirical question as an opportunity to think through our skeptic's contention as well as the implications of our own assertions in more detail.

First, our skeptic's claim has a crucial, embedded assumption: targets of protest measure their reaction and weigh the significance of a protest based on the costliness of the participation. Indeed, it is the almost-effortless nature of highly facilitated e-tactics that make our skeptic so pessimistic about their impact. But if this assumption were true, the most effective of all forms of protest would be something like civil disobedience, which requires substantial effort, or individual or collective acts that hurt the body, such as standing up in the face of a repressive force (think of the student standing in front of the Chinese tank in Tiananmen Square), hunger strikes, or self-immolation.

And yet, there is no suggestion that this is true in the social movement literature on "movement outcomes." Rather, according to Verta Taylor and Nella Van Dyke's review of the literature on tactics and consequences (2004), things that might be as true of classic street protests as of our e-tactics, such as novelty, have been shown to influence effectiveness. Also, things that would be more common among some kinds of street protest than most Web protest—such as disruptiveness—have been found to both increase and decrease effectiveness, leading to no clear evidence of an advantage for street versus online actions. The same could be said of culturally resonant tactics. The size of mobilizations has been shown to affect effectiveness as well, which would presumably give our flash activists an advantage, but most of that research is based on conventional street protest.

Our skeptic has another embedded assumption that reveals a somewhat dirty secret about offline protest: our skeptic assumes that offline protest is effective and that researchers can show that conclusively. To the contrary, empirically documenting the causal influence of protest on policy (Giugni 1998; Earl 2000; Amenta and Caren 2004) or culture (Earl 2004) is notoriously hard. While some have demonstrated that various combinations of factors matter (e.g., as Edwin Amenta and Neal Caren have shown of the Townsend Movement; for a summary, see Amenta and Caren 2004), empirically evidencing the effects of major movements or specific protests is a tricky business. By failing to acknowledge the real state of the literature, our skeptic has unfairly set the comparison bar higher than is empirically known. It might be fairer to say that the consequences of both conventional street protest and e-tactics are relatively unknown at this point.

Another way to approach this issue might be to ask whether there is some meaningful middle ground between skepticism and faithful optimism. For instance, are there some efforts for which short blasts of action might be quite effective at achieving the goal, even if other campaigns or movements might have goals that are longer term in nature, and therefore might be presumed to require more enduring mobilizations (either through classic street organizing or e-mobilizations)? We have noticed that a large number of case studies of successful e-tactics have been about opposing a particular decision or policy (Gurak and Logie's research [2003] is a perfect example, as is Carty quotation from a Nike representative [2002] discussing the impact of a Web campaign on Nike's decision making). Opposition to a specific decision or efforts to stop a specific thing may well benefit more from flash activism than campaigns aimed at longer-term and more consistent changes to individual behavior or larger government or corporate policies. Instead of indicting all Web protest, we encourage our skeptic to ask what kinds of efforts might decisively benefit from powerful bursts of participation.

We would also note that our skeptic may not have noticed some of the other potential advantages of e-tactics. For instance, David Liben-Nowell and Jon Kleinberg's study of online petition signing (2008) suggests that petitions continued to circulate despite rather large levels of nonparticipation. But because so many people were exposed to the online petitions, the petition could still gather signatures quite successfully. Even the most sanguine proponents of e-tactics could not claim that low costs translate into 100 percent participation, but Liben-Nowell and Kleinberg show that some kinds of online actions (such as the petitions circulated via email that they study) can hang on with lower rates of mobilization, because the number of people who can be exposed to the action and offered an opportunity to participate is so large.

For social movement scholars, the insight that even with super low costs one could not expect or achieve 100 percent participation opens new questions that were historically always resolved with recourse to costs and resources. For example, Klandermans, Jojanneke van der Toorn, and Jacquelien van Stekelenburg's recent review of the literature on social movement participation (2008) argues that five factors robustly affect participation: grievances (i.e., the things that people are upset about), efficacy, identity, emotions, and network embeddedness. All of these could be markedly impacted by declining costs, since most are likely important in some large measure because of costs.

For instance, when resource mobilization was created as an approach, McCarthy and Zald (1973, 1977) contended that grievances were ubiquitous but social movements were not. They reasoned that while grievances may be required to create and support a social movement, they would not be enough on their own. Resources were also needed. In the case of e-tactics, one wonders how severe a grievance has to be for individuals to be willing to consider such low-cost participation. Similarly, the emotions that Klandermans, van der Toorn, and Stekelenburg most focus on as motivating participation are not those produced through participation but rather the anger that may precede it. Must one be as outraged and angry to bear low costs of activism as to attend a march? Efficacy and identity investments have mattered in part because they provide returns for bearing the substantial costs of action. If individuals think they or their group can be successful, and/or their self-perceptions and social identity are reinforced by bearing the costs of participation, they may be more willing to assume those costs. We wonder whether people are more willing to try different styles of activism if there are low costs before they make assessments of efficacy, and whether identity investment needs to be as heavy when the costs are so low (a topic that we revisit in chapter 6). Network embeddedness, finally, has been tied to participation through two paths: having a literal personal or organizational route through which to find out about protest, and/or the provision of social support for participation. The Web supplies a wide array of ways to find out about activism, and social support might be irrelevant for encouraging a few mouse clicks and button pushes (but social pressure to participate when you can see your friends are participating might be a different issue online). On a broader level, all of these potential changes to protest participation on the Web—including the role of network embeddedness, efficacy, identity, emotions, and grievances in compelling participation—would be theory 2.0 changes.

Social movement scholars can now vary the costs of participation by studying e-tactics, and start to gain substantial theoretical and empirical leverage over an empirical question that could never be precisely studied: How much do wide cost variations matter? As we explore in the chapter on copresence and participation (chapter 6), we wonder whether e-tactics can create a category of participants without a shared collective identity and whether collective identity is even necessary for online action. In that chapter, we note that when costs (and hence investments) are low, and one is not necessarily participating at the same time as others, the feel of participation could change substantially.

Of course, social movement scholars are not the only ones interested in the changing dynamics of participation. Organizations that offer online activism also wonder about online and automated participation along with their meaning. Although we do not include a survey of organizations or analyze such data here, our contacts within the nonprofit industry suggest that larger organizations running activist Web sites with e-tactics have one of two views about online participation through e-tactics: e-tactics are important and can be effective in their own right; or e-tactics are a "gateway" participation format. In the former, e-tactics are offered in hopes of achieving the goals expressed in the individual actions.

In the latter, much like marijuana has been argued to be a gateway drug that leads to harder-core drug usage later, e-tactics are thought to be a way to pull people into an organization's orbit, leading them toward "harder-core" activism (e.g., street protests) or at least donations. Indeed, a number of for-profit firms that build and sell platforms of e-tactics try to sell potential SMOs on the ability to build their (contact and development) "lists" and increase donations. And there is some evidence that small contributions may prime people for larger contributions later (Garrett 2006).

Perhaps a less cheeky way of putting the same point would be that some organizations envision a ladder of participation where low-cost forms of engagement like e-tactics are the bottom rung, and an effective Web presence gets people on to the ladder, and then facilitates and encourages their climb upward. In contrast, sites without the gateway view see e-tactical participation as a worthwhile destination. We suspect that SMOs that deploy e-tactics as gateway forms of engagement use e-tactics in different ways, and position them in their campaigns differently than those that view participation in e-tactics as a goal in and of itself. Future research on this subject would substantially advance the study of Web protest. The next chapter turns to consider organizing, or the "supply side" of protest (Klandermans 2004), more fully.

5 Making Action on the Cheap: Costs and Organizing

To the extent that resources have been important to understanding individual participation in social movements, they have been even more critical to understanding the empirical rise in—and attendant academic interest in the rise in—SMOs. Interest in SMOs began in the 1960s (think Olson, although he wasn't focused on social movements in particular) and 1970s. For instance, Oberschall (1973) contended that movement participation would depend on the calculation of costs versus benefits accrued through participation. He further claimed that while grievances could affect the pace of insurgency, they could not account for the form of insurgency. Similarly, Tilly's mobilization and polity models (1978) included resources, and were based on a rational actor approach. Tilly (1978) asserted that mobilization could be measured by the amount of resources controlled by or dedicated to a movement and its organizations. Jenkins and Perrow (1977) argued for a rational actor approach and the role of external support in movement emergence in their study of the farmworkers' movement.

Still, McCarthy and Zald's work (1973, 1977) is widely recognized as the watershed that created resource mobilization and its attendant focus on SMOs. Their clear articulation of resource mobilization as a coherent approach gave a common voice to nascent trends and laid out a research agenda that would help to drive social movement scholarship for the next several decades (and still does today).

As the last chapter noted, resource mobilization represented a substantial break from prior social movement theorizing. While grievances might have been necessary conditions for social movement formation or protest, they alone could not explain protest. Instead, resource mobilization pointed to the individual participation problem identified through the free-rider dilemma, and maintained that this problem must be addressed in order for social movements to form and thrive. Resource mobilization, following Olson ([1965] 1998), argued that the solution to this problem was the provision of selective incentives. The resources required to provide these selective incentives would need to be gathered, consolidated, and strategically deployed, which could be done effectively by SMOs.

Specifically, resource mobilization researchers held that large influxes of resources make for stronger movements, more movement organizations in any given movement, more product differentiation between SMOs (that is, a wider variety of goals and tactics across SMOs in a movement), and improved odds of overall movement success (McCarthy and Zald 1973, 1977). These claims were exciting to many scholars and represented a clear research agenda guided by a focus on SMOs as part of the solution to the free-rider problem. Scholastic interest in organizations bloomed.

Although not all social movement scholars subscribe to resource mobilization, even major theoretical competitors have tended to stipulate the growing importance of SMOs while honing in on other sources of disagreement. For instance, political process scholars contended that resource mobilization improperly focused on the flow of external resources, such as from foundations, to social movements instead of on indigenous resources (McAdam 1982). Aldon Morris (1981, 1984) makes a similar critique of external resources (for an evaluation of these arguments, see Jenkins and Eckhart 1986) and extends this further to talk about the role of indigenous organizations in movement formation.

Similarly, scholars who concentrate on the framing processes of social movements are more interested in subjective meaning making and motivations than many classic resource mobilization theorists, but framing scholars still turn to SMOs as social entities capable of creating and promoting frames that could motivate as well as guide participation (Snow 2004). Scholars interested in collective identity, whose theoretical traditions seem most at odds with the rational choice beginnings of resource mobilization, have also noted the ways in which SMOs could play important roles in creating and maintaining collective identities.

Perhaps the only major approach that does not consider SMOs to be central is the new social movements approach, which worries that certain formations for *organizing*—particularly more informal, open, and network-based styles—are improperly underplayed through the focus on SMOs. In fact, aside from debates about whether resources flow from outside into movements or from within aggrieved communities, as discussed above, critiques of resource mobilization have largely been concerned with whether professional SMOs are the modal and/or most effective type of organization (Jenkins 1983).

That debate has looked at alternatives to professional SMOs, like Luther Gerlach and Virginia Hine's decentralized, segmented, and acephalous networks (1970). These were cell-based networks that lacked central leadership, and were thought to be highly adaptive and able to mobilize wide nets of people quickly. Jenkins (1983) asserts that in reality, most social movements feature both professional SMOs and decentralized networks, and even federated local groups; Jenkins and Eckhert's empirical examination (1986) shows that for the civil rights movements, professional SMOs were not the modal organizational form.

Nonetheless, as Elisabeth Clemens and Debra Minkoff (2004, 155–156) summarize in their review of social movement research on organizations: "For the past two decades, resource mobilization theory has been a workhorse of social movement research, fueling an impressive literature in which organization plays a central role." Indeed, research on SMOs gained speed quickly after resource mobilization's introduction, and became a dominate means for identifying social movement actors, measuring social movement health and viability, and as a prism through which scholars viewed the dynamics of organizing and social movements generally. Whether in case studies of particular organizations (e.g., Zald 1970; McAdam 1988), more qualitative examinations of major organizations within a movement (e.g., Staggenborg 1988, 1991), or quantitative examinations of organizational "birth," "death," and transformation (e.g., Minkoff 1999; Minkoff, Aisenbrey, and Agnone 2008), studying organizations became a vehicle for studying movements themselves (Minkoff 2002). In a synecdoche between SMOs and social movements, social movement scholars began to identify, track, and study SMOs as if these organizing forms represented the most important components of social movements.

As scholars dug into SMOs and their dynamics in this research, it became clear that in addition to the resource collection and management functions described by resource mobilization and the "middle-management" functions explored by Shirky (2008), SMOs helped to accomplish a wide variety of other tasks and goals for movements (although we do not undertake an exhaustive review of this literature here). Most relevant to this book, SMOs are cast as critical to creating and organizing opportunities for participants to engage; that is, SMOs are responsible for the "supply side" of protest by organizing protests and other ways to be involved in activism (Klandermans 2004). Research has empirically assumed that SMOs are the central creators of protest opportunities (although few tests exist of this assumption, save Jenkins and Eckhert 1986). For instance, McCarthy and Clark McPhail (1998), among others, discuss the increasing reliance on professionalized SMOs for organizing events, even when those SMOs are radical (e.g., Queer Nation or ACT UP). Thus, not only do organizations help to motivate people to participate through selective incentives (i.e., help to create "demand" for protest) they also create the moments in which people can collectively participate (i.e., create a supply of protest opportunities; Klandermans 2004).

Further, SMOs can help to organize other organizations and their members, thereby increasing turnout to events to an even greater degree, in a process known as "mesomobilization" (Gerhards and Rucht 1992; see also Morris 1984). In this process, umbrella organizations or key brokering organizations enlist the support and activity of other SMOs, all of which work to turn out their members to a specific action. The size of the actions that can be organized is increased, as is participation in those actions.

SMOs have been seen as providing a critical training ground and respite for protest organizers across time, too. The future leaders of tomorrow's SMOs are expected to be involved in activism today as they work their way up the ranks, learning how to organize and operate within as well as control the reins of an SMO. Having been duly trained and dedicated themselves to activism, activists find that SMOs provide a place of work and community during low times so that the most dedicated activists can stay connected and committed to the movement while they wait for interest and activity to rise again. Social movement researchers refer to this as an abeyance function of SMOs (Rupp and Taylor 1987; Taylor 1989).

Moreover, the organizational forms of SMOs help to structure how these activist leaders engage their organizations and make decisions. Schussman and Earl (2004, 443) argue that the literature on organizational forms and decision making is clear in finding that "the actions of leaders, and their capacity (or lack thereof) for independent decision making depends on the organizational structures in which they are embedded" (for a similar point, see Klandermans 1989). For instance, hierarchical organizational structures helped to empower relatively structured and closed leadership (Eichler 1977), whereas collectivist organizations tended to adopt more consensus-based decision making, and have less centralized leadership and/or decision making (Brown 1989; Stoecker 1990; Mushaben 1989).

SMOs also serve as effective spokespersons for movements. Todd Gitlin (1980) has shown how destructive competition between individual spokespersons can be to a social movement. Professional SMOs simplify this process, and help connect a social movement to the press on a more regular basis and in more effective ways (for instance, by being in tune with the news cycle as well as the daily routines and deadlines of reporters). As David Snow, Soule, and Kriesi have pointed out in a range of work, SMOs can work to frame a movement to bystanders, potential supporters, and opponents (for the most pointed discussion of this, see Snow, Soule, and Kriesi 2004, 387–390).

Supersizing versus Theory 2.0

From trade books (e.g., Benkler 2006; Shirky 2008) to scholarly articles (Earl and Schussman 2003; Bimber, Flanagin, and Stohl 2005), work by Web observers has generally agreed that costs can be dramatically reduced online whether one is talking about organizing a business or a social movement. That there is a cost-reducing affordance of Internet-enabled technologies is not the new element to our story. What is new is tracing out the consequences of this theoretically and empirically by determining which effects are essentially business as usual with a marginal twist (supersizing), pie-in-the-sky optimism that is supported in only a few cases (notice, there is still only one Wikipedia), or seemingly robust effects across a range of Web sites (theory 2.0 changes).

A supersized approach to SMOs would suggest that SMOs are able to effectively (perhaps with some variation) adopt new technologies, including ICTs, and use them to further existing goals. In effect, the Web would become another resource for SMOs that could be mobilized (Peckham 1998). Below we review research taking this position. Meanwhile, a theory 2.0 approach argues that if the cost-based affordance of the Web is leveraged, the need for, and therefore reliance on, SMOs may decline. It follows that if SMOs exist to handle costs but costs can be suddenly made much lower, then the value of SMOs to movements or the return on the resources that they absorb may be diminished. Alternatively, investments in SMOs may become more tailored to contexts in which the value they deliver is clear.

Because of the variability in leveraging the cost-reducing affordance for organizers, we expect some supersized effects and some theory 2.0 effects, underscoring the significance of considering degrees of leveraging as the leveraged affordances approach calls for. For instance, while some SMOs may survive and thrive (through supersize effects), the variability of forms that organizers produce to facilitate their organizing may vary more widely, from single-person operations to increasingly diverse organizational forms, reflecting the declining hegemony of SMOs as an organizing form for

Web-based protest and requiring theory 2.0. We discuss these possibilities in more detail in the next section.

Supersizing SMOs

Supersize theories would expect the fundamental place of SMOs as the primary facilitator of protest to be unchanged when activism takes place online, and that SMOs would incorporate ICTs that reduce their marginal costs into their everyday workflows. This is generally consistent with how existing organizations are expected to adopt and use new technologies, including the Web (on both points, see DiMaggio et al. 2001).

A range of scholars has found this to be true where Web-related activism is concerned. Fisher and her colleagues (2005) studied street protest participation and assert that the Web presences of organizations provided additional ways to market protest events, but other than adding a new and decidedly inexpensive media outreach channel, were business as usual. Ayres (1999), Joanne Lebert (2003), Daniel Myers (1994), and Markus Schulz (1998), among many others, second this view: the Web can cheaply expand the reach and speed of communication, but it doesn't change the necessity of SMOs, what SMOs do, or substantively how they do it. Tetyana Pudrovska and Myra Marx Ferree (2004) go so far as to treat SMOs' Web presences as virtual organizational brochures that are meant to inexpensively convey the groups' framing of events, but are only educational and representational. Halfway around the globe, Guobin Yang's study of Chinese civil associations' use of the Internet (2007) seconds Fisher and her colleagues' business-as-usual finding, although he does find that younger organizations see possibilities in Internet use that older, more established organizations do not.

This is not to suggest that cheap and fast communication is unimportant; practically, it can make a huge difference. The numerous studies of Web use by the Zapatistas to publicize their cause as well as gain international support shows the practical muscle of a fast and cheap media like the Web (for a particularly good study of the Zapatista movement, see Garrido and Halavais 2003). But making a large practical difference is not the same as changing the fundamental causal processes underlying activism.

When organizational or activist behavior is thought to change from these lowered costs, it is largely in the service of preexisting goals and issues (again, supersizing at work). Horton (2004), for example, finds that email helps activists stay connected to multiple groups, and allows groups easily and cheaply to educate and update their members; he doesn't find substantial changes in activist behaviors, though, or changes in the presence or behavior of organizations.

Bennett (2003a, 2003b, 2004a, 2004b) argues that ICT usage can allow SMOs to connect with one another more easily (much as Horton [2004] claims is true for activists). These connections do not cause fundamental ideological reorientations and convergences but rather allow SMOs to form ephemeral coalitions or temporary umbrella organizations that help drive mobilization for specific, large, planned protests. This works through a process often referred to as mesomobilization (mentioned briefly above), in which SMOs work to mobilize each other, and in doing so, mobilize the base membership of several SMOs at once. The goal of this is to produce larger events through the coalition or umbrella group than any single SMO could produce. Mesomobilization is not a new process, and Bennett's point is primarily that Web-facilitated contacts can help spur more mesomobilized events even though ideological convergence is not occurring.

We could go on with other studies that discuss SMO behavior online, but most play the same tune: the Web helps SMOs reach further, do that faster and cheaper, and sometimes even work better. But the fundamental processes and dynamics are not changed. There are a few writers and researchers who march to a different drummer, and they have been thinking about more fundamental shifts, as the next section describes.

Theory 2.0

As we explored in chapter 2, early writing on ICTs and social life, and Web protest in particular, was bifurcated between darkly pessimistic concerns about anomic and addictive technologies and widely optimistic forecasts about technological panaceas and Guttenberg-style shifts. As Paul DiMaggio and his colleagues (2001) pointed out, neither camp was right; reality tended to be somewhere in between and had important variation.

As "search" has matured, and Web 2.0 "social software" has been developed and refined, a new round of strong-selling, optimistic books have been written (recall that early optimists and pessimists alike were writing about things that now seem technologically anachronistic like dial-up bulletin boards and text-based multiplayer games). The approachable *Here Comes Everybody* by Shirky and the lengthy yet still well-selling *The Wealth of Networks* by Benkler are two such works. In both cases, the authors give wide-ranging examples of the revolutionary possibilities of Web 2.0 and search technologies, which they show can be thrilling for the winners and harrowing for the losers. For instance, it is a gross understatement to say that "old media" has been shaken up by online tools; Benkler focuses more on the music industry and other intellectual property powerhouses, and Shirky concentrates more on the decline of the newspaper industry because of blogging, craigslist, and other amateur onslaughts.

Importantly, both books touch on a theme that has been developing among researchers on Web activism for several years: with innovative uses of the Web, organizing doesn't necessarily require organizations anymore (for an early treatment of this in reference to street protest and the first use of the phrase "organizing without organizations" that we can find, see Tarrow 1994; for an early application of this distinction for Web-based activism, see Earl and Schussman 2003). We will discuss this more in a moment, but the central idea for Shirky is that organizations developed largely to play the role of managers so that coordination costs that had been inherent in collective social action could be consolidated and paid.

Shirky argues that whenever those costs were worth the benefit of bearing them, you would see organizations grow and satisfy that demand; where the benefits did not outweigh the organizing costs, no social action was organized or taken. He contends that we see far more social collaboration and social production (read: collective action) today because technologies have driven the costs of organizing to all-time lows. Essentially, far more ends are now worth more than the costs, leading to organizing around far more things.

As Shirky (2008, 22) notes: "The current change, in one sentence, is this: most of the barriers to group action have collapsed, and without those barriers, we are free to explore new ways of gathering together and getting things done." Shirky (2008, 48) sees Internet-enabled technologies as clearly revolutionary, and maintains that seemingly disconnected changes in social and economic life are actually all driven by common technological effects on costs: "The collapse of transaction costs makes it easier for people to get together—so much easier, in fact, that it is changing the world. . . . [L]ike a chain of volcanoes all fed by the same pool of magma, the surface manifestations of group efforts seem quite separate, but the driving force of those eruptions is the same: the new ease of assembly." If we translate this to protest as a particular kind of collective action, SMOs developed and thrived in part to consolidate resources, as resource mobilization tells us, but also to coordinate the management of movements. If the costs to organize and coordinate can be brought to rock-bottom lows with innovative uses of the Web, then we would expect to see relatively fewer organizations running the show yet more organizing.[1]

While there are many things to admire about Benkler's and Shirky's books (and other works like them), and many points on which we agree—

like the rise of organizing without organizations—there are a few things that should give social scientists pause. Perhaps most crucially, both books tend to cream the top off reality by choosing to discuss exemplary cases that best demonstrate the potential of innovative technological uses. But reality is more of a mixed bag: there are few truly revolutionary sites and/ or uses of Web technology, a small number of pretty darn innovate sites and uses, a large number of sites that go with the technological flow and follow a peer pressure model of adoption and use, and a not-insignificant number of mundane users and uses.

Our approach is therefore more akin to other researchers who have tried to think through (e.g., Bimber, Flanagin, and Stohl 2005) and empirically study (e.g., Earl and Schussman 2003) wider fields of (mixed) action. Embracing the idea that variation is the lifeblood (methodologically and theoretically) of social science, this brand of scholarship steps back from the edge of social software-induced revolution to note both the potential and the real variation. In other words, while we will point to evidence of theory 2.0 claims and consequences, which are consistent with some of Shirky's and Benkler's assertions, we are not arguing that the shifts we find will be ubiquitous. This is the case because the leveraging of the cost affordance we discuss varies widely. Further, we don't disregard the supersizing effects examined earlier in the chapter (we suspect they are right on target for less leveraged uses) but rather also expect to observe some theory 2.0 effects.

Organizing without Organizations

The most significant theory 2.0 effect that we expect to find, foreshadowed in our brief discussion of Shirky's work above, is that when costs become variable, the things that depend on cost for their social import will also become variably important as a consequence. Here, this means that while the necessity of organizations has always been a constant in social movement theory and research, we think it can be rendered variable by ingenious uses of technology that leverage the low organizing cost affordance of the Web. Existing research already shows early signs that this is true. For example, Earl and Schussman's study of the strategic voting e-movement (2003) found that it was organized around a core group of less than two dozen Web sites. They interviewed the owners and operators of the majority of those sites and discovered that "of the 13 sites from which we were able to interview representatives, 6 were built by and run by solo designers, 3 were built and run by two designers, 2 were built and run by three designers, and 2 were built and run by a group of seven and a group of ten respectively. This yielded an average of 2.7 organizers per site and a mode of 1 organizer per site" (Earl and Schussman 2003, 160). Now that is organizing without organizations! Similarly, Gurak (1997) and Gurak and Logie (2003) studied online movements that were coordinated by a small group of people, sometimes through a single blog or a one-off Web site on the issue. Bennett and Fielding (1999) remind us that the now-venerable MoveOn started out as two people trying to make a difference who ran a company that sold flying-toasters screen savers—and it was viable and successful as a two-person organization, although it has since grown to include paid staff.

Bimber, Flanagin, and Stohl (2005) as well as Bimber, Stohl, and Flanagin (2008) offer a theory that is compatible with our approach for why organizing without organizations might be possible. Specifically, they argue that communication technologies reduce the division between public and private life. With fewer barriers between public and private, the risk of free riding and the need for physical organizations are also reduced. Looking back to Olson's ([1965] 1998) assertion that the major barrier to social action was free riding, or people taking advantage of the public goods produced through the action of others, these three scholars contend that his free-rider dilemma was really a special case of collective action, not universal. In this special case, the costs to cross from private to public action were particularly large, and therefore required selective incentives to overcome. But the ease with which communication technologies publish information has, if anything, flipped the problem on its head: with Google trolling the Web and making many, many things on the public Web available through searches, and Facebook pushing your every digital move to your friends, it is harder than ever to keep the private from becoming public. They claim that in such cases, the classic free-rider dilemma doesn't apply and the importance of formal organization is diminished.

Like Benkler, they discuss cases in which people even become unwitting contributors to public goods. Referring to this as "second-order communality," they argue that people contribute to repositories with little or no knowledge of other participants and their contributions, including posting to Web sites, participating in an electronic bulletin board, participating in credentialing services (e.g., rating services), forwarding useful emails, and forwarding useful email addresses. More generally, innovative technologies can be used to reduce the costs of contribution to an extent where decisions over participation become relatively minor or even entirely unnoticed.

And when people want to collaborate, the cost reductions in going from private to public are still helpful. Pointing to open-source projects, online social movements, and "smart mobs," they maintain that "micro-" and "middle" media diminish the need for organization because communication tasks that organizations historically have been responsible for can be done simply and inexpensively using newly available technological aids.

Much as we argue that reality is a mixed bag, Bimber, Stohl, and Flanagin similarly do not argue that organizations are on their way out entirely. Rather, they propose increasing "organizational fecundity" in which a wide variety of organizing forms are used to forward collective action:

> The contemporary media environment provides many opportunities for emergent forms that combine the characteristics of traditional organization forms with non-hierarchical networks resulting in new forms of relations among members, leaders, and other stakeholders. A theory of collective action organizing must simultaneously account for the efficacy of bureaucratic as well as network forms of organizing and the possibility that organizations exhibit several types of structures across time and constituencies. Indeed, in the case of the internet and politics, there is mounting evidence for coexistence of a myriad of organizational structures. (Bimber, Stohl, and Flanagin 2008, 76)

They go on to outline different dimensions of organizing forms that they regard as important to understanding how those organizing vehicles behave.

We consider this a promising line of work, but would split one hair: organizational fecundity points to a wide variety of organizations—including informal networks—but nonetheless positions the organizing of collective action as happening through collective efforts. We think it might be more appropriate to say organiz*ing* fecundity because it is the process of organizing that is becoming more varied to include even "parties of one" organizing collective actions (as we discuss in more detail in chapter 7). Sure, organizational fecundity is a consequence of that, but we suggest the more expansive claim that the process itself is being opened up, not just the variety of units that participate in it.

In examining these theoretical claims, we have an ace in the hole in that our data collection strategy allows us a unique forest-level view. As we have noted, a number of researchers have approached the study of Web protest by studying particular organizations. But since this strategy rests on SMOs, it necessarily precludes the opportunity to observe protest that is not organized by SMOs. By asking a broad question—How are people using online petitions, boycotts, and letter-writing and email campaigns?—

and then tracking a random sample of those e-tactics, we are able to get a unique bird's-eye view of these phenomena.

The Rise of Warehouse Sites and the Decline in SMO Dominance

All of the foregoing discussion is well and good, but what do we see in the proverbial meeting of the rubber and the road? Empirically, do SMOs play as dominant a role on the Web as they have in traditional street protest? Supersize advocates would answer "Yes," and describe the Web-based tools that SMOs are using to do their job better. But we argue that in clear and important ways, e-tactics are not always organized the same way as their offline progenitors. Changing these underlying processes is like changing how an engine actually works, and leads to shifts that are both practically and theoretically critical. In our leveraged affordances approach, we are interested not only in supersizing protest but also in these underlying shifts in process—places where the engine of collective action operates differently than it has in the past—especially because understanding such shifts is integral to continuing to understand protest as it evolves in a technology-rich environment.

The most obvious and substantial evidence that the low-cost affordance of the Web has heralded changes in the way that protest is organized comes in the presence of warehouse sites. Warehouse sites are clearinghouses for protest where the production of protest is completed by users themselves, rather than by the Web site operators. In contrast to offline protest, where organizers tend to be regular and established players in protest, warehouse sites open the door of protest organizing so that individual users can easily become organizers. And these users can easily organize a single protest action or a whole series of actions, reducing the significance of having previous experience for current and potential organizers.

While warehouse sites made up only a small fraction of the sites in our study (15 of 184), they hosted or linked to a volume of e-tactics that dwarfed the protest opportunities on nonwarehouse sites, illustrating that warehouse sites indeed drive a substantial quantity of protest. We estimate that warehouse sites offered over twenty-five times as many e-tactics as the nonwarehouse sites in our sample. That means that the distribution of e-tactics on the Web is heavily weighted toward warehouse sites. This, in turn, means that a large amount of protest is being organized by anyone who wants to go on a warehouse site and create an e-tactic. We look at some implications of this as we proceed through this chapter by, for instance, trying to identify differences between what SMO and non-SMO sites are able to organize online. And we also extend our thinking on the topic in chapter 7 when we consider the additional effects of "anyone" being able to organize e-tactics (e.g., effects on the causes they choose to organize around, on who organizers consider their peers, etc.).

But before we get ahead of ourselves, we first ask: Are there other indications that SMOs are not the only organizing game in town? Definitely. Among nonwarehouse sites, seventy-five were affiliated with SMOs, but ninety-four were not.[2] This means that over half of the sites were not SMO affiliated. SMOs are not only not the only game in town: in our data they are not even the dominant game in town.

Non-SMOs as Competitors

While thus far we have focused on how necessary SMOs are to protest organizing—whether via classic resource mobilization theorizing or in the day-to-day practice of offline organizing—there is a latent claim hidden in this discussion that SMOs are better able to organize than other individuals and groups. As we investigate online protest, we must ask the important question of whether this is empirically true where e-tactics are concerned. Our data suggest that it is not, at least not in most of the ways that we can measure the claim. That is, the return on being an SMO versus not being one is not clear from our data, with only one major exception—when organizing costs are higher—which we consider later in this chapter.

Comparing Patterns in Hosting and Linking to E-tactics

First, as table 5.1 shows, Web sites run by SMOs were no more likely to host or link to e-tactics than were other sites. SMOs hosted e-tactics on their Web sites 84 percent of the time, while non-SMO sites hosted e-tactics just as frequently, at 83 percent of the time (table 5.1). For instance, the Web site for the Center for Reclaiming America, an SMO devoted to prolife and antigay causes, hosted petitions furthering issues it cared about,

Table 5.1
Hosting and Linking Patterns for Nonwarehouse Sites

	Hosted e-tactics	Linked to e-tactics	Hosted offline protest
SMO sites	84% (N = 63)	47% (N = 35)	60% (N = 45)
Non-SMO sites	83% (N = 78)	46% (N = 43)	44% (N = 41)

including one protesting federal funding for human embryo stem cell research and another calling for the prohibition of late-term abortions.[3] Non-SMO sites hosted e-tactics, too, such as the site of a man who calls himself The Simpleton.[4] The Simpleton's Web site hosted one letter-writing and one email campaign, both calling for change at his local newspaper.

The same is true for linking to e-tactics, with 47 percent of SMO sites linking to e-tactics and 46 percent of non-SMO sites doing so (table 5.1). Among the non-SMO sites that linked to online protest opportunities was a blogger who encouraged visitors to follow a link to an online petition protesting George W. Bush's and Tony Blair's nominations for the Nobel Peace Prize because of their involvement in waging war on Iraq.[5] SMO-affiliated sites also linked to e-tactic opportunities—indeed sometimes about the same causes as their non-SMO counterparts. For instance, Corp Watch, an SMO, featured a call for an end to the war in Iraq and provided a link to an email campaign on its Web site.[6]

These values examine the overall hosting and linking trends, though, and so we might ask, What happens if you look at specific e-tactics? The story is largely the same: non-SMO organizers are able to produce similar numbers of protest opportunities, and protest opportunities that have similar features, when compared with protest opportunities produced by SMOs. This is especially true for email campaigns and boycotts. When looking at the percentages reported in table 5.2, it appears that SMOs hosted email campaigns more frequently than non-SMO sites, but the difference is not actually statistically significant (using a chi-square test with a p-value level of 0.05). The same goes for boycotts, with non-SMOs and SMOs hosting boycotts at essentially the same rate (table 5.2). Non-SMO and SMO Web sites hosted boycotts of everything from the city of Cincinnati to specific businesses, for reasons ranging from support of free speech to gay rights.

Table 5.2
Rates of Hosting the Five E-tactical Forms by SMO Affiliation for Nonwarehouse Sites

	Petitions	Letter-writing campaigns	Email campaigns	Boycotts	Fax campaigns
SMO sites	29%	56%	41%	23%	37%
	(N = 22)	(N = 42)	(N = 31)	(N = 17)	(N = 28)
Non-SMO sites	18%	43%	31%	22%	18%
	(N = 17)	(N = 40)	(N = 29)	(N = 21)	(N = 17)

Similarly, whether a site was run by an SMO or not did not affect the likelihood that it would host a petition or letter-writing campaign. As table 5.2 shows, petitions were hosted on 29 percent of SMO sites and 18 percent of non-SMO ones. This looks like a big difference, but it is actually not statistically significant (using a chi-square test with a p-value level of 0.05).[7] The Web sites of SMOs like the National Association of African Americans for Positive Imagery, the Christian Family Coalition, and the Citizens Commission on Human Rights all hosted individual petitions, just as did sites run by individuals.[8] One non-SMO site, for instance, called for an investigation of the practices of the U.S. Securities and Exchange Commission and hosted an online petition requesting a congressional investigation.[9]

The rate of hosting letter-writing campaigns was also similar on SMO (56 percent) and non-SMO (43 percent) sites. Again, although this seems like a notable difference, it isn't statistically significant (using a chi-square test with a p-value level of 0.05). While SMO sites like Amnesty International and the Committee to Protect Journalists hosted letter-writing campaigns on their Web sites, non-SMO sites did as well.[10] For instance, one site pushed for the historic preservation of planes used in World War II and was run by a single individual.[11] The hosting rates of petitions and letter-writing campaigns for SMO sites, in other words, do not dramatically differ from those of non-SMO sites.

The story is the same when we look at the SMO and non-SMO patterns of linking to e-tactics (table 5.3). Across all five e-tactical forms, the rates of linking to each differed by fewer than 7 percent between SMO and non-SMO sites, and these differences were never statistically significant. SMOs linked to email campaigns 12 percent of the time and letter-writing campaigns 13 percent of the time. The Tucson chapter of the National Organization for Women, for instance, linked to a letter-writing campaign

Table 5.3
Rates of Linking to the Five E-tactical Forms by SMO Affiliation for Nonwarehouse Sites

	Petitions	Letter-writing campaigns	Email campaigns	Boycotts	Fax campaigns
SMO sites	31%	13%	12%	1%	11%
	(N = 23)	(N = 10)	(N = 9)	(N = 1)	(N = 8)
Non-SMO sites	36%	10%	5%	1%	4%
	(N = 34)	(N = 9)	(N = 5)	(N = 1)	(N = 4)

in support of national health insurance.[12] Meanwhile, non-SMO sites linked to email campaigns 5 percent of the time and letter-writing campaigns 10 percent of the time. Examples include a non-SMO group against the intellectual property rules of the Recording Industry of America Association that linked to a letter-writing campaign forwarding its cause.[13]

Non-SMO sites linked to petitions 36 percent of the time (table 5.3), like the Web site of a group of students at a Washington State public school that linked to a petition protesting Columbus Day being a national holiday.[14] SMOs linked to petitions 31 percent of the time, as in the case of the Global Response Web site that linked to a petition to save the Saemangeum Wetlands in South Korea.[15] Like the linking patterns for the other e-tactical forms, SMO and non-SMO sites linked to petitions at essentially equivalent rates.

It is interesting to note that unlike the other four e-tactical forms, petitions from nonwarehouse sites that were not run by an SMO had a higher rate of being linked to than hosted (tables 5.2 and 5.3); while 18 percent of non-SMO sites hosted a petition, twice that percentage linked to a petition. Given that several of the warehouse sites that we studied specialized in petitions and indeed hosted a large number of petitions, it makes sense that a non-SMO, nonwarehouse site might more frequently link to a petition than host one. In fact, over one-third of the e-tactics that non-warehouse sites linked to were found on warehouse sites, and all of these were petitions. Due to the presence of warehouse sites specializing in petitions, the cost to a nonwarehouse site of linking to an online petition is particularly low. Table 5.3 shows that non-SMO sites especially take advantage of this reality.

We found few linked boycotts on nonwarehouse sites. Those few we did find were often associated with an additional e-tactic. For example, the Web site of the SMO Rock Out Censorship called for the protection of the First Amendment, and linked to a series of pages on other domains that contained simultaneous calls for boycotts and petitions.[16]

Both SMO and non-SMOs sites linked to fax campaigns at low rates, with SMOs (11 percent) linking to fax campaigns slightly more frequently than non-SMOs (4 percent), although this difference is not statistically significant. The Campaign for Labor Rights SMO, for instance, linked to a fax campaign against Starbucks calling for fair wages and working conditions for coffee plantation workers.[17] Examples from non-SMO sites include one woman's personal Web site that linked to a page with information, a letter-writing campaign, an email campaign, and a fax campaign targeting the German consulate because of alleged animal cruelty in Germany.[18]

Both SMO and non-SMO sites demonstrate that they are capable of producing a diverse array of protest opportunities. We found no significant difference in their patterns of hosting or linking to petitions, letter-writing campaigns, email campaigns, or boycotts. For producing these kinds of protest, it doesn't appear that SMOs are at an advantage.

Variety of Protest Opportunities
We did find a few ways in which SMO and non-SMO sites differed in producing online protest opportunities, although we discuss these as differences in the extent to which sites deployed their organizing ability, not their demonstrated capacity to organize. First, SMOs tended to host larger numbers of different e-tactical forms while non-SMO sites more frequently hosted only a single e-tactical form (48 percent of non-SMO sites hosted a single e-tactical form versus 24 percent of SMO sites; see figure 5.1). SMOs averaged 1.9 different hosted e-tactical forms and non-SMO sites averaged 1.3 different hosted e-tactical forms (and this difference is statistically significant). It may be that SMO sites' commitment to particular causes encourages them to offer several different e-tactical forms in support, making their claim through as many different means as feasible. For example, SMOs most frequently hosted three different e-tactical forms (39 percent of the time), like the Web site of the SMO Fairness and Accuracy in Reporting, which hosted letter-writing, email, and fax campaigns.[19] Meanwhile, most non-SMO sites were like the site that provided resources

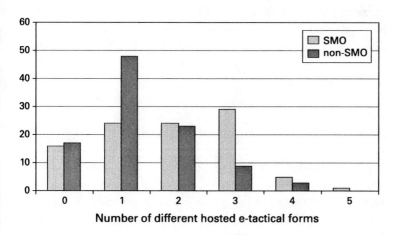

Figure 5.1
Comparison of diversity of hosted e-tactical forms for nonwarehouse sites, by percent.

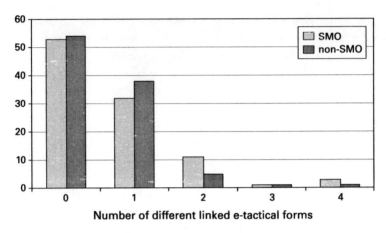

Number of different linked e-tactical forms

Figure 5.2
Comparison of diversity of linked e-tactical forms for nonwarehouse sites, by percent.

for adopting families, which hosted only one e-tactical form—in this case, a letter-writing campaign.[20]

Patterns in linking, on the other hand, were essentially indistinguishable between SMO and non-SMO sites. The average number of different forms that SMOs linked to was 0.7, while non-SMO sites that linked to e-tactics averaged 0.6 forms. As figure 5.2 depicts, non-SMO sites more often restricted themselves to linking to only a single e-tactical form (38 percent for non-SMO sites versus 32 percent for SMOs), while more SMOs linked to two e-tactical forms than non-SMOs. Eight SMO sites (11 percent), such as the Mexican Solidarity Network's site, linked to two different e-tactical forms, while only five non-SMO sites (5 percent) linked to two different e-tactical forms.[21]

Volume of E-tactics
Moving beyond the e-tactical forms—that is, the classes of e-tactics—to the individual e-tactics themselves—the actual petitions, letter-writing campaigns, etc.—we find that SMO and non-SMO sites show some differences in the sheer volume of e-tactics that they host or link to. As we argue above, this is not because SMOs have a leg up in organizing certain kinds of online protest opportunities, but it does appear that they are deploying their e-tactic organizing ability more frequently than non-SMO sites.

Non-SMO sites hosted an average of 2.4 e-tactics, and SMOs hosted an average of 6.6.[22] As can be extrapolated from the first columns of figure

5.1, a portion of both SMO and non-SMO sites did not host any e-tactics (i.e., they only linked to e-tactics). Of those that did host e-tactics, many more non-SMO sites stopped at just a single e-tactic (54 percent) than did SMOs (19 percent). SMO sites tended to host a larger volume of e-tactics overall, peaking with the American Muslims for Jerusalem site, which hosted 65 individual e-tactics: 18 letter-writing campaigns, 22 email campaigns, and 15 fax campaigns.[23] Meanwhile, only two non-SMO sites offered more than 8 different e-tactics.

SMO sites also, on average, linked to a higher number of actual petitions, boycotts, letter-writing campaigns, email campaigns, and fax campaigns than did non-SMO ones. Linking SMO sites linked to an average of 5 individual e-tactics (although 60 percent of the linking SMO sites linked to only one e-tactic). The highest number of linked e-tactics on an SMO was on the Rock Out Censorship Web site, which linked to 11 petitions and 22 boycotts.[24]

Non-SMO sites linked to a smaller average of 2 e-tactics. Again, most (70 percent) linked to just a single e-tactic like a petition or email campaign, for instance. The high for e-tactics linked to by a non-SMO site was 25, lower than that for an SMO site, on a site devoted to patriotism that linked to 25 petitions.[25]

To summarize, SMO and non-SMO sites are equivalent in their ability to produce online protest opportunities, as shown by the rate at which they host or link to any e-tactics. Yet SMO sites were more likely to scale up this ability, offering more different kinds of e-tactical forms and simply more individual e-tactics than did non-SMO sites. We regard these differences, though, as relatively minor, particularly compared to the differences between SMO and non-SMO sites in their relationship to offline protest, which we examine in the next section.

The SMO Difference

It is important for us to be clear here that we are not arguing that SMOs never matter in the Internet age. We are claiming that they matter most when costs are higher and they matter least when costs are lower (or at a minimum, that SMOs must return other rewards aside from cost management to be useful in low-cost environments). Therefore, we expect that SMO sites would only "outperform" non-SMO sites when the costs of organizing are higher.

That is precisely what we found. Offline protest is the most expensive form of protest, so one might suspect that SMOs would have an advantage there, and that any SMO with a Web presence would be well advised to advertise its offline protests on its Web site, to make them e-mobilizations. That is empirically correct: SMO Web sites noticeably differ from non-SMO sites in their discussion and endorsement of offline protest; this difference is statistically significant at the 0.05 level. As table 5.1 shows, 60 percent of SMO sites contained information about offline protest actions such as rallies, marches, and vigils. Examples include the Coalition for Peace Action's Web site, which featured information about a rally, the Campaign for Labor Rights site, which encouraged participation in a strike, and the National Grassroots Peace Network, which endorsed a vigil and a strike, among other offline actions.[26]

In contrast, the nonwarehouse sites in our sample that were not run by an SMO were far less likely to host or link to e-mobilizations. Only 44 percent of non-SMO sites hosted information about street protest. That is nearly a third fewer non-SMO sites than SMO sites with information on offline actions. Non-SMO sites that endorsed offline protest included a site that opposed the expansion of public land closures to motorized vehicles.[27] The site called for a protest rally at senate offices. Similarly, a blog by an Irish expatriate housing a letter-writing campaign also encouraged participation in a march against the Iraq War, along with other posts containing computer advice and musings on news articles in the Irish press.[28] Again, this difference is neither surprising to us nor problematic to our theoretical account. As we observed above, organizing offline protest is expensive, even when some coordination takes place online as in an e-mobilization, and so it makes sense that SMO sites would be better able to produce opportunities for street protest.

Likewise, there were other places where costs appeared more important and thus SMOs also appear more important. For instance, of the e-tactical forms we discussed, most showed no real, or at least no substantial, differences between SMO-run and non-SMO sites. But fax campaigns displayed a larger difference between hosting rates for SMO (37 percent) and non-SMO sites (18 percent), and this difference was statistically significant. Web sites run by SMOs hosted fax campaigns such as the Physicians for Human Rights campaign to release six arrested doctors in Cuba.[29] Non-SMO sites also hosted fax campaigns, such as one to oppose charging fees at U.S. national parks.[30] Although present in our data, fax campaigns such as this one, hosted by a non-SMO Web site, were less common than similar campaigns on SMO sites.

Faxing is more costly to organize than petitions, boycotts, and letter-writing and email campaigns, with the requirement that the message be sent over a phone line to a terminal fax machine, and it follows that SMOs, with their access to financial and labor resources, would be better able to launch fax campaigns. A campaign that hoped to generate a high volume of faxes would need multiple fax machines and operators, or a Web-based service provider that could process outbound faxes for a fee. SMOs are more likely to have the resources to absorb these costs. Still, we remind readers that because we did not independently draw a sample of faxes, these data are more speculative.

Benefits and Risks of Organizing without Organizations

We close the chapter by focusing on the major implication that we have been exploring thus far: a change in the dominance of SMOs both practically and theoretically. For folks not from a social movement tradition, the heresy of this claim may not be evident, while for students of social movements, this probably looks like we are betraying our research traditions.

We are not scholastic Benedict Arnolds, however. Instead of throwing out SMOs and theories that put organizations at the center of the theoretical map like resource mobilization, we are actually arguing for a more nuanced approach to organizations and their role. We are suggesting that something we have never really seen vary in any meaningful way—the costs of organizing—can now vary substantially under some circumstances. And when that constant is transformed into a variable, we are able to better understand when and why organizations matter, and when and why they matter less.

In addition to contextualizing the role of organizations in a theoretical and practical way that has been difficult to do before now, this shift offers a chance to study whether organizations return other benefits that don't have to do with costs, or at least with the costs of producing collective action. For instance, it may be that the collective identity work that SMOs regularly engage in or the framing work they do are critical, and are tasks not well picked up by uncoordinated organizers of specific protest opportunities.

On a broader level, it could also be that a healthy social movement requires that some well-heeled SMOs exist in order to create an environment in which other organizers can be successful. We don't have many empirical cases of movements where there are no SMOs, but if the trends we look at in this book continue, we might well have the chance to watch movements grow without the aid of formal organizations. If SMOs are exclusively important because of their cost management and selective incentives functions, then those movements without SMOs will do well. Yet if they decay because SMOs did more than manage costs, selective incentives, and people, we will get a new window into the role of SMOs in the larger ecology of social movements.

There might also be other reasons that SMOs maintain some level of heightened importance, at least within a broader social movement ecology. We discuss two extensions of cost-based arguments here. First, there is some reason to believe that organizers who are pulled in by lower costs can be pushed out if repression by the state or private actors increases the price of organizing. For instance, Earl and Schussman (2004) found that when the potential costs to organizers (none of which were SMOs) for their actions were increased by threats from state-level authorities, many organizers stopped organizing. Easy in, easy out was the story for some (although others took advantage of the ability of Internet users to "route around" censorship and continued their campaigns). More generally, this at least suggests a potential vulnerability to a movement ecology that is devoid of SMOs: it may be easier to squash.

Second, our foregoing discussion has focused on costs that are accrued in order to create an event. But what if those costs go away while the costs of cleaning up from an event remain? A frivolous day of partying in Santa Barbara illustrates this concern. In 2009, over twelve thousand mostly college-aged people met up at the beach for a day dubbed "Floatopia." Organized entirely online and allegedly largely through Facebook, the day drew unexpectedly large crowds. With no organization sponsoring the event or in charge, some key details were overlooked. There were no extra bathrooms for twelve thousand people, nor was there emergency water. No special law enforcement, paramedic, or life guard details were arranged in advance (although all showed up once people started swimming while drunk and falling from the bluffs abutting the ocean). There was no cleanup crew for all of the trash that was created and not taken away. Summed up, there were many costs during and after the event that public entities had to assume liability for because there were no organizers to hold responsible. Applied to protest, it will be critical to examine not just the up-front costs of organizing but also the follow-up costs, and how those are spread across different actors.

Keeping in mind the impact of the low-cost affordance of the Web on both participating in and organizing protest, we now turn to our second leverageable affordance: protest without copresence. In part III of this book, we analyze the way that the asynchronous structure of action on the Web affects participation in and the organization of protest online. We begin by thinking through what happens when people no longer need to be in the same place at the same time to engage in collective action.

III From Copresence to Coordination

In part III, we switch gears to examine the copresence affordance of the Web for allowing action without the need for copresence. Importantly, we think about copresence as both the need to share physical space and the broader expectation of collectivity in participation and organizing. In both chapters, we chart how differently leveraging this affordance can produce either supersized or theory 2.0 protest, and underscore the value of thinking about the leveraged uses of Web affordances in analyzing online protest.

Chapter 6 starts this analysis with an investigation of what the decreasing need for copresence means to participation in collective action. We examine how and when collective action is represented when actions take place online as well as consider some of the ways that actions may benefit from *not* representing collective participation. Thinking about how the dynamics of participation can change without the need for physical togetherness, we discuss the potential consequences for social movement theory, particularly on collective identity.

Then, in chapter 7, we drill further into the consequences of this Web affordance to explore how the Web makes it possible for individuals and small teams to organize protest, further decreasing the requirement for SMOs in online collective action. As more organizers emerge from outside the social movement tradition, we see trends that look different from what scholars have historically considered protest—specifically, the rise of nonpolitical causes and private collective actions.

6 Being Together versus Working Together: Copresence in Participation

If you ask almost any social movement scholar what defines protest or a social movement, one of the first elements of their answer will be that people are working together. Certainly, individuals resist things that they don't like and try to effect change on their own with some frequency— think of any uncomfortable conversation that you have been a part of or witnessed when someone says something that is racially or sexually offensive, and another person challenges the speaker. Think of politically inflected graffiti. Think of trying to be more carbon neutral or energy conscious in your own life. Think of foot-dragging at work when your boss or company has upset you. As James C. Scott's classic work on the weapons of the weak (1990) shows, people often resist power and/or attempt to better their world on their terms as well as in their own constrained ways. But individual resistance is not the stuff of social movement studies. It never has been.

Even before social movement studies was social movement studies— when it was still the study of collective behavior and crowds that began in the 1800s—the focus has always been on people acting collectively, typically marked by their copresence in space and time. Yet people did not look so kindly on crowds back then. In fact, early work feared the crowd, attributing monstrous powers to it. Gustave Le Bon ([1895] 1960, 12), one of the earliest theorists of collective action, believed that people lost themselves in a crowd: "By the mere fact that he forms part of an organised crowd, a man descends several rungs in the ladder of civilization. Isolated, he may be a cultivated individual; in a crowd, he is a barbarian—that is a creature acting by instinct." Work on crowds continued into the twentieth century, still considering the crowd to be a dangerous social entity. Then, in the 1940s and 1950s, work on collective action added a new reason to be concerned as collective action began to be tied to fascism and Communism. As late as the 1960s and 1970s, many scholars still saw crowds and collective action as dangerous. Riots were rocking the nation (McPhail 1994), and even gatherings like rock concerts had experienced deadly stampedes (see Johnson 1987, although this work disputes the animalistic vision of crowds).

But in the 1960s and 1970s, the tide turned as some scholars began to consider more positive aspects of collective action. For instance, observers of mass movements like the civil rights movement started to see the positive possibilities that protest offered for political equality. Crowds were no longer special because of their destructive power, but rather collective action was special by virtue of the pressure it could create for change. Indeed, it was quite clear that individual action could not generate civil rights for African Americans, or full and equal political and social citizenship for women, for example.

This is about the time when social movement studies, as we know it today, was really taking shape, and distinguishing itself from the study of fads, fashions, and other forms of collective behavior. Social movement scholars imported a belief in the "specialness" of crowds into this emerging area of study, but attributed the specialness to the positive potential of collective action, not the dangers that crowds represented in the past. As Tarrow's *Power in Movement* aptly summarizes through its title, social movement scholars saw power in people working together for change. Social movement scholars also became interested in the complex dynamics that allow people to work together for change and ones that result from group efforts.

Historically, the togetherness that made collective action collective was quite literal: people were together in cause, space, and time. So fundamental was this physical togetherness that scholars studied the "assembling process" (McPhail and Miller 1973)—that is, exactly how people come to arrive at the same time and place for a protest event or other gathering.

Assumptions of physical togetherness can even be found in the data used by many social movement scholars. For instance, a prominent way of studying social movements involves studying "protest events," typically as reported by the media. In media reports, protest events are often identified by scholars in part by the presence of two or more people working together for change (e.g., Earl, Soule, and McCarthy 2003). Social movement scholars lack a particular turn of phrase to describe this physical sense of copresence, and this makes sense given that the necessity of physical togetherness wasn't really variable before now.

In this book, though, we do think of physical togetherness (and in chapter 7, togetherness at all) as a variable. We use the term copresence to refer to the collectiveness of collective action—that is, the idea that collective action requires the coordinated efforts of many people—and the physical togetherness that marks that face-to-face togetherness as a specific way of working together. In this chapter, we are focused on the participation-related dynamics of collective action when the second aspect of copresence, physical togetherness, is removed.

Where participation is concerned, the physical togetherness represented by copresence brings with it both costs and rewards. The costs may be somewhat invisible because they have been so constant, but they are there. For instance, people have to spend time, money, and effort to physically come together. Whether arriving home from work in time to attend an antiwar candlelight vigil or traveling to Washington, DC, for a march, actually making it to a common locale culls the proverbial herd immediately. If people could act together without the necessity of copresence, they might gain important flexibility and reduce the costs of participation. In this way, one could see the two affordances that we discuss—costs and copresence—as intimately linked.

In addition to time and other costs, in practice, physical copresence also associates or identifies people with a movement, which can lead to stigma and/or more directed reprisals. Early gay activists certainly faced stigma when they effectively came out by publicly demonstrating. Civil rights activists risked late-night (and some daytime) reprisals for being seen at civil rights protests. As a wide literature on the repression of protest shows, protest events can be dangerous places for protesters.

To be sure, there is another, and more positive, side of physical copresence and the immediate identification that it brings: forming and sustaining a collective sense of "we-ness," or as social movement scholars refer to it, collective identity, has been thought of as a powerful benefit of copresence in prior research. Collective identity and collective action are theoretically as well as empirically separable, although they are often seemingly connected: collective identity might result from participation in a collective action, or participation in a collective action may result in part from a feeling of we-ness. Collective action can theoretically occur without collective identity, however. Given that, we discuss collective identity more in this chapter after reflecting first on the collective nature of participation itself.

As is hopefully evident now, it is bold to claim that one could have protest or collective action at all without copresence. Yet research on online engagement shows that with the right Internet-enabled technologies, people can collaborate quite effectively, with real common purpose and effort, without copresence in time or space. This may be surprising for some social movement scholars, unless they reflect on their own academic collaborations, which have probably included some asynchronous and distant collaborations facilitated by digital technologies. Further, while many worried about pasty, asocial, isolated, and tech-addicted computer users when the Web was first growing in popularity, research has soundly established these fears as unfounded. Indeed, Web 2.0 technologies are fundamentally about their sociability along with their ability to use technology to help connect, bind, and associate people. The "killer apps" of today are all about creating and maintaining togetherness without necessarily requiring copresence (with sites like MeetUp as notable exceptions).

We argue that truly meaningful collaboration—the power of collective action—can be created and facilitated without copresence for protest as well. Certainly we are not referring to the physical marches and rallies that we have seen before. We are instead referring to the hundreds, thousands, or hundreds of thousands of people signing a common petition online to express their outrage about some issue. We are talking about massive letter-writing and email campaigns. We argue that these people are using Internet-enabled tools to collaborate without copresence for social change in meaningful and potentially transformative ways.

Pushing a little deeper, we are trying to challenge the conflation of collective action and copresence in this chapter by asserting that innovative uses of Internet-enabled technologies can allow for meaningful collective action without copresence. We are also claiming that those collective engagements need not be online transfigurations of offline collaborations. That is, one need not try to recreate a march in a virtual space (although some have tried to do so in virtual spaces like Second Life). In fact, given that the facilitation of asynchronous communication and long-distance collaboration are some of the most distinctive capacities of Internet-enabled technologies, it would seem that forms of Web activism that reestablish time or space constraints on their participants actually undo some of the cost reductions that can lead to theory 2.0 changes. What we are arguing for here, instead, is a redefinition of collective action that focuses more on collaboration and common purpose, and less on physical togetherness.

Supersizing Copresence versus Theory 2.0 Models

We should emphasize that this is not the argument that supersize researchers have made. To the contrary, a wide array of scholars interested in the relationship between the Web (or Internet-enabled technologies more broadly) and protest and activism have asked how these technologies can be used to facilitate even greater levels of copresence. For instance, Fisher and her colleagues (2005) examined the impact of Web outreach on offline protest mobilization. Similarly, Horton (2004) found that email and other digital forms of communication allowed environmental activists to manage a broader array of physical engagements, or what we would call e-mobilizations.

Moreover, scholars who have argued for no real lasting impact of ICT usage on protest and social movements (which is to argue against even a supersize effect) have made this claim on the grounds that physically copresent protest is the only real, true, or effective form of activism. They assert that copresence is required to build the mutual trust needed to support activism (e.g., Diani 2000; Rucht 2004).

Whether one argues for a supersize effect or no effect, the idea that copresence is a prerequisite for collective action is a fundamental assumption. Certainly the two camps differ in the extent to which each imagines Internet usage as positively contributing to copresence, but neither imagines collective action occurring without physical copresence.

A theory 2.0 approach, as we outline it, considers copresence from a fundamentally different angle. Specifically, a theory 2.0 approach maintains that: action can be considered collective without copresence (or with limited copresence); collective action can be identified without copresence, although copresence is still often a convenient offline marker for collective action; and we can identify what the consequences of collaboration without copresence might be for participants and social movement processes. In the following sections, we evaluate each claim in light of our data.

Can Collective Action Take Place without Copresence?

As we suggested earlier, we and several other scholars of new media believe that action that is meaningfully collective can be undertaken online. By meaningfully collective, we're contending that these actions are collective even though the way that collectivity is enacted looks a bit different in online as opposed to offline protest. Importantly, here we are not trying to reengage the hypothetical critique of e-tactics introduced in chapter 4 by asking whether the collective action engaged in online is meaningful in some philosophical way or effective in some practical sense. Rather, we are interested in something more basic: Can participation in e-tactics and other forms of online protest participation be considered *collective action*? We claim that it can.

A superficial case is easy to make: offline protests are thought to be effective because of the "power in movement," and e-tactics and other forms of online protest participation can also generate large numbers of participants that represent power through their collective expression. Further, people participate knowing that others may also participate by taking similar actions. This coordination is crucial, and as we will assert, is the point that delineates the distinction between individual resistance and collective action. Of course, the format of expression in online collective actions is different, and the implications of their expression may differ, but people do not sign online petitions or send emails as part of an email campaign, or otherwise participate in e-tactics, because they think they are participating alone. Instead, they participate with the implicit understanding that collectivity can exist—that collective action can take place—when people are engaged in the same expressive act (e.g., signing a petition).

While the e-tactics that we study are for the most part cheap and easy to participate in, more elaborate collaborations also take place online to build private and public goods. For instance, some who develop opensource software see themselves as part of a larger movement against intellectual property and proprietary information. Their participation in open-source software development is their way of enacting their beliefs, and the collaborations that result can be quite impressive (Okhuysen and Bechky 2008).

We contend that whether as easy as coordinated action or as taxing as collaboration, though, both kinds of online actions are collective. Indeed, what would it mean exactly to argue the opposing position—that these actions are not collective? It would mean that people see themselves engaged in isolated and uncoordinated actions, much like Scott's weapons of the weak. It would also mean that the dynamics involved in collective action are absent online. The processes required for organizing and coordinating the participation of multiple people (from tens to millions) would be absent. And the processes related to how participants come to understand themselves in relation to a cause, their participation in a coordinated action, and others' participation would all be irrelevant. Problems that can be created by coordinated action would be absent. It would mean that social movement theory has little to contribute to the understanding of, or learn from, these actions. Clearly this is not the case.

Yet, to say that both are forms of collective action certainly should not imply that there are no differences that follow from achieving collectivity through copresence versus through distributed coordination. For instance, while physical copresence has always allowed participants to see and hear other participants, something different is happening online. Offline, standing shoulder to shoulder, participants can roughly estimate the extent to which others are also dedicated to their cause. While most rally participants, for example, are probably not experts at estimating the size of a crowd, they can recognize that a large number of other people share their concerns and are taking action, or that only a few do. How do online participants learn that their actions are part of collective actions? That is, when people act in a coordinated fashion online, are they able to glimpse some proverbial view of other participants?

A Data-Driven View of Acting Together without Being Together

A reasonable starting place in examining collective participation and copresence is to ask how collective the actions that we studied (i.e., e-tactics) were, and whether they required synchronous participation or physical copresence. The answers are straightforward: our data make a prima facie case for considering e-tactics as collective actions, and also show that physical copresence is not required. In fact, despite the potential to design digital tactics that at least require synchronous participation, even if that participation is geographically distributed (e.g., Flood Net), physical and temporal copresence were never required for the e-tactics that we studied. Sympathetic site visitors instead could participate in the e-tactics in our sample at any time, from any place.

And work together they did. For example, a Consumer Freedom petition calling for the cancellation of People for the Ethical Treatment of Animals' tax-exempt status reported 28,878 participants.[1] Following the petition statement, the site provided fields where interested participants could enter their contact information. Importantly, there were no restrictions on these entries; they could be made on any date, at any time, from any computer with an Internet connection. A petition targeting the U.S. Supreme Court that opposed a ban on the pledge of allegiance in public schools was formatted the same way and had garnered 248,388 signatures—an impressive number for any protest action—all captured asynchronously.[2] It would be difficult to allege that e-tactics like these are not a kind of collective action, even though people did not have to come together at the same time and place to participate.

The language used in many of the e-tactics in our sample suggests that their authors and participants saw these actions as collective actions, too. The pledge of allegiance petition, for example, implored site visitors to "join the 284, 388 who have already signed the petition," thereby signaling collaboration. Other actions were even more explicit in referencing a collective. Numerous e-tactics employed the pronoun "we" to frame their claims as collective ones. For instance, a petition targeting the minister of foreign affairs in South Africa with a call not to recognize Somaliland as an independent country stated: "We the undersigned Somalis and other Africans plead with the Minister and the ANC government . . . "[3] Another, opposed to the war in Iraq, read: "As historians, teachers, and scholars, we oppose the expansion of United States empire and the doctrine of pre-emptive war that have led to the occupation of Iraq."[4]

Although the e-tactics that we studied varied in what kind of data they reported on participants (as we discuss below), we can glean some information about the breadth and diversity of participation in online actions by more closely analyzing what information they did publish. For example, we found clear evidence that the Web facilitated participation globally, unrestricted by geographic distance and thus physical copresence requirements. One petition in support of therapeutic cloning listed all participants and their U.S. state of residence.[5] States on the East Coast, the West Coast, and in between were represented, along with Hawaii and Alaska, illustrating how online actions can circumvent state boundaries. On an even larger geographic scale, on a petition to free former Yugoslavian president Slobodan Milošević, signers reported their nation of origin.[6] Citizens of Greece, New Zealand, Germany, Ukraine, Belarus, England, and the United States, among others, were listed among the five hundred thousand signatories. This mirrors the breadth of participation found in Earl and Schussman's study of PetitionOnline petitions related to entertainment issues (2008).

On one warehouse site, ThePetitionSite, the facility of e-tactics to essentially cross the boundary of time was also evident with users signing on to petitions even after they were formally over. Extending protest actions beyond the initial deadline that organizers specified, participants signed on to petitions after they were purportedly "closed." For example, a petition to the Los Angeles superintendent of schools against tearing down a local bowling facility and building an elementary school in its place listed an official end to the petition of March 5, 2004.[7] Nonetheless, the petition remained available after its close date, and sympathetic site visitors continued to sign on through May of that year. While the extension of an online action beyond its initially stated duration is relatively easy, such a thing is not possible for offline actions like rallies and marches.

One cannot show up for a march a day, week, or month later and be a participant.

Even though all of the e-tactics we studied depended on collective participation—sometimes the collective participation of tens or hundreds of thousands of people—representations of the specific scope of collective participation were often absent (an issue that we will discuss in more depth shortly). So while rhetorical flourishes about "joining" and uses of the pronoun "we" imply that these actions are collective, reported participation figures were frequently not available. For instance, a site calling for a rule change at the Securities and Exchange Commission asked visitors to sign its petition and "seek out others to do the same," building a collective call for change.[8] The authors appeared to have a specific volume of signatures in mind; the site stated, "When we reach a number that serves our goal we will submit the entire package to Congress for review." Yet participation numbers were not reported anywhere on the site. Likewise, a letter-writing campaign denouncing anti-Semitism characterized its claim as "urgent," and beseeched users to "urgently click here to sign and request others to sign this petition," conveying the importance of large-scale participation, but it did not publish the participation numbers.[9]

Identifying Collective Action without Copresence

While we acknowledge that more elaborate collaborations are possible, we argue for a definition of collective action focused on coordinated action, not the physical marker of copresence or the high standard of online collaboration (indeed, most of what we would think of as collaborative would fall under the bailiwick of organizers, which we turn to in the next chapter). Indeed, this is what the e-tactics that we just looked at all had in common: they required the collective and coordinated actions of many people. We argue that a theory 2.0 approach to collective action requires us to recast copresence as a variable instead of an immutable constant. When copresence is removed as the constant identifier of collective action, we contend, one can peel back the onion to the deeper sense in which protests have been collective all along: they were coordinated actions that required the participation of multiple people.

Far from entirely novel, this view is similar to the definition of collective action taken in literatures outside of sociological social movement scholarship that are focused on collective action (Oliver 1993; Macy and Flache 1995). In that larger literature on collective action, protest is only one type of collective action. Further, what all collective action shares is not necessarily copresence but instead concerns for cooperation, coordination, and conflict. This is also the view of collective action that is associated with protest in disciplines such as political science and communication (e.g., Flanagin, Stohl, and Bimber 2006).

Looking for coordinated action and participation by multiple people, rather than for just copresence, makes identifying collective action akin to scholars studying how many protesters showed up at an offline protest event, with the decided advantage of recognizing important ways in which people can act together in an online context. Still, this begs the question, How are representations of collective action accomplished (aside from rhetorical moves similar to the examples above) for e-tactics, and what kinds of e-tactics were more and less likely to make explicit size representations? In other words, one way to represent the collective in collective action is to showcase participation figures. In the next two sections, we first examine which e-tactics are more likely to do this and consider the implications of this way of representing collective participation. Many sites, however, did not report their participation figures and represented collective participation in other ways, and so, second, we explore these sites and consider the implications of their decisions.

Representing the Collective through Reporting Participation

Many e-tactics did publish information on participation, although the amount of information they published varied widely. For instance, a small minority of e-tactics listed information on participation, but did not give specifics. An email campaign targeting presidential hopefuls in an effort to inform their political agendas, for example, stated that over 1,500 emails had already been sent.[10] Similarly, a petition in support of the First Amendment claimed participation of "over 20,000."[11]

Other e-tactics published what we might consider minimum participation numbers. As we discussed in chapter 4, some warehouse boycotts allowed participants to register their support. Registering was an additional action, not integral to participation in a boycott, so one might imagine that some people participated in boycotts without registering for them. On KarmaBanque, one of the boycott warehouse sites where users could register their support of actions, 163 people registered for a boycott of Exxon-Mobil for its contribution to global warming and 141 registered to boycott McDonald's for its deforestation practices.[12] These numbers are not too much different than those reported for some of the petitions that we sampled: thirty-three e-tactics in our sample had lower reported participation than either of these registration counts. Yet we also sampled two

KarmaBanque boycotts with only a single registrant, boycotting Boeing and Cadbury, and one boycott that had no registrants.[13] The boycott with no registrants was of a company that the boycott claimed produced toxic salmon for human consumption.[14] These extremely low registration numbers—lower than the participation numbers reported for any other e-tactic in the sample—suggest that perhaps not all participants registered for the boycott. Nevertheless, we can use the registration numbers to determine a floor of actual participation.

But the bulk of e-tactics that reported any information on participation levels did so by reporting the exact numbers of participants. For instance, some actions listed an exact number on the Web page, such as a petition condemning statements made by Senator Trent Lott.[15] Along with the text of the petition and fields that the participants could complete to sign on, the page stated, "Signatures gathered: 31." Across the e-tactics that reported exact participation levels, there was a high participation mark of 375,420 participants and a low of just 3, with a median of 1,054. Even the petition with only 3 signers, however, communicated a sense of collective action, beginning its claim with, "We the undersigned, endorse the following petition."[16]

In addition to reporting the overall number of participants, some e-tactics also supplied specific information on the most recent participants in the e-tactic. Petitions on the warehouse site ThePetitionSite, for example, published the most recent 25 signatures along with listing the total participant count. So users could see the name, city, state, zip code, country, and any comments provided by a signer, along with the date and time they participated, for the last 25 of 256 signers on a petition against a business merger that would allow a monopoly over broadband Internet services.[17]

Other e-tactics published the names of all the participants, as was the case with a petition asking the European Parliament to take a stand against software patents.[18] A signature page contained the names of the 317,299 people who had signed the petition so far. All of the petitions on Petition-Online fell into this category. Every petition on the site was accompanied by a series of signature pages, listing 50 signatures per page. All 3,222 signatories on a petition to Lions Gate Home Entertainment regarding its DVD release policies, for instance, were listed on the signature pages.[19] Along with their names, as the signers provided them, the pages published the signers' reported location and any comments they entered.

Other sites went further still by requesting and publishing a larger amount of information about participants. For example, to sign a petition calling for Amnesty International to label as a human rights violation the raising of Palestinian children to become suicide bombers, the participants were asked basic information (e.g., names and locations) consistent with other e-tactics just reviewed as well to provide their age, gender, and religious affiliation.[20] Moreover, the participants were asked to answer three questions: What are you willing to do to stop the raising of children to be homicidal? Do you believe in the war against terrorism? Can a state of Israel and Palestine live side by side peacefully? The 2,610 participants' answers were listed on the site along with their names.

E-tactics that reported on participation were different from those that tended to not report participation in patterned ways. As we can see in table 6.1, e-tactics from warehouse sites were far more likely to report participation than e-tactics from nonwarehouse ones: 78 percent of the e-tactics associated with warehouse sites reported participation numbers. For example, a petition on the warehouse site thiscause.org demanding representation for a U.S. prisoner being held in Cuba reported 82 signatures.[21] But only 6 percent of nonwarehouse e-tactics represented participation on their sites. Included in this category was a petition supporting a university's investment in Israel. At the time that we coded the site, the petition had garnered 9,506 signatures.[22]

The story may be as much about the e-tactical form as it is about warehouse versus nonwarehouse, though. In fact, if one breaks down the numbers by form, petitions are about the only e-tactical form that had

Table 6.1
Reported Participation by E-tactical Form, by Web Site Type

	Nonwarehouse e-tactics		Warehouse e-tactics*	
	Don't know participation	Reported or estimated participation	Don't know participation	Reported or estimated participation
Petitions	72% (N = 110)	28% (N = 43)	12%	88%
Letter-writing campaigns	100 (212)	0 (0)	100	0
Email campaigns	99 (151)	1 (1)	100	0
Boycotts	100 (82)	0 (0)	100	0
Fax campaigns	100 (149)	0 (0)	100	0
Total	94 (704)	6 (44)	22	78

*Percentages reported for warehouse e-tactics are weighted and therefore are shown without Ns.

regularly reported participation values. The other four e-tactical forms, regardless of whether they were found on a warehouse or nonwarehouse site, tend not to report participation.

As table 6.1 shows, 88 percent of warehouse petitions published information on participant volume. This category includes petitions on several warehouse sites, such as PetitionOnline and ThePetitionSite. For instance, a petition on ThePetitionSite against the use of motorized boats on lakes, ponds, and streams in the Adirondack Park reported that 489 people had signed the petition to date.[23] Other petition warehouse sites also publicly tracked participation, like the site e-the-people. In one case, users could sign on to a petition hosted on e-the-people calling for the prosecution of welfare cheats, knowing that 156 others had already endorsed the petition.[24]

A smaller percentage (28 percent) of nonwarehouse petitions informed visitors about the rate of participation. Site visitors could see, say, that 274 people had already signed the nonwarehouse petition calling for the inclusion of local citizens in future talks to resolve the Kashmir dispute.[25] And they could learn the participants' names, email addresses, and locations on the same page. On another nonwarehouse petition, the site boasted of 8,642 signatures to date on a petition against funding Michael Moore's film *Fahrenheit 911*.[26] In addition, a single nonwarehouse email campaign—the one described above that targeted presidential hopefuls about their political agenda—estimated participation.

Clearly a strong determinant of reporting participation is the e-tactical form, with petitions being more likely to have reported participation values and warehouse petitions especially likely to report. If you are looking at a warehouse petition, the betting odds are far in favor of reported participation. Why might this be the case?

To begin with, in order to report on participation levels, you need to be able to accurately measure participation. While counting participation at an offline protest like a march is as straightforward as counting the number of people present, when participants aren't physically copresent, counting is more difficult. Indeed, one of the first casualities of untethering collective action from physical copresence is our ability to easily assess participation. Not only is it harder to count participants in online actions but it is more expensive as well. And so which e-tactics tend to report participation levels is strongly influenced by how easy and inexpensive it is to count participation.

We found two features of e-tactics that can make it easy to count participants: automation and high virtualness (or the extent to which participation can be completed online), which were characteristics of e-tactics

Table 6.2

Reported Participation by E-tactic Feature, by Web Site Type

	Nonwarehouse e-tactics		Warehouse e-tactics*	
	Don't know participation	Reported or estimated participation	Don't know participation	Reported or estimated participation
No automation for participation	99% (N = 550)	1% (N = 3)	100%	0%
At least some automation of participation	77 (131)	23 (39)	13	87
Entirely or mostly online participation	86 (252)	14 (41)	14	86
Mostly offline participation	92 (23)	8 (2)	100	0

*Percentages reported for warehouse e-tactics are weighted and therefore are shown without Ns.

introduced in chapter 4. Both of these features make it easier for sites to track and hence report participation.

First, we found that the degree to which participation could take place online was linked to higher rates of reporting participation (table 6.2). In the terminology we introduced in chapter 4, we referred to this as the virtualness of an e-tactic. When the bulk of the participation in an action required an Internet connection, it was considered mostly online; when all of the participation in an e-tactic required an Internet connection, it was considered entirely online. It is much easier for sites to directly track (and therefore count) participation when it takes place online, rather than offline, and in turn, report participation. For instance, when a petition is signed virtually, it creates action on a server that can be logged, counted, and summed. Similarly, when an email is sent through a Web site, there are server-side logs indicating that activity, which then can be used to track and count participation. The same cannot be said for a letter that someone downloads and sends—there are ways to record the downloading of the letter, but not the actual sending.

Warehouse e-tactics that could be completed entirely or mostly online had a high rate of tracking participation; 86 percent of entirely or mostly online warehouse e-tactics published participation. For example, 3,820 participants were reported on a petition against tobacco use by children on the warehouse site ThePetitionSite.[27] Petitions on this site could be completed entirely online, without any independent action by the participant.

For nonwarehouse e-tactics, 14 percent of actions facilitated entirely or mostly online published participation numbers (table 6.2). For example, to sign a petition protesting the depiction of people with neuromuscular diseases as childlike, helpless, and pitiful, users entered their contact information directly on to the Web page, without any offline action.[28] And the site, in turn, published that information for the 992 people who had signed already.

In fact, only a single nonwarehouse e-tactic that took place mostly offline reported participation, although the number was actually a hybrid of both entirely online and mostly offline e-tactics. One petition, by Historians against the War, could be signed on the Web page itself, as an entirely online e-tactic, while a second petition could printed, signed, and returned by mail in a mostly offline action.[29] Since there are two distinct mechanisms for signing the petition—and indeed, the wording is slightly different on the two petitions—we consider these two separate e-tactics (for more detail on determining e-tactics, see the methodological appendix). In reporting participation in these actions, however, the site offered only a single, combined number: 688. In other words, the site reported participation in a mostly offline e-tactic when it was already easily tracking participation in a similar, entirely online action.

Having some automation gave nonwarehouse e-tactics an even higher rate of publishing participation—more than nonwarehouse e-tactics that were highly virtual. We can understand this by remembering that when e-tactics featured some aspect of automation, the tasks that their back-end servers performed could be logged, counted, and reported. For example, to participate in some e-tactics, users could simply enter their contact information and the site itself would populate the letter or email with that information as well as deliver it to the named target. It follows that more automated actions should be much easier to count since the site can track all aspects of participation, leading to more frequent reporting of participation for automated e-tactics. Nonautomated e-tactics, on the other hand, required the user to complete all aspects of participation, making it relatively more difficult for a site to track participation; when an e-tactic requires independent action by the user, completion of the action becomes much trickier to ascertain. And if a site cannot track participation, it certainly cannot publish reliable participation numbers.

We found that nonwarehouse e-tactics with at least some automation were more likely to report participation than those that were not at all automated: 23 percent of the former tracked participation while only 1 percent of the latter did so. For instance, a nonwarehouse petition in support of development in India that was automated, allowing users to sign the petition by entering contact information into fields on the site, published the names and locations of all 8,040 signatories.

The rare cases of nonautomated nonwarehouse e-tactics that reported participation included a petition that users were asked to print and mail to a central location.[30] Supporters of keeping the Boy Scouts of America religiously affiliated instructed site visitors to print, sign, and return by mail the petition. The site tracked the signatures on the mailed petitions and so far has reported 375,420 signers. As this example makes clear, it was possible but uncommon for nonautomated e-tactics to track and report participation.

Warehouse e-tactics that automated some aspect of participation, too, had a high rate of tracking participation (table 6.2): 87 percent of warehouse e-tactics that had at least some automation of participation published participation information, while none of the nonautomated warehouse e-tactics did. So warehouse petitions that automated at least some aspects of participation, like the PetitionOnline petition against a federal broadcasting law covering television viewing in private homes, often publicly tracked participation.[31] Even before signing themselves, visitors to the petition could see the names and locations of all of the previous 2,466 signers.

One way to simply summarize the trends in table 6.2 is that e-tactics are likely to report participation when organizers can easily track it themselves. E-tactics whose participation takes place entirely online and/or is facilitated by the Web site itself through automation are easier for Web sites to monitor and therefore track.

Since some kinds of e-tactics are more likely to be automated or be completed entirely online, the patterns in table 6.1 are even easier to understand. For instance, this helps to explain why petitions more frequently report participation levels than other e-tactical forms, and warehouse e-tactics generally represent some kind of participation more often than do nonwarehouse e-tactics. As we discussed in chapter 4, e-tactical forms such as petitions are more likely to automate participation and more likely to take place entirely online. Nonetheless, for letter-writing, email, and fax campaigns (save one nonwarehouse email campaign), neither automation nor entirely online participation led to reporting participation, suggesting that e-tactical form itself is still important to understanding these patterns.

Further explaining table 6.1, given the economies of scale on warehouse sites, we can see how warehouse sites would be more likely to overcome the hurdle of counting participation. While it may be relatively inexpensive for warehouse sites to track participation across e-tactics they host, nonwarehouse sites with significantly lower numbers of e-tactics may not put resources into tracking participation and thus may be unable to report participation. We see evidence of this in the rates of reporting participation among warehouse petitions as compared to nonwarehouse ones.

The Ups and Downs of Reporting Participation

The fact that coparticipants are not easily visible to each other in online actions (as they would be at, say, an offline rally) means that sites make the decision to report or not to report participation—that is, to represent the level of collective participation or not. As we discuss above, in some cases this choice is made based on the nature of the e-tactics themselves; it is much harder to track and then report participation in, for example, nonautomated, mostly offline e-tactics. We can also think about other reasons that organizers may struggle with whether or not to report participation, even if they have the technical capacity to count and report values at low marginal costs.

For one, while an e-tactic may be attractive to new participants if a large number of people have already participated, the converse is also true. E-tactics with small numbers of participants may have trouble mobilizing other sympathetic individuals. For example, potential signers on a petition demanding the federal government legalize marijuana might want to know how many others had already signed before adding their name and exposing themselves to possible government surveillance.[32] If there were few participants, it might make them less willing to participate. The site published no participation information, however, so these potential participants would not know if the signature count was low.

A second concern that sites may experience involves the authenticity of the participants. Given the low cost barriers to participation, a passionate participant might be motivated to sign a petition more than once, under false names or even anonymously. Many signers on warehouse sites, for instance, can opt to sign a petition anonymously. We will go into more detail about e-tactic policies on the privacy of participants' information in the next chapter, but here we point out the difficulty of assessing the legitimacy of an anonymous signature. On a warehouse petition against the U.S. Department of Defense's Total Information Awareness program, protesting the increasing government surveillance of "ordinary Americans," six of the most recent twenty-five participants were anonymous.[33] Given the petition's privacy topic, we might not be surprised that some signers were reticent to publish their names online, but anonymous participation may also appear fraudulent. When a site chooses not to publish participation information, it avoids this risk.

It is also possible that an opponent might participate in an e-tactic using a fraudulent identity, even an absurd one, in hopes of undermining the action altogether—or maybe just making a joke. Offline, we have seen groups like the Billionaires for Bush attend their opposition's protests in hopes of subverting the protest's claims. The Billionaires for Bush, for example, vociferously campaigned for George W. Bush, asserting that he would protect the rights of billionaires if elected. The intent of their theatrics was to mark Bush's broader agenda as more beneficial to the ultrarich than to average Americans and hence decrease support for the candidate.

Several of the signers on a petition asking the U.S. government to accept the right of the Kurdish people to self-determination, for example, were clearly fraudulent.[34] Of the 25 most recent signatures displayed on the Web page (out of a reported total of 980 signatures), only 1 appeared legitimate. The rest of the entries in the name column included obviously fictitious entities along with negative statements about Kurds (e.g., "Deport Kurd Terrorists"), thereby allowing opponents of the claim to use a petition in support of the group as a platform to oppose it. Dagwood Bumstead, of the comic *Blondie*, and Tweedle Dee, a character from *Alice in Wonderland*, purportedly signed the petition. The support of patently false participants can serve to weaken the claim itself.

Some sites included mechanisms to verify the identity of participants. The petition mentioned above calling for an end to childlike depictions of people with neuromuscular diseases, for instance, required the participants to follow instructions in a confirmation email, after submitting their name, in order to be published as a signer of the petition.[35] While such a procedure cannot verify that participants are who they say they are, at the least it can assure that each signature represents a unique email address.

Other sites opted to publish only overall participation numbers, but not specific data on participants. For example, the petitions on the warehouse site WebPetitions.com published a total number of signatures for each petition, but not data on individual signers. Such a strategy can avoid the problems associated with obviously fake participants, although it still risks the first issue raised above of reporting small numbers of participants.

Other sites sidestepped the twin risks of having to report low participation values and/or having apparently fake participants signing on by not reporting participation at all. In the next section, we examine which sites were likely to represent collective participation in ways other than reporting on participation numbers and examine the risks associated with that strategy.

Implied Collective Action: Participation Nonreporting

Although a significant number of e-tactics did report participation, the bulk of the Web sites in our sample did not. For these sites, collective participation was implied yet not concretely represented through counts. On one nonwarehouse site, for example, visitors could participate in five petitions, three letter-writing campaigns, a boycott, an email campaign, and a fax campaign in support of civil rights, but not a single one of these e-tactics tracked participation.[36]

Most e-tactics on nonwarehouse sites did not report participation. In fact, 95 percent of nonwarehouse e-tactics had no representation of participation numbers. E-tactics on nonwarehouse sites run by everyone from the Columbia Action Network to a fan of the television show *A Country Practice* encouraged large-scale participation, but did not inform visitors of the volume of participants to date.

In contrast, only 22 percent of warehouse e-tactics were missing participation numbers (table 6.1).[37] A standout site that looked more like nonwarehouse sites in this regard was iPetitions.com, which never published participation information. So we don't know how many people signed the petition encouraging Senator Diane Feinstein to run for president in 2004 or one calling for African leaders to release incarcerated journalists, despite the fact that participation took place entirely on the Web site, and the site presumably knew the participant count.[38]

Building on the finding from above that petitions were the only e-tactical form that regularly reported participation, no boycotts, fax campaigns, or letter-writing campaigns on nonwarehouse sites reported participation. Participants in a fax campaign protesting South Korea permitting dogs and cats to be raised for human consumption did not know how many other faxes had already been sent, nor did those who engaged in a letter-writing campaign to President George W. Bush supporting the distribution of HIV/AIDS medications in Latin America know how many letters had gone out to date.[39] And 99 percent of email campaigns on nonwarehouse sites did not report participation at all, including an email campaign calling for the release of Christians imprisoned in Saudi Arabia for practicing their religion.[40] Although emails were sent through the Web site itself, and so we could expect the site to know the actual number of participants, no participation numbers were reported.

And although there was at least some reporting of participation for nonwarehouse petitions, 72 percent of nonwarehouse petitions still did not publicly track participation. Site visitors therefore did not know, for example, how many others had signed a petition to the Pope to revoke a 1493 Papal Bull or who else had participated in a petition to the Wisconsin legislature against a hunting rights amendment to legislation protecting the rights of all citizens to safely use public land.[41]

The warehouse versions of these e-tactical forms, save petitions, never reported participation either (except for one email case). Both a letter-writing campaign and an email campaign targeting the governor of Tennessee in a plea to grant clemency to a death penalty prisoner, for instance, aimed for a high rate of participation, but we do not know from their published information whether they were successful.[42] Similarly, a fax campaign on a warehouse site specializing in conservative issues decrying police violence did not tell site visitors how many faxes had been sent as part of the campaign.[43] Warehouse boycotts, too, never reported exact participation numbers, just like their nonwarehouse versions, with the partial exception noted above of warehouse boycotts that allowed users to register for a given boycott.

Bucking the trend, only a minority (12 percent) of warehouse petitions were also missing participation numbers (table 6.1). Like the iPetitions cases described earlier, for this small set of petitions, site visitors had no way of knowing how many signers a petition had received. But for most warehouse petitions, you could see how many people had already signed on.

To better understand these trends, we should remember that things that make it harder to count participation—nonautomated e-tactics and ones that are mostly offline—will also make it less likely that participation is ultimately reported. As table 6.2 shows, none of the nonautomated warehouse e-tactics publicly tracked participation, and 99 percent of the nonautomated nonwarehouse e-tactics also failed to report on participation levels.

Looking at the three exceptions to this trend—nonautomated nonwarehouse e-tactics where participation was published—underscores the importance of the extent to which the action took place online for tracking and reporting participation, as we discussed above. In two of the three cases, participation occurred entirely online, although it wasn't automated. To sign a petition to keep a television show on the air or protest the prosecution of Milošević, participants emailed their name and contact information to the Web site administrator, who in turn posted the signer's name on the site and reported the overall participation.[44] In the third case, already mentioned, a mostly offline petition by Historians against the War, reported the combined participation in the mostly offline petition and an entirely online one.

Along these same lines, we found that nonwarehouse e-tactics whose participation took place mostly offline rarely reported participation and mostly offline warehouse e-tactics never did. For instance, a site encouraged visitors to write a letter of protest to international oil companies investing in a new oil pipeline in Burma.[45] The site provided the names and addresses of the targets along with a sample letter of protest. Nonetheless, participants had to write out or type the letter themselves and put it in the mail. With all of these steps taking place offline, the site had no reliable way of counting participants, and as might be expected, did not report participation numbers.

There are a series of potential consequences of missing participation numbers. First, there are the potential impacts on participation levels themselves that need to be examined by future research. Are people more likely to participate in an action if the number of other participants is shown, and is relatively large and/or growing? Brunsting and Postmes (2002) found that cognitive factors (e.g., efficacy) mattered more to online participants than to offline ones, but it is not entirely clear how efficacy and other factors might be assessed by potential participants. Also, without a record of participants, potential participants do not know *who* else has participated. If social networks or shared social identity encourage participation in protest, not knowing who has participated already may have an impact on whether a user opts to participate in an online action.

Second, collective identity, or roughly the sense of we-ness generated by protest, may be affected by how collective action is represented to participants. While stigma is the negative side of copresence for some participants, collective identity is often understood as a powerfully positive result of (and contributor to) collective action. In fact, collective identity can be so powerful that a number of social movement scholars have argued that the collective identity produced by copresence and collaboration helps to buffer the costs of protest, or at least make them more worth weathering.

Verta Taylor and Nancy Whittier (1992), for example, show that the lesbian feminist community's success in sustaining a collective identity encouraged members to mobilize for social and political change despite often hostile responses, even from other (heterosexual) feminists. Echoing the work of other theorists of new social movements (e.g., Melucci 1989), they explain that in movements on behalf of dominated groups, including women and sexual minorities, participants' experience of collective identity makes the risks of protest worth it. And scholars have shown that collective identity has helped movements survive periods of demobilization or abeyance (Taylor 1989). Similarly, Rick Fantasia (1988) argues that collective identity helps to buffer the effects of repression (i.e., when state or private actors try to stop protest). For instance, it is easier to endure negative actions by employers in a strike if you feel connected and committed to other strikers.

Collective identity has also been shown to be furthered by the emotion generated when people come together. In fact, an increasing number of scholars are contending that a range of emotions is generated through copresence and participation that help to bind people even as it further commits them to the cause (Goodwin, Jasper, and Polletta 2004).

In the cases we examine, reporting participation levels hardly assures or even necessarily builds a sense of collective identity, and one could reasonably suspect that collective identity is fostered even less when no information on other participants is available. In work on collective identity, scholars often begin from the assumption that the production of collective identity is premised on face-to-face interaction (Melucci 1989; Mueller 1994). Collective identity emerges in physically shared spaces, like the black church for the civil rights movement, and is sustained through in-person group activities, such as consciousness-raisings during the women's movement, not only knitting together participants, but helping them weather the risks and stigma associated with protest, too. Without physical copresence, as in online actions, it is unclear that collective identity can be forged. Some research on online chat rooms has even explicitly challenged the ability of participants to form a collective identity online (e.g., Ayers 2003; Nip 2004).

We are not convinced, however, that failing to build or support a sense of collective identity is as problematic for e-tactical participation as it would be for e-mobilizations, or actions entirely disconnected from Internet use or facilitation. A large part of why collective action has been so critical is that the sense of common cause helps people to endure the costs associated with their activism: prodemocracy activists in Communist Eastern Europe, say, sustained themselves against severe repression through their participation in literary circles (Johnston 2005); Taylor and Whittier's analysis of collective identity formation (1992) focuses on lesbian feminist identity in a period of U.S. history where lesbian identification, with or without protest, was marked negatively. With the option to make participation, even when published, anonymous, participants in e-tactics may be able to entirely sidestep the stigma accrued to the makers of some claims.

But in most cases, e-tactics are not only *not* dangerous, they are virtually costless to participate in. In fact, coordinated action without copresence, particularly when also asynchronous, can reduce the costs of acting even further. To the degree that this drives participation costs down further, all of the trends that we discussed in our chapter on costs and participation would be furthered. If protest is low cost, the bar that must be met for participants to engage in action is significantly lower, and people may no longer need to have a strong identification with a cause—that is, a sense of collective identity—in order to be mobilized. Indeed, this mirrors what Brunsting and Postmes (2002) found in their research on online activism: efficacy was a relatively more important determinant of participation, while collective identity was relatively less important online. And because low costs can lead to episodic rather than sustained mobilization (as we explored in chapter 4), movement survival in abeyance (Taylor 1989), which is sustained by collective identity, may also be less important.

The dynamics of online protest suggest new wrinkles in how we theorize collective identity. If your sense of others' participation changes, especially when you don't have a representation of that participation, we might expect that the processes driving collective identity would change, too. Or collective identity itself might change, emerging from places other than face-to-face interactions, and encouraging different kinds or levels of mobilization than previously studied. These are theory 2.0 effects, differing from both supersize assertions and claims of the negative effects of online action that argue for Web usage simply increasing or decreasing levels of collective identity.

Looking into the Future

Not all of this is new, of course: some offline tactics do not require physical copresence nor do they always represent collective action through reported participation. Participation in offline boycotts—for example, of tuna that isn't dolphin safe—and letter-writing campaigns—such as those coordinated by Amnesty International—has been hard for organizers to track.

And of course, some of this may change as changes in technology occur, such as advances in connection speed and the use of ICTs for synchronous communication. We might see a rise in sites that represent online copresence (i.e., through chat) and thus variation among online tactics

We certainly do not pretend to have written the final word on these topics or to have exhaustively outlined the potential consequences of a theory 2.0 approach for understanding collective participation. In fact, we suspect that researchers will need to spend years, if not decades, to thoroughly answer the questions raised by collective action without copresence. But we hope that we have made some progress in understanding the opportunities and challenges raised by collective actions that unfold in virtual spaces and often asynchronously.

In the next chapter, we will extend these arguments further. For instance, private collective action has always been an oxymoron where copresence-based collective action was concerned. With rare exceptions, such as groups like the Ku Klux Klan whose members wore robes and masks to shield their identities when they acted publicly, most protest is explicitly public, and one's presence at an event precludes any sense of private allegiance. This is not so when copresence is no longer required. Indeed, people can participate in meaningfully collective action relatively privately. In the next chapter, we examine the privacy of participation among the e-tactics that we studied, while we try to understand why organizers might create ways for people to privately participate in public collective actions.

7 From Power in Numbers to Power Laws: Copresence in Organizing

In the last chapter, we questioned what the collective in collective action means when protest participants don't have to physically come together in order to work for political, social, or cultural change. In this chapter, we turn our attention to the changing nature of collectivity in organizing. As we have conceptualized copresence, it includes not only the expectation of physical togetherness but also the expectation that activities require collective efforts. Just as we showed with participation, if properly leveraged, Web tools dispense with the need for physical togetherness among protest organizers. Simply put, people can organize without coming together physically.

We also go one step further here: we question whether organizing even needs to be collective at all. Can innovative uses of Internet-enabled technologies reduce the necessity of collective organizing altogether? We argue that some innovative uses of the Web can allow individuals or drastically smaller teams to organize. Even if the collectiveness of participation is still integral on the participation side (albeit redefined in terms of collectivity without physical copresence), we contend that the ubiquity of *collective* organizing is a different story.

Standing Shoulder to Shoulder to Organize for Change

Historically, organizing protests has taken the work of many hands and was often coordinated by SMOs. This hard work was usually done by people who were working shoulder to shoulder in physical spaces, or at least had frequent face-to-face contact with one another. Organizers met to coordinate messaging, brainstorm about goals, and determine strategy. Organizers have also generally been busy with the job of running the day-to-day operations of their SMOs. And perhaps most important in our view, they create and manage the protest opportunities that people engage in.

In a grounded way, this means that organizers have decided the date and times of protest events, negotiated with police and garnered permits (when necessary), led marches down a march route, and so on. Online, organizers also create and maintain protest opportunities, whether those opportunities are online petitions, denial-of-service actions, or other online actions.

The collective nature of organizing is recognized within the social movement literature. For instance, just as collective participation leads to dilemmas and opportunities that have been studied extensively by social movement scholars, the collective nature of organizing, too, poses dilemmas and creates opportunities that scholars have studied, both explicitly and implicitly.

In fact, assumptions about the collectivity of leadership run throughout social movement theorizing. We won't rehash the history of the most obvious collective representation of organizing, the SMO, since research on SMOs has been covered extensively in prior chapters. But it is worth noting that even the alternatives to SMOs discussed in the social movement literature represent variously constituted collectivities. For example, consider acephalous, cell-based networks, first discussed in chapter 5. These are fairly flat and disconnected organizing structures designed to be resistant to various types of repression. Even these networks and cells are still understood to be meaningfully collective; they are dependent on many people, even if those people are connected through a different set of relationships than in standard SMOs. Research questions on cells touch on how cells communicate, how they are led, and the effects of repression on cells and groups of cells. The same could be said for loose networks. Scholars have asked questions such as, How does the distribution of labor work in these networks? How is leadership accomplished?

None of these alternative forms contemplate the possibility that meaningful organizing could be accomplished by a single person, or by such small groups that the labels of networks or cells would seem to grossly overstate their size. Considered in relation to a major theme in this chapter—whether you consider the big fish of SMOs or the alternatives to SMOs suggested in the social movement literature—research on organizing has assumed that organizing, like participation, is a collective phenomenon.

The assumption of collectivity even bears on thinking about how organizations work together. In social movement research, the mesolevel is often the level of organizations or loose networks (with individual participants at the microlevel and the entire movement at the macrolevel). As introduced in earlier chapters, research on mesomobilization examines how organizations or organization-like networks come together to try to mobilize one another, and through that, mobilize each other's members and participant networks. Scholars studying mesomobilization argue that effective mesomobilization allows an even larger organizing team to work together, thereby producing an even larger turnout to major events. This theoretical concern suggests that collectivity is also presumed at the meso-level: collectivity is not just about getting organizers to work together, it can also be about getting their SMOs to do so.

With the Web, however, we find opportunities for organizing by individuals (which certainly doesn't qualify as collective) and small teams that stretch the meaning of collectivity up to the breaking point. To understand the consequences of noncollective organizing, we need to understand what exactly collectivity accomplishes for organizing, aside from historically having made it possible to organize large numbers of people. We highlight two ways in which collective organizing has affected organizing behavior, based on prior research.

Leadership Is Developed and Structured by Organizations

It would not be too much of an overstatement to claim that much of the literature on social movement leadership is really a literature on organizational leadership. Scholarship examines how leaders are developed through organizations and movements (e.g., Reger 2002; Oberschall 1973; Rejai and Phillips 1988; Marullo 1988), different levels and kinds of leadership within organizations and movements (e.g., Robnett 1997; Herda-Rapp 1998; McNair Barnett 1993), conflicts between leaders in organizations and movements (e.g., Gitlin 1980), and the leadership practices in organizations and movements (e.g., Reger 2002; Staggenborg 1988, 1991).

One thing that is clear from this research is that there is collective work that goes into identifying and developing young would-be social movement organizers and leaders. Another thing that is clear is that this development process socializes would-be leaders to core values and action routines of the movement(s). As we discuss later in this chapter, while the effects of socialization may not have been noticed in full before, we think it is consistent with existing work to argue that socialization ensures a level of predictability to leader's actions.

A brief aside makes this clearer. If you have ever had to stand facing the back of an elevator or violate some other social norm as part of a sociology class assignment, you have experientially learned that some ubiquitous things are best observed when they are disturbed. This is referred to as studying something "in the breach" because the existence of a norm may only be truly evident when you breach it; it is often tacit when you comply with the norm.

By analogy, scholars don't know much about leadership that has not been presocialized to social movement norms because such a high percentage of social movement leaders have been brought up through the ranks. We look at how some organizers of e-tactics allow us to examine the impact of organizational socialization by studying its importance in the breach. We won't allege that the leadership is unstructured but will instead suggest that it may be structured by norms from social systems not involving protest (e.g., norms from e-commerce or cybersecurity).

Decision Making Is Also Structured by Organizations

Scholarship shows that organizational structures also affect organizer decision making within movements (Klandermans 1989; see also Eichler 1977). That is, participants and organizers have expectations about how an organization will operate based on its form (e.g., hierarchical, distributed, professionalized, or informal). Those expectations are difficult to deviate from without alienating participants. This is even true when the organizational structure is relatively flat and/or informal, as is the case with some forms of "distributed leadership" (Brown 1989; Mushaben 1989; Stoecker 1990).

To give an example: if you joined a women's group that shared a core belief in consensus, you would not expect to see decisions made hierarchically. If they were, you would expect people to leave that group, disillusioned by the mismatch between the group's belief and leadership style, or work toward reestablishing a consensus process in the group. Because there are often many groups that you could join, some of the product differentiation between SMOs has to do with their organizational character and decision-making style. This can be true of informal networks as well.

The assumption of collectivity is obvious here. What will soon also be obvious is that if there is no organization or even loose network (because the organizing is being done by parties of one or two), that organizational structuring or constraint on decision making is absent. The consequences of this absence can be quite interesting.

Supersize Visions of Collectivity in Organizing

A supersized take on collectivity in organizing argues that ICTs can be used to more effectively collectivize the organizing process, by either expanding that process or solving various dilemmas that are impeding the dynamics of collective organizing. So a supersize model is not about the breach of theoretical findings above but instead how those processes are augmented by innovative uses of ICTs.

For instance, consider Bennett's work on the growth of broad yet "ideologically thin" coalitions involved in large mesomobilizations (e.g., Bennett 2003a, 2003b, 2004a, 2004b). He contends that Internet connectedness allows organizations with similar short-term goals to ignore larger ideological differences as they create short-term coalitions. These coalitions then mobilize larger numbers of participants together than they would have alone for specific events or time-limited campaigns. Importantly, Bennett is not claiming that these coalitions alter the ideology of each group in the process; rather, loose and temporary connections between organizations, facilitated by Internet-enabled tools, have become more common. Essentially, he is asserting that mesomobilization can be more effectively accomplished in the Internet age and using Internet-enabled tools.

Other research examines how ICTs can be used to resolve impediments to collective organizing. For example, R. Kelly Garrett and Paul Edwards (2007) offer a wonderful example of computer-aided communication enabling better organizational communication and coordination. Specifically, they examine how a novel computer- and telephone-based communication system was developed to allow expatriated leaders of the South African antiapartheid movement to coordinate the actions of the lower-level field leaders who were operating within South Africa. The system allowed messages to be encoded in computer tones, recorded, transmitted via recordings played over a phone line (including pay phones), recorded on the receiving end, and then decoded by computer. The alternative had been messages carried by personal couriers, which was slow and allowed no real-time adaptation of instructions given local conditions. The computer-aided system allowed in-country operatives to provide feedback and get updated instructions from their expatriated leaders. While not a Web-based technology, this system doubtlessly has many analogous online communication protocols (whether in stenography, private chat rooms, etc.). Even using commonly available encryption techniques can facilitate faster but still-safe communication, making the collective work of organizing flow more smoothly and/or effectively.

Theory 2.0: Organizing without Organizations, Part II

A theory 2.0 approach does not disregard the importance of Bennett's and Garrett and Edwards' arguments, or arguments like theirs. We agree that collective organizing can at times be facilitated by some uses of ICTs, including Web-based communication, especially where e-mobilizations are concerned. Where we differ is in whether or not supersize phenomena make up the whole story; we think they do not.

Most important, there are a number of examples in existing research showcasing the ability of solo organizers and parties small enough to scarcely be called teams starting and running protest campaigns and/or movements. This means that collectivity in organizing may not be necessary under the right conditions. As reported in prior chapters, Earl and Schussman (2003; Schussman and Earl 2004) found that individuals and pairs were the most common strategic voting organizers. Some of the movements that Gurak (1997, 1999) and Gurak and Logie (2003) studied were led by single pivotal individuals and their Web sites.

Such findings are certainly unanticipated by social movement scholarship and resource mobilization. So how can we explain these empirical observations and others like them? First, as we already discussed in chapter 5, the costs of organizing have dramatically dropped, which allows the labor and resources of a single person to go much further than in the past. Second, we have to appreciate the costs or burdens that collective organizing imposes: it takes time to find like-minded others to help, agree on what is to be done, and coordinate the work toward that goal. Indeed, perhaps we have seen so much collective organizing because organizing has always been expensive enough that it was worth overcoming the costs that building collectivities create.

But if organizing were to become cheap enough, it should be possible to find an inflection point where it could cost more to set up and maintain the structures to manage coordination among people than it would to just have one or two people shoulder the whole load. For instance, let's assume it took Katrina two hours to create and then one hour a day to maintain a Web site that she is very passionate about. In seven days of operation, she would have spent nine hours. If she wanted to form a group to build and maintain the site, she might spend that much time just in finding others who are willing to help her, agreeing on what they would do together, and coordinating with them about what she would do versus what they would do, and so forth, before they even launched the site. In short, when the costs of working in a group outweigh those of not working in a group, we could expect solo or small organizing teams. (Of course, a potential downside is that Katrina might become burned out over time, leading to spurts of organizing. Where true, though, this simply feeds into the other pressures for episodic organizing and activism, which we have explored in previous chapters and will return to in chapter 8.)

Our argument thus far in this chapter has strong similarities to the one about the expense of middle management that Shirky (2008) makes and our discussion in chapter 5, prompting the thoughtful reader to wonder what an analysis of collectivity in organizing e-tactics can add. In a nutshell (which for many readers won't be interpretable for a few more paragraphs), we contend that innovative uses of the Web can allow organizing to follow a power law such that drastically smaller parties can organize, including parties of one. Indeed, there are conditions under which parties of one might be far preferable as organizing units.

OK, let's step back: What is a power law? Shirky (2008, 125) explains it as an imbalance in participation that grows more extreme at higher levels of participation:

[A] power law describes data in which the nth position has 1/nth of the first position's rank. In a pure power law distribution, the gap between the first and second position is larger than the gap between the second and third, and so on. In Wikipedia article edits, for example, you would expect the second most active user to have committed only half as many edits as the most active user, and the tenth most active to have committed one-tenth as many. This is the shape behind the so-called 80/20 rule.

Researchers have found that a range of online phenomena follow power laws, including the popularity of blogs, linking behavior, posting behavior, and editing behavior, to name only a few (for several examples of power laws online, see Shirky 2008, 122–130). Of course, Shirky is not the first person to note the potential significance or apparent frequency of power laws; power laws are interesting in large part because so many researchers have found them in research on Web-based participation phenomena.

The "so-called 80/20 rule" that the above quotation alludes to basically says that 20 percent of your users will account for the vast majority of activity on your site (although it can be applied elsewhere too). So, in the Wikipedia case, not only is the most active person twice as active as the second user, three times as active as the third most active user, and so on, but by the time you get through the top 20 percent of active users, the other users are barely contributing any activity at all.

We are arguing that innovative uses of the Web can make organizing inexpensive enough that it can begin to follow power-law dynamics in some situations. When that happens, one person will bear the majority of the costs, the next most active organizer has to bear substantially fewer costs, and so on down the line, so that quickly there are no organizing costs left to bear at all. When an active organizer either cannot bear all of the costs alone or cannot find an extremely small number of people to bear increasingly smaller costs, the organizing effort will miscarry or fall apart. But when an active organizer can bear all of the costs, or the vast majority of them (consistent with an 80/20 rule), the organizing effort can move forward.

Crucially, we don't expect to observe power-law phenomena when organizing is expensive. We aren't predicting the rise of superhero organizers who can single-handedly carry high costs; we are claiming that costs can become so low that mere mortals can often handle them on their own.

As Shirky points out, while many people think of something having to do with "imbalance" as a bad thing, power-law participation rates can be quite successful online. Certainly some will fail, but many collectively organized activities also fail; that some individual efforts fail, too, does not distinguish them.[1] Indeed, when one of these efforts fails, there is often only a captain and no crew when the ship goes down.

Our power-law explanation of organizing is certainly consistent with the findings that we cited above of online protest efforts being led by single individuals, pairs, or drastically small teams. But what are the follow-on implications of a radical reduction in the organizing person power needed to start and maintain a protest effort? How are protest-related processes altered by solo, pair, or drastically small organizing teams running the show? We begin to trace those implications here.

First, we think this dramatically changes who is likely to become an organizer. Schussman and Earl (2004) started thinking about how organizers (or leaders, if you prefer) come to run protest campaigns or movements, and we follow their thinking here. For more expensive organizing efforts, which will probably still be disproportionately organized by SMO or SMO-like organizing forms, there is a clear vetting and mentoring process that happens (as mentioned earlier in the chapter). This means that leaders tend to be well socialized into the patterns of protest in general and the specific organization in particular, by the time they are making major organizing contributions.

But who vets and then trains the solo organizers, pairs of organizers, or drastically small teams that we are interested in? In fact, no one does. And no one is charged with training them before they begin organizing either. Participants may effectively vet organizers by deciding whether or not to participate, and hence whether or not to collectively make an organizing effort popular, but that happens after an organizer has already put in time. There is far less constraint on who becomes an online organizer, for good or ill. Instead, that constraint operates in terms of whether their action is successful *after* they have already effectively become an organizer. (Here we mean externally imposed constraints; of course, there are lots of skill, time, and aptitude constraints that may dissuade any given person from becoming an online organizer even for a cause they care about.)

We argue that when you dramatically change who can become an organizer by throwing open the doors to anyone who wants to invest the time, you are invariably opening the door to many new organizers. There are good reasons to expect that these new organizers will behave differently from their vetted, trained, and disciplined (in the Foucauldian sense) predecessors. Recall, as we discussed above, that the social movement organizers who social movement scholars are so accustomed to studying are recruited and socialized before they begin to lead, and their leadership and decision making are tightly structured by both their past and their organization's structure. In a party of one, there is no such constraint. We suggest several hypotheses about what will happen when power-law organizing through parties of one, two, or a few takes place.

First, we hypothesize that people will organize around a much wider array of causes and concerns. We don't just mean that within environmentalism (or other mainstream causes), for instance, there will be more specific issues raised. We mean that we expect people to bring their own, sometimes far-from-standard political concerns into the world of Web protest. We expect e-tactics about saving television shows, supporting boy bands, and challenging corporate game producers. We expect that things social movement scholars never dreamed of studying a protest about will be things that some new organizers decide to pursue online. In fact, we expect that things social movement scholars never dreamed of considering as protest will be things that some new organizers pursue using e-tactics. These might not be things that organizers would organize around if the costs were high, or if they had to recruit and maintain large teams of organizers, but we argue that individual and small party organizers will use low-cost protest forms to pursue their passions.

Second, we hypothesize that their decision making will not be strongly structured by classic social movement concerns, reflecting instead the paths outside of social movements that they traveled prior to organizing. If you ask a social movement organizer or a social movement scholar about decision-making processes and organizational priorities, you will probably get similar responses. People will discuss the importance of fund-raising (à la resource mobilization), framing and media outreach, and knowing who your peers, allies, competitors, and opponents are (and knowing that sometimes peers, allies, and competitors aren't that different), among other high-priority topics. Prior research suggests that the new organizers we discuss are not as concerned with these things (Earl 2007; Schussman and Earl 2004). In essence, if you are not socialized to care about these things and your costs are low enough, you may pay little attention to them.

Does that mean that new organizers are socially unstructured? Not at all. Rather, we expect that new organizers are likely to import concerns and issues from the areas in which they were socialized. Put differently, these new organizers are coming from somewhere, and that somewhere has its own socialization patterns, logic, and priorities. Instead of vanquishing those concerns and learning about the norms of protest, we argue, these new organizers bring their existing concerns, processes, and tools with them. As we explore in our data below, sometimes this means that the logics they import are actually at odds with standard social movement concerns. Specifically, below we examine the development of private, collective protest and the rise of privacy policies.

Distributed Organizing

Of course, it is not that all organizing will all of a sudden be conducted by one-person operations. And some of the one-person operations that start organizing will grow larger over time for a variety of reasons. Are there theory 2.0 changes possible when moderate or large teams work together to produce protest opportunities? We think so. We believe that the same kinds of uses of ICTs that have allowed business to distribute workloads and coordinate projects will allow protest organizers to engage in what we could think of as distributed organizing in which several people engage in coordinated organizing without needing to come together physically.

An important potential implication of this style of organizing is that the pool of people with whom you might collaborate, should you need help, grows substantially when you include people you can work with without ever meeting face-to-face or even over the phone. You don't have to find someone physically close to you that cares about your issue; you just have to find someone somewhere who also cares enough about your issue to be willing to work on it with you. Although it might be hard to immediately create high-cost alliances with strangers, these are not high-cost engagements. Unlike organizers working on e-mobilizations, organizers of e-tactics are often on the cusp of being able to do it alone, so the risks of working with someone who you don't know are presumably much lower.

Organizers without Organizations

We can evaluate many of our claims using data from the Web sites and e-tactics that we studied along with responses from the interviews (introduced in chapter 3) with organizers of Web sites that hosted or linked to e-tactics. All of these respondents operated a Web site that hosted or linked to an e-tactic—that is, they were organizers of e-tactics. These interviews were designed to shed light on the back-end human dynamics of organizing. From these data, we find that while participation is still collective, it appears as though organizing is not similarly always collective.

Parties of One

More than a few sites in our sample appeared to be organized by a single person. We call these parties of one lone-wolf organizers to express both their solitary nature and less constrained position as organizers who are unfettered from coordinating (or even agreeing) with others. Our interviews confirmed our suspicions that lone wolves were at work creating e-tactics. For instance, one respondent said that he was motivated by his dislike of the mainstream media to start his Web site, explaining that the entire site was the result of his own work, save for a few of the graphics that a friend had helped design.[2] Another respondent explained that her site "arose out of frustration."[3] She elaborated that she started using the Web for political expression "and that lead me to some of the bigger participatory blogs, and then I just started my own because I felt like I had more to say than what I was posting on other people's sites." In essence, she felt restricted by the existing opportunities for activism and so decided to create her own. She was surprised by just how easy it was to build her site, even without the help of others. It was, she explained, "a one-woman show."

Tales of lone-wolf organizing were echoed throughout the interviews and usually mentioned without fanfare. Respondents who created these Web sites solo or in small teams did not see this as a rare or daunting task. Instead, the small number of organizers was related matter-of-factly. Some even pointed to the advantages of having unconventionally small organizing teams. Mentioning first the advantages of a large number of organizers, one administrator who had worked with several activist Web sites ultimately came down on the side of having a notably small organizing team:

If you have more people who are actively involved in producing and maintaining the site, I think that's generally a plus because it means the material can be fresher, you can just get more content, and you can build a better vehicle. On the other hand . . . the more people—you know, too many cooks in the kitchen—there can be clashes over ideas. . . . My experience has been that this can be extremely detrimental. . . . Sometimes the smaller outfit who's directly involved with doing the Web site—and in my case, very involved—I think is an advantage.[4]

Sometimes these lone wolves still saw themselves as connected to broader social movements even though they were acting alone. For example, one site administrator identified his site as affiliated with the veteran's movement, but not with a specific SMO, explaining that he was the only person involved in organizing the site: "I've been the only one who's worked on it."[5] As we discuss shortly, however, Web sites not affiliated with SMOs often lacked any language that pointed to affiliations with a larger movement. This suggests that either few lone wolves see themselves as parts of "imagined" social movement communities (à la Benedict Anderson 1983), or when they do, they don't necessarily include language on their Web site that represents that connection.

"Doubles" and "Triples" Organizing

Other sites were the work of just two people, or originally the work of a pair that added a third hand into the mix, and not collectively organized using traditional SMOs. These pairs and triplets are hardly what we would term a group of organizers. One activist site, for example, was founded by the respondent and one friend, although they had recently added a third member to their organizing team. Motivated by a strong dislike of a national drugstore chain, this organizer turned to the Web to express his claim: "I was very disgruntled with some of their business practices in my city, and I was trying to think of ways that I could try to get my disdain for them kind of out in space in some sort of legitimized fashion."[6] He began to create the site but hit a few technical obstacles, at which point he described his idea to a friend: "I once expressed my idea to a friend of mine—and he was a little better at the back-end stuff. He just went home and made the whole back part of it. Then I just did the front design on it. . . . [H]e greased the track for it." As the respondent explained in the interview, consistent with a power law of organizing, his contribution as the first organizer was larger than that of the second organizer, and both did more for the site than the recently added third organizer.

Drastically Small Teams

Other sites that we studied were run by drastically small teams—groups far smaller than social movement scholars usually think about when they think about core groups of organizers. For instance, one administrator of a Web site in our sample explained that the entire site was the work of just four people, none of whom were paid for their effort. Explaining what each person did for the site, he said, "I'm basically in charge of everything that happens there: paying for the domain, posting on a daily basis, any link checking, promotion, and so forth. The other three people are contributors whose input varies from quite frequently, sometimes they'll post daily, and sometimes they'll post once a week."[7] Another respondent collaborated with a few friends to found an activist site. All of them had received an email with an action plan for creating social change, noted the respondent, and "I liked it. Several friends of mine had received the same email. We decided to make a Web site about it. We could not contact the originator of the email originally, so we did it on our own. And it grew from there."[8] At the time of the interview, three people were involved in the production of the Web site, the primary arm of the group's social change efforts, and about two dozen other people supported it through their participation in media work for the site.

Another site that was initially founded by a pair expanded by adding organizers as the project grew: "As we progressed and expanded we actually had to bring on chairpeople, and we ended up having about a dozen chairpeople located across the country."[9] In sum, whether we are discussing lone wolves, doubles, triples, or a handful of organizers, one thing that came through clearly in the interviews is that there is much organizing happening not only outside of SMOs (as we showed in chapter 5) but even without meaningful collectivity at the organizing level.

Organizing Outside of Social Movements

As we saw above, some organizers felt connected to larger social movement causes even though they were acting alone as organizers, with their sites hosting or linking to e-tactics. In this section, we examine how connected e-tactics organizers seem to traditional social movements, and their norms and practices.

Movement Affiliations Represented on Web Sites

One way to get a measure of how much organizers see themselves as being connected to larger social movements (versus being really, really lone-wolf organizers) is to measure whether Web sites in our data set tended to include rhetoric or other representations that connected the site or specific e-tactics to larger social movements. That is, just because an antiwar e-tactic was linked to from a Web site doesn't mean that the Web site itself discusses or affiliates with the antiwar movement.

In fact, our data suggest that SMOs almost always make some representation of association with a larger movement, but non-SMO sites don't. Among nonwarehouse sites, while 80 percent of the SMO sites in our sample affiliated with a social movement, only 30 percent of the non-SMO ones did. On its Web site, the SMO PEN American Center, for example, explicitly affiliated itself with the free speech movement.[10] Non-SMO sites, on the other hand, far less frequently affiliated with social movements, even though they often organized protest around causes associated with social movements. For instance, a site run by an individual hosted a letter-writing campaign in support of intellectual property rights, but the site itself did not contain any language of affiliation with the broader social movement around intellectual property.[11]

Self-identification of Organizers

Remarkably, not only do the vast majority of non-SMO Web sites fail to represent an affiliation with a larger social movement, in our interviews with site organizers a number of them questioned whether they should even be considered activists or organizers, despite the fact that every respondent worked on a Web site that hosted or linked to at least one e-tactic. Seeming to believe (much like the hypothetical skeptic we introduced in chapter 4 and many social movement scholars) that you are only an organizer if what you do to create protest opportunities is costly, often personally and certainly in terms of time, these organizers believed that what they were up to was too easy to consider organizing. As one respondent flatly explained, "Online activism, I would have to say no. . . . I don't have any involvement in that."[12] He elaborated that, in his view, "[what I do] is not activism; that is artistic expression" and further:

Even though we have been talking for a while, it is still not clear to me what online activism is in contrast to personal expression. The way I am thinking about this, activism has more to do with a motivation to convince people as opposed to expression which could be a very private thing and my impression of the vast majority of blogs and Web sites that I have had contact with is that most people they just want to talk as opposed to convincing people.

Imagining a certain definition of organizer, formulated on his experience with street protests, this respondent denied that he organized protest and that his site was activist, despite the fact that his Web site contained an e-tactic.

Another interviewee described his perceived distance from being an organizer by citing his motivation for starting a Web site.[13] He commented that he was motivated by personal interest rather than a desire to be an activist. Moreover, his role in the evolution of his site was more passive—people sent content to him—rather than active, as the organizer label would suggest:

I didn't start with the idea that I will start an activist Web site. That's not how I started. I just wanted to write about things that were important to me. I wanted to sort of make public and it kind of developed from that, and a lot of things have just come to me rather than me go to them. So areas in which I am very active have kind of dropped in my lap as opposed to me going and finding them, and people have picked up on that, and I have kind of just gotten involved and have just taken off from there. It was kind of the opposite way around of you starting something like an activist blog.

Another site operator maintained that he couldn't appropriately be called an organizer because he did not really know how to be one.[14] The bulk of his activist experience, he said, "has been as a participant and an organizee, not an organizer, so I can't speak with great authority to all the ins and outs of organizing."

Still another respondent drew a distinction between what he did and "true activism."[15] Contrasting his own site with a site that he helped set up for an SMO, he argued that the SMO site was true activism:

I just see from the way they conduct it. [It] is so different from how I do this one. They're really invested in it. They do advertising, they sell stuff, they have multiple volunteers contributing to it. They get all kinds of hate mail. That feels more like the activism model. I think it's neat what we did. I'm proud of what we did, [but] if you told me I had to spend three hours a day on it, I'd be like, "You got to be kidding me." The site would be down the next day. So I guess the traditional activism that I see in other people . . . mine just feels real different from them.

In all of these cases, the Web sites that these organizers produced either hosted or linked to an e-tactic. Thus, whether these respondents had a self-identity that included activism and organizing or not, they were in practice creating and connecting participants to protest opportunities, which is perhaps the most basic trait of a social movement organizer.

Peer Recognition

Organizers in the social movement tradition are trained to be keenly aware of potential competitors, collaborators, and opponents. So in our interviews, we asked which Web sites the Web site operator saw as peers and which they saw as setting an industry standard. Their answers were telling in several ways.

First, as a result of their lack of either movement affiliation or training, some interviewees had trouble even naming example peer or industry standard sites. One site owner, hard-pressed to name an industry standard activist site, stated, "To be honest, I think my site is pretty unique."[16] He elaborated that the nature of the Web itself meant that there simply could not be such a thing as an industry standard for activist Web sites: "[The Web] is largely formless and shapeless and standardless; and industry standard seems silly, for lack of a better term." Another site operator had a similar response, insisting on the uniqueness of his site: "I'm afraid that I'm not able to answer [who would be a peer site] because I don't know anybody who does what I do exactly. I just can't answer that."[17] Online organizers clearly did not always see themselves as part of the social movement tradition, with the attendant models of activism that it would include.

Second, while the majority of respondents were able to name peers or industry standard Web sites, they did not tend to name peers or industry leaders because the other Web sites were involved in activism. This suggests that organizers saw themselves as similar to others, even if those others did not include people who have traditionally been considered organizers. When they did offer examples of peer and industry standard sites, respondents frequently identified sites with a similar ideological perspective, size, and style, departing from social movement models. For instance, one administrator explained that he chose peer sites "from an issue perspective, and from a scope and size and number of visitors [perspective] in general. So what I'm looking at is sites that are similar in visitors, in political bent, in kind of scope of things that they cover, and so forth."[18] For the operator of one activist blog that contained e-tactics, determining a peer site was straightforward.[19] She named a blog that used the same blogging software as her own:

[The peer site] is set up under Blogger as well. And the way Blogger functions, looks, and feels is very similar across everybody who uses Blogger as their blogging service. The comments function [is] the same. And the person who runs [that site] and I have very similarly aligned political views. We've actually collaborated at times so that I would post one part of a story while that person posted another part of a story.

These respondents drew the boundaries of their field based on content and style, aligning themselves with other sites whose message and presentation were similar.

A handful of respondents named peer sites not only for their similarity in content and style but also for the technical mechanisms that they used for engaging in online activism. One site founder, for example, stated that he identified peer sites that had similar foci on issues of social justice and human rights, and "are involved in various campaigns that are conducted online and employ other technologies such as texts and email technologies."[20] Another site operator pointed to a site that used similar methods to his own site as a peer: "And they've been having similar methods . . . sending letters, sending emails, doing that type of activity, reaching out to people at conventions, trying to get them involved."[21] A different respondent drew on a similar process of analogy based on technical structure, identifying an industry standard activist Web site "because they provide the means to contact federal officials through faxing and email and/or phone numbers."[22]

Finally, in early 2006, when we were collecting our interview data, MoveOn seemed to be the most talked about activist Web site in the United States. Going into the interviews, we expected that it would receive a fair share of nods from other Web site organizers as an industry leader. We were wrong. In our interviews, MoveOn was rarely mentioned. Instead, respondents appeared to be identifying peer and industry standard sites based on other metrics, like the ones discussed above.

To summarize our claims thus far, we are arguing that parties of one, two, and three, and drastically small teams, can now organize online using e-tactics. We expect that these organizing efforts will follow a power-law distribution where SMOs are not involved. We have also shown that these new organizers aren't as connected to overall social movements as their SMO counterparts, which can be seen not only in the ways that they represented relationships (or the lack thereof) to movements on their Web sites but also in their views on what constitutes a peer site. One more thing is worth noting before moving on to examine various impacts of this shift in organizing structures: while our data are cross-sectional (i.e., we observed Web sites at one point in time) and cannot speak directly to changes over time, there is reason to believe that this power-law structure to organizing should allow organizing to emerge quickly. We might also expect that many organizers will fade away over time, and that others will succeed in their quest and therefore complete their campaign. If this is true, we should expect that sporadic, episodic, and periodic organizing will become more common over time. We have much more to say about this in chapter 8, including a look at the relationship of our argument to abeyance structures. But for now, we point out this potential implication and note that it is consistent with findings from a good number of studies on online organizing (e.g., Bimber 2001, 2006; Bimber, Stohl, and Flanagin 2008; Earl and Schussman 2003, 2004; Gurak and Logie 2003; Schussman and Earl 2004).

Broadening the Scope of Claims

Thus far we hope we have made a strong case that organizing can be less collective online, and that the new types of organizers we studied—pulled in by their interests coupled with the low costs of action—are less connected and socialized into social movement ways of thinking even though they use classic social movement tactics. In this section, we begin to analyze data that provide a window into a set of consequences that may follow from the lack of social movement mooring and training.

Specifically, we predicted that lone-wolf organizing or organizing by drastically small teams would result in organizing around a much wider array of issues. Simply put, there are many things to get upset about in politics, institutional decisions, and everyday life. In Western democracies, scholars have noted, people tend to turn to protest to ameliorate these upsets. Our data confirm that e-tactics covered a broad range of claims (and targets) in two distinct ways. First, a wide array of standard political issues was given voice online. Second, some new and decidedly nontraditional issues were raised in other e-tactics. We find, in fact, a veritable explosion of causes and the proliferation of the use of e-tactics for issues that many social movement scholars might not have previously considered "true" protest.

Political Outsiders: A Fecundity of Claims

Thinking back to chapter 3's introduction to the claims made in the e-tactics that we studied, there is clear evidence that people are organizing protest around a broad range of political issues. Recall that we found 71 unique issues addressed on the main pages of the sites coded and 86 different issues on specific e-tactics (interested readers should refer to figure 3.2). And drilling down to the different positions that could be taken on the same issue (i.e., support or opposition for the same issue), we found 88 unique stances on the sites and 110 unique stances in the e-tactics themselves.

Even more intriguingly, recalling the table on the distribution of claims across nonwarehouse sites (interested readers should refer to table 3.1), we find an extremely varied online claims sector (i.e., a wide sector) where any particular claim was unable to dominate the claims-making activity (i.e., a thin sector). We found a broad distribution of claims across the sites in our data set with no claim found in more than 15 percent of the sample. Further, only six claims appeared on more than 10 percent of the non-warehouse sites and only one claim appeared on more than 10 percent of the warehouse sites as a main claim of the site itself. Clearly no claim dominated the sample; even as a large number of claims were invoked, only a handful were invoked with any notable frequency.

Similarly, few issues appeared on a large number of tactics: only a small number of claims appeared on more than 10 percent of any of the subcategories of e-tactics that we investigated (i.e., nonwarehouse petitions, nonwarehouse boycotts, etc.), while a large number appeared infrequently in the data, on only one to a few e-tactics. For instance, only one claim appeared on more than 10 percent of the nonwarehouse boycott campaigns and there were only five claims that appeared on more than 10 percent of the nonwarehouse letter-writing campaigns. In contrast, thirty-five different claims were discussed on less than 2 percent of the nonwarehouse letter-writing campaigns and thirteen different claims were discussed on less than 2 percent of the nonwarehouse boycotts. Looking at these values, it is clear that no single or even small number of issues dominated our data; instead, a diverse array of issues was championed, but each issue was championed through only a small number of e-tactics.

Even some of these larger frequencies may hide additional diversity, therefore serving to understate our evidence for this contention. For example, "Government Policy, not elsewhere classified" is a claim category that is coded when a claim is made about a government policy that is not elsewhere classified in the coding scheme. In practice, this means that about 12 percent of the nonwarehouse sites that included such a claim may have been discussing different government policies from one another, thereby understating the diversity in our data.

Just as the types of causes engaged in protest actions are widespread with no dominating issue, online organizers named a range of targets for their e-tactics (Earl and Kimport 2008). To briefly review our more detailed description in chapter 3, we note that e-tactics were aimed at government officials and departments as well as private actors. As with the spread of claims, analysis of the targets of these e-tactics reveals a wide, thin protest sector around political issues.

Outside Politics: Newbies Do the Craziest Things

In our data, all five e-tactical forms—and petitions and boycotts in particular—were used to handle problems outside the purview of traditional social movements. About 11 percent (N = 104) of all the e-tactics in our sample were organized around claims that noticeably depart from historical social movement uses of protest tactics (see also Earl and Kimport 2009). For instance, a consumer of Hong Kong films organized a petition to Disney to depart from its current procedure and release these films uncut.[23] As committed to this cause as the organizer might be, it is hard to imagine there would be enough interest to sustain a formal organization around this cause, not to mention incur the costs associated with creating one. Yet on the Web, a single individual could author this petition at minimal to no cost and hope to find like-minded supporters online. In this case, the organizer was highly successful: his petition had 13,069 signatures.

The bulk (N = 91) of these divergent claims related to entertainment, including television shows, movies, and video games.[24] For example, fans of the Nickelodeon network show *Salute Your Shorts!* petitioned the network to play reruns of the series, and fans of *Firefly* petitioned to keep the show on the air despite its low ratings.[25] Other supporters of movie series, such as *Halloween*, used e-tactical forms to make their claim, as did video game users for the release of specific games for use on certain game systems.[26] Fan activism is not a wholly new phenomenon (Jenkins 1992; Scardaville 2005), but scholars have documented a rise in the use of social movement practices to forward these claims (Earl and Kimport 2009).

Other nonpolitical e-tactics focused on sports figures, such as a World Wrestling Entertainment (WWE) wrestler. A self-described "18-year-old fan of WWE" wrote a petition asking that a specific wrestler be removed from the WWE and promised to take his petition to the owner of the company.[27] The main reason offered for the wrestler's removal was that the petition authors and signers were not interested in watching him wrestle. In other words, he was no longer entertaining to this audience. A far cry from traditional political claims, this petition nonetheless made a claim for change and named a target.

These e-tactics also diverged from traditional social movement actions in the targets they named. Just as the causes of these actions were nontraditional, some of the targets they named show the migration of protest into the mainstream as a way of creating all kinds of change. One petition named parents as its target, demanding that they work to keep their children from smoking.[28] Although other antismoking efforts have been aimed at tobacco companies or government, asking these institutions to make it more difficult for teens to smoke, this petition chose a target that in theory can more closely monitor children's behavior. In making this nonpolitical, cultural claim via a petition, the organizer deployed a practice that was historically used for political protest.

Some e-tactics even named private individuals, as with a petition in support of personal gun ownership that named a specific private citizen as its recipient.[29] And a petition to convince someone to take a trip to Ottawa was another example of e-tactics that targeted individuals with no apparent institutional authority.[30] These e-tactical forms are a way of making a broad range of claims directed at an array of groups and individuals, both political and private.

Interestingly, we found the most divergent claims—that is, claims that were the furthest afield from traditional social movement concerns, including all thirteen of the nonentertainment, nonpolitical claims—on warehouse sites where organizing an e-tactic is particularly easy to do. As we have noted before, warehouse sites often automate the production of e-tactics, allowing would-be organizers to create an e-tactic for free in just minutes. The immense range of causes that these organizers in turn engage is evidence of their freedom from socialization into the norms of social movement organizing. We can imagine that people might not be motivated to organize an e-tactic demanding the release of uncut Hong Kong films by Disney, as mentioned above, if the costs were high. And they might be less likely to call for a boycott of the movie *Chicago* because of its overzealous media promotion if they had to recruit and maintain a large team of organizers to implement the boycott.[31] But when the costs are low, we do find organizers using these e-tactical protest forms to address all manner of grievance.

As we have argued elsewhere (Earl and Kimport 2009), there is a line of social movement theory that helps make sense of this. According to research on "movement societies" (see contributions in Meyer and Tarrow 1998a, 1998b; Rucht and Neidhardt 2002; Soule and Earl 2005; Earl and Kimport 2009), as social movements become mainstream, movement practices become standard vehicles for handling grievances, even when those grievances are far from political.

The structure and ease of organizing protest on the Web should further accelerate this trend. In movement societies where e-tactics are available, not only do movements become the go-to instrument for making griev-ance-related claims, e-tactics in particular will flourish, becoming a sort of standard operating procedure for grievances. So concerns raised in every-day life, such as a hope that the most recent season of your favorite televi-sion show will be released quickly on DVD, are communicated through practices that have historically been reserved for political issues. In other words, movement practices—the means—become decoupled from tradi-tional movement causes and claims—the ends. And the lowered obstacles to organizing protest online that we have described serve to amplify this trend.

The Birth of Private Collective Actions

The presence of privacy policies on the Web sites that we studied illustrates an institutional model at play in e-tactics, but generally absent from entirely offline protest, pointing to theory 2.0 changes. Counter to the historical publicness of participation in protest, many of the sites discussed the privacy of users' information.

This was particularly pronounced among warehouse e-tactics: 94 percent were accompanied by some kind of privacy policy. Signers of a warehouse petition on WebPetitions.com in support of current library procedures for selecting books at the Montgomery County Memorial Library, for example, could click on a link to learn about the privacy of any information that they shared online.[32]

These policies for warehouse e-tactics fell into two broad categories. In the first, covering 45 percent of warehouse e-tactics, participation was completely public. Digging into the varying e-tactical forms, 50 percent of warehouse petitions made participation information completely public. PetitionOnline, for one, spelled out in its privacy policy that all submitted content was available to the general public: "Please remember that any information that is disclosed in these areas becomes public information."[33] This meant that information about petition organizers and participants was visible to any site visitor. Another warehouse site, iPetitions, had a privacy policy for e-tactic authors and another one for participants. Authors were apprised that any information they provided would be solely owned by iPetitions, while signers learned that all of their information would be made public when the petition was delivered. The site explained the logic of this policy by writing that "a petition is far more likely to be effective when its recipients receives [sic] a list of signatures rather than simply an aggregated number of signatures."[34] So the manufacturers of Cover Girl cosmetics would receive personal information for all signers of a petition against using animals for cosmetics testing.[35]

All of the warehouse letter-writing and email campaigns in the data set with privacy policies made participation information completely public, although, as we discussed in the previous chapter, this did not always mean that these e-tactics reported their participation numbers on the Web site (table 7.1). Participants in a letter-writing campaign demanding the release of a political prisoner in Lhasa or an email campaign requesting clemency for a death row prisoner in Texas were apprised that all participant information would be made public to the recipients of these actions.[36] Interestingly, none of the warehouse boycotts with privacy policies made participant information completely public.

The remaining 49 percent of warehouse e-tactics with privacy policies, all of which were petitions or boycotts, were governed by a patchwork of different policies. On ThePetitionSite, for example, participants were required to give the site identifying information, but could choose to have their signature listed as "anonymous."[37] The warehouse site Petition Petition.com allowed users to opt to make their participation publicly anonymous yet still available to the petition sponsor.[38] Thus, signers on the petition demanding that corrupt Child Protective Services staff be investigated could choose to let the petition organizer know their contact information, but no one else.[39]

All of the warehouse boycotts with privacy policies fell into this patchwork category. These policies, however, were unclear as to how the privacy of participation would be handled. Instead, warehouse sites like Karma-Banque contained extensive language about user data and the importance of user privacy, but did not expressly address how information on boycott registration—a partial proxy for participation, as we discussed in chapters 4 and 6—would be handled.[40]

Nonwarehouse sites were much less likely to have a formal privacy policy; only 14 percent contained any sort of policy (table 7.1). No nonwarehouse boycotts had a privacy policy, and 5 percent or less of letter-writing, email, or fax campaigns did. Those few exceptions included a letter-writing campaign calling for debt relief in countries facing health crises that explained that any information supplied by participants would be forwarded to the action's target.[41] Like this campaign, all the privacy policies covering these e-tactics made participation information completely public.

Nonwarehouse petitions, in contrast, were more likely to have a policy than not, and 46 percent made participation information completely

Table 7.1
Privacy Policies by E-tactical Form by Site Type

	Nonwarehouse e-tactics				Warehouse e-tactics*		
	No privacy policy	Private to Site	Completely public	Other	No privacy policy	Completely public	Other
Petitions	46% (N = 70)	3% (N = 4)	46% (N = 70)	6% (N = 9)	2%	50%	48%
Letter-writing campaigns	97 (205)	0 (0)	3 (7)	0 (0)	65	35	0
Email campaigns	95 (145)	0 (0)	5 (7)	0 (0)	67	33	0
Boycotts	100 (82)	0 (0)	0 (0)	0 (0)	18	0	82
Fax campaigns	95 (141)	0 (0)	5 (8)	0 (0)	100	0	0
Total	86 (643)	1 (4)	12 (92)	1 (9)	6	45	49

*Percentages reported for warehouse e-tactics are weighted and therefore shown without Ns.

public. A petition against cuts to school budgets that was sponsored by MoveOn, for instance, bluntly detailed that "we treat your name, city, state, and comments as public information."[42] The privacy policy for a petition from the Center for Reclaiming America advocating a ban on second-trimester abortion similarly noted that by signing a petition, users consented to having their names published and "deliver[ed] to President Bush and others we feel will help further the cause."[43]

An additional 3 percent of nonwarehouse petitions kept participant information private to the site, as with a petition calling for the impeachment of Attorney General Janet Reno.[44] This petition emphasized how strongly it would protect the privacy of its signers, simultaneously characterizing the attorney general as likely to abuse her power and thus in need of removal, saying, "This information will never be sold or given away for any other purpose. If her agents storm our office, we will wipe the disk."

The remaining 6 percent of nonwarehouse petitions' privacy policies fell into the category of "other." As with some of the warehouse petitions with uncategorized privacy policies, some nonwarehouse petitions were accompanied by privacy policies, but the policies themselves did not articulate how participant information would be handled. A petition by Working for Change calling for greater accountability in electronic voting systems, for instance, made clear in its privacy policy that email addresses would not be sold, traded, or released, but did not detail the privacy or publicness of signers' other information.[45] Other petitions with privacy policies that fell in this catchall category allowed users to opt to make their information either public or private, putting that choice in the participants' hands. A petition sponsored by UFPJ, for example, that expressed outrage at the surveillance of domestic protesters, gave signers the option to choose whether to have their name displayed publicly.[46]

It is an interesting puzzle to find privacy policies for such a high number—or even any—online actions, and some of the solution to this puzzle lies in looking to the socialization of organizers through nonactivist channels. Since participation in protest has historically been considered entirely public, organizers cultivated through traditional SMO means are unlikely to have been encouraged to worry about participant privacy. That we see so many privacy policies for these e-tactics suggests that organizers are being attuned to this concern from other socialization processes. As Earl (2007) and Earl and Schussman (2003; see also Schussman and Earl 2004) found in a study of strategic voting, many organizers of online activism who came from nonactivist backgrounds considered it "natural" to have a Web site privacy policy.

Table 7.2
Presence of Privacy Policy on Nonwarehouse E-tactics with Automation

	Privacy policy	No privacy policy
E-tactics with some form of automation	58% (N = 99)	42% (N = 71)
E-tactics with no automation	1 (6)	99 (547)

A perception that having a privacy policy is a legal requirement may also lead to their increasing presence on Web sites. Although there was no federal mandate that Web sites have a privacy policy in the United States at the time of our study, some states had taken proactive steps to ensure the privacy of personal data submitted online. California's Online Privacy Protection Act of 2003, to cite one case, specifies that any Web site that collects personally identifiable data on California residents has to conspicuously post and comply with a privacy policy detailing how those personal data are handled. Other countries have also mandated published policies about how user data will be handled, such as the Data Protection Act of 1998 in the United Kingdom.

Consistent with this explanation for the presence of privacy policies for online protest actions, we find that automated e-tactics were far more likely to have a policy than their nonautomated counterparts. Nearly 60 percent of nonwarehouse actions that had some form of automation had a privacy policy, compared with just 1 percent of nonautomated nonwarehouse actions (table 7.2). And the dramatic majority (98 percent) of the automated warehouse e-tactics included a privacy policy. If we remember that automation generally entails a Web site capturing participant information and facilitating some portion of the action's completion, we can see how organizers familiar with the legal requirements about data privacy might be more often compelled to include a privacy policy.

Putting the Pieces Together

There's no question that the process of organizing an online action can look very different from organizing an offline one, and in this chapter, we've tried to underscore just how different the two processes can be. With the copresence affordance of the Web, organizers don't need to stand shoulder to shoulder as they create protest opportunities. Even more dramatically, organizers don't have to be a "they"; a not-insignificant number of e-tactics can be and are organized by a single individual. Once the process of organizing is unhitched from social movement traditions, all sorts of changes can occur. In our data, we see organizing around nonpolitical causes and increased concern about the privacy of participation—something that has never been of concern before. And there's every indication that these changes will continue, especially as social networking sites make it increasingly easy to share and show protest, all within the privacy of the site.

These findings present scholars not only with a chance to think about the ways that uses of the Web may change what we know about protest but also with opportunities to build bridges to other literatures. For example, although social movement scholars have historically had little to say about entertainment-related claims like those we found in a segment of our data, sociologists of culture and media scholars have a tradition of analyzing fan activism. These discrete literatures can be usefully brought into dialogue with each other (Earl and Kimport 2009). Similarly, research in Internet studies might be able to speak to user expectations of privacy online in ways that enrich social movement understandings. As people socialized to different norms and expectations become organizers of online protest, scholars of protest can benefit from collaborating with scholars familiar with those different processes of socialization.

This is not to say that social movement scholarship does not have a great deal to say about protest on the Web, and indeed we think this analysis of e-tactics through a leveraged affordances approach is both in line with and an extension of one of the overarching theoretical trajectories of the field. Specifically, we suggest that online protest may be ushering in a new repertoire of contention. It is to this discussion that we turn in the next chapter.

IV

8 A New Digital Repertoire of Contention?

Our arguments thus far can be boiled down to a few central propositions. First, the affordances of reduced costs for participation, reduced costs for organizing, reduced need for physical togetherness in order to participate in collective action (one component of copresence), and reduced need for both collectivity and physical togetherness in organizing (both components of copresence) are critical to understanding Web activism. Second, there are two broad kinds of effects that the use of Web tools can have on Web activism (aside from no effect, of course): supersize effects, which may be of practical importance, but don't change the underlying dynamics of either participation or organizing; or theory 2.0 effects, which may be both practically and theoretically significant, because the underlying processes driving participation and/or organizing are altered. Third, according to our leveraged affordances approach, supersize effects will dominate when people don't leverage, or at least don't leverage well, the key affordances we discuss, while theory 2.0 effects will dominate when Web usage does skillfully leverage one or both of our key affordances. Finally, reality is likely to always be a mix of supersize effects and theory 2.0 effects because some people don't notice key affordances, others don't want to or can't leverage them even if they do notice them, and still others notice and leverage these affordances quite skillfully.

In parts II and III, we aimed to provide evidence that could both evaluate these claims as well as hint at what some of the actual theory 2.0 changes might be along with their implications. In chapter 4, which focused on reduced costs for participation, we asserted that low-cost participation would make it easier to participate and would drive surges of participation that we referred to as flash activism (even if low costs might not drive longer-term affiliations with movements, causes, or groups), and also that e-tactics varied in the extent to which they employed tools that helped to drive down the costs of participation. In a loose way, we were able to show that for the e-tactics that used cost-reducing tools, participation was higher.

In chapter 5, we turned our attention to costs and organizing to contend that the unparalleled dominance of SMOs as the producers of protest opportunities is imperiled on the Web. The Web affords low-cost organizing options that allow organizers to get in the game at very low start-up costs and with quite low recurring costs. As our data showed, SMOs were better at offering protest opportunities than other types of organizers where the costs for organizing were still high, such as with e-mobilizations, but SMO and non-SMO sites were equivalent in their capacities to create and/or link to e-tactics.

In chapter 6, we argued that meaningfully collective action could be undertaken without copresence. And because collective participation is not automatically represented through copresence, we maintained that e-tactic designers had to decide whether and how to represent the collective nature of the e-tactics they were offering. Where tracking participation was easy and cheap, we saw that organizers often represented collective participation by reporting on participation and even specific participants. Where tracking participation was relatively harder, we saw organizers resort to more rhetorical flourishes to suggest the collective aspect of the action to be undertaken. Neither option is trouble free. For those who publish participation information, there are risks such as having to publish low participation numbers or data that may call into question the veracity of participation of some participants. For those who did not publish information, questions about how motivated people may be to participate are more severe, although we claim that for low-cost participation, things like collective identity are probably less influential in determining participation.

In chapter 7, we saw that low costs allowed organizing to look like a power-law phenomenon at times, where one or a small number of people did all of the work involved in organizing. The combination of low costs pulling in new organizers, low levels of socialization to social movements for these new organizers, and low organizational pressures on them meant that their behavior as organizers differed from what social movement scholars have observed before. For instance, they were willing to organize about causes that few social movement scholars had ever considered legitimate topics for protest (e.g., a protest over the cancellation of a television show), they organized against a range of targets, and they were concerned about things that haven't historically been considered by the social movement tradition such as the privacy of participation.

We hope that the driving force of all these changes—the leveraging of key affordances—has been clear. But what may be harder to glimpse so far is whether the products of those forces—the resulting changes themselves—culminate in some meaningful way. We believe that it is quite likely that they do. Specifically, we think it is worth considering whether e-tactics that well-leverage cost and copresence affordances represent a kind of Web activism that is actually creating a new repertoire of contention.

Traditional, Modern, and Digital Repertoires

The set of tactics available for use at a given historical moment as well as the characteristics that those tactics fundamentally share constitute what scholars have called the "repertoire of contention" (Tilly 1977). The motivating idea behind a repertoire of contention is that would-be organizers and activists don't exist outside the historical moment that they are living in; they are not blank slates, nor do they choose from an infinite array of tactical options. Instead, they must learn how to perform protest, and they therefore choose tactics from a culturally and historically specific set: the repertoire of contention. The tactics included in a repertoire may change over time as people innovate and develop new tactics, and/or as older tactics fall out of fashion. There are two parts to this term, though. Repertoires of contention are both the actual set of tactics that are culturally available and the common characteristics shared by that pool of available tactics (Tilly 1977, 1978, 1979, 1995). While many social movement scholars look at the addition of new tactics to the existing repertoire, such as the rise and diffusion of shantytowns as a protest tactic (Soule 1997), far fewer have explored the latter.

If we focus on the shared characteristics of tactics within an overall repertoire, we find that what its tactics have in common is generally stable, defining fairly durable repertoires. In fact, Tilly's research on repertoires (1995) suggests that there have been just two, with a single major historical shift dividing them. First, there was the traditional repertoire of contention, which characterized the forms that conflict and contestation could take prior to and during the early nineteenth century. Tactics included actions such as food riots, "seizures of grain, tollgate attacks, disruptions of ceremonies or festivals, group hunting on forbidden territory, invasions of land, orderly destruction of property, [and] shaming routines" (Tilly 1995, 33). These tactics shared three defining characteristics; they were

parochial, particular, and bifurcated. It was *parochial* because most often the interests and action involved were confined to a single community. It was *particular* because forms of contention varied significantly from one place, actor, or situation to another. It was *bifurcated* because when ordinary people addressed local issues and nearby objects they took impressively direct action to achieve their ends, but when it came to national issues and objects they recurrently addressed their demands to a local patron or authority who might represent their interest, redress their grievance, fulfill his own obligation, or at least authorize them to act. (Tilly 1995, 33)

By the middle of the nineteenth century, that "traditional repertoire" had been replaced by the "modern repertoire," which is what most contemporary social movement scholarship examines. Tactical forms in the modern repertoire shared a distinctly new set of characteristics. They tended to be: directed at national or state-based targets (i.e., what Tilly termed "national"); used across a range of movements (i.e., "modular"); and directed at political elites, eschewing patrons or intermediaries (i.e., "autonomous"). Clearly, this is a quite different set of shared characteristics than what historians and social movement scholars interested in the eighteenth or early nineteenth century are studying.

Tilly's work on these two repertoires does a wonderful job of articulating the differences between them, but here we want to highlight some of their unacknowledged similarities. For instance, both the traditional and modern repertoires identify participation in collective action through physical copresence at an event (as shown in table 8.1). Similarly, both the traditional and modern repertoires have posited a coupling between tactics and movements such that tactics are a means to an end (and an explicitly economic and/or political end at that).

Additionally, another unexamined feature of the modern repertoire is its strong belief in the enduring nature of protest. Protests (i.e., the use of tactics) in the modern repertoire mark different levels of mobilization along the life course of a movement that has ups and downs. (This is not shared by the traditional repertoire because of pronounced differences in industrialization and urban versus rural life in their respective time periods.)

We explore each of these below in more detail, and argue that these characteristics of the modern repertoire (two of which are also shared with the traditional repertoire) may be changing in important ways with innovative uses of the Web or other ICTs. A different way to think of the same issue is that there are things that have been treated as constant in the social movement literature—particularly about how social movements are defined and how tactics are related to social movements—that may now be able to vary.

We think of this new constellation of characteristics as a new "digital repertoire of contention." Noting that repertoires are defined by both their

Table 8.1
Traditional and Modern Repertoires of Contention

	Traditional repertoire	Modern repertoire	Digital repertoire
Time frame	Through mid-1800s	Mid-1800s to present	Present
Copresence is a feature of the repertoire	Yes	Yes	No; coordinated collective action possible with or without participant copresence
Tactics associated with long-term campaigns (i.e., social movements)		Yes	No; short, sporadic, episodic, and enduring campaigns are possible, as are campaigns disconnected from larger social movements
Tactics are politically oriented	Yes	Yes	Not necessarily; tactics are used widely as a means of redress

tactics and the shared characteristics of those tactics, we do not mean only that new tactics have been added, such as online petitions, denial-of-service actions, or hacktivism. Rather, we contend that when the key affordances that we outline are leveraged, the sum of the effects is not just to add new tactical options but to *entirely change what is common between tactics* and hence the fundamental repertoire. Of course, while in important ways it is too early to know conclusively whether this is a new pivot in history that is ushering in a new, digital repertoire of contention, the data examined here and extant research on other online protest both strongly suggest that scholars need to seriously examine this possibility. In the following sections, we marshal evidence from prior chapters to demonstrate how we are connecting these dots.

Copresence versus Coordination

As we mentioned earlier, in both traditional and modern repertoires of contention, the collectivity of participation was defined and marked by people gathering in time and space. Whether townspeople were coming together to threaten a local elite in the eighteenth century or civil rights protesters were marching across a bridge to challenge segregation, collectivity in participation has (thus far) always been marked by physical togetherness.

In chapter 6, however, we showed that collective participation no longer requires copresence in time and space. Participants can now participate in online actions in the ease, luxury, and privacy of their homes (or anywhere else a wireless or wired connection to the Internet exists). Instead, the importance of physical togetherness to the execution of a tactic now varies between tactics, most markedly between e-tactics and offline mobilizations (although readers should recall that some online tactics, such as distributed denial-of-service actions, can be designed to require temporally synchronous participation). And as we showed in chapter 7, organizing doesn't even need to be collective anymore, and when it is collective, it can benefit from all of the Web tools that allow distributed work teams to be productive. Lone-wolf organizers can produce actions independently, and the groups that are organizing collectively can share the burden without meeting face-to-face.

As a result of these changes, the spaces in which participation and organizing occur are also being decoupled: many of our e-tactic organizers will never meet any of the people who participated in the actions that they organized. This is in marked contrast to organizers' experience only decades ago, even if they had been simply gathering physical signatures for a (offline) petition. Just as the lack of copresence between participants has potential consequences for collective identity, so too does this growing separation between organizers and participants. Organizers can't create a sense of connection through their own physical interactions with participants.

Although these changes may seem somewhat innocuous after reading about them for so many pages, this move away from physical copresence as a key shared characteristic among tactics is nothing less than a rupture from practically all of extant thinking about collective action. In the place of physical copresence, we offer coordinated action among participants as the new shared trait that binds tactics that are part of the digital repertoire. Importantly, (coordinated) collective action by participants is still required, but not collective organizing.

The Rise of Sporadic, Episodic, and Enduring Challenges

Social movements are often defined by their "enduring" nature. If you think of civil rights, the women's movement (and different feminist "waves"), or even conservative movements such as antitax movements, they all have been around for a while. Sure, there are ebbs and flows in their level of activity—sometimes the civil rights movement is strong and sometimes it is weaker, for instance, but it's around. In fact, there is a concept in social movement studies called abeyance that is meant to explain how social movements endure through the hard times of low mobilization levels (i.e., low protest levels). Taylor (1989) introduced the concept in order to show that the women's movement did not disappear between periods of high mobilization but rather was maintained during these periods of low mobilization by a cadre of lifelong activists. When the conditions for feminist protest improved, this group of diehards sprung into action and supported resurgent mobilization.

Occasionally, what people generally recognize as a movement is of comparatively short duration, but this is usually because of a clear success or failure. For example, if there is a controversy about the siting of a toxic dump, within a year or two a decision will be made, and people fighting the dump will have either won or lost. This sort of contention is of much shorter duration than, say, the civil rights movement, but still long enough for scholars to easily accept its legitimacy as a social movement.

In contrast, collective behavior has been academics' foil to social movements where length is concerned. Social movement scholars have argued that contention that only lasts for a few hours or days is too much of a flash in the pan to be a social movement. A bit of background adds some important context to this claim. When resource mobilization was busy convincing people that social movements were rational and potentially positive, most of the negative beliefs that scholars had shared about crowds didn't just dissipate, they were instead refocused. While social movements became the proverbial good child of collective action, collective behavior became the proverbial bad child of collective action. All of the positive things associated with collective action were suddenly social movement characteristics, and all of the negative aspects were suddenly characteristics of collective behavior. Perhaps worse yet, the status of scholarship on collective behavior was often considered lower than that of social movements. With these incentives in place, fewer people wanted to study collective behavior while a good number of people were interested in social movements.

So when we say that short or sporadic incidents of contention are labeled as collective behavior, while long and enduring mobilizations are considered a proper social movement, we are implicitly saying that the line between collective behavior and social movement scholarship is heavily policed. What's really surprising about this policing is that there are actually many relatively ephemeral collective engagements that have been studied in social movement scholarship. For instance, campaigns about specific local issues tend to be fairly short lived. A campaign to stop a toxic dump might take years, but one against a Wal-Mart siting might only last months. Likewise, a campaign against a proposed city policy might be quite short, yet is political and collective, and likely has dynamics that could be usefully unpacked using social movement concepts. But if something is too short (with "too" being a subjective description), social movement scholars are often quick to suggest that it might be better classified as a case of collective behavior, or at least not as the stuff of social movement studies.

As a reader will quickly see, e-tactics complicate this picture quite substantially. As we have shown, flash activism, which is a model underlying at least some uses of e-tactics, is not about a steady and long stream of contention. Instead, it is about the effectiveness of overwhelming, rapid, but short-lived contention. And whether or not organizers have flash activism in mind, there are a range of reasons to believe that the time horizon for campaigns that use e-tactics will be much shorter in duration, particularly when campaigns rely solely on e-tactics.

On the participant's side, there has never before been an opportunity to be a five-minute activist who navigates between participating in an e-tactic, checking Facebook, and doing job-related work on a computer. There have only been opportunities to spend hours or more coming together with people and put oneself in harm's way. This dramatic drop in participation costs means that participants are able to easily and quickly respond to calls for well-designed e-tactics, especially when facilitated by some level of automation (recall that these were crucial findings in chapter 4). And they are likely to be willing to consider participation even if they have not developed a substantial sense of collective identity with other potential participants and/or organizers (see chapter 6).

We expect that the ease of participation, then, could produce quick rushes of participation when a call for participation is made. Further, these rushes of participation don't require high relative participation rates; Liben-Nowell and Kleinberg's (2008) research on online petitions shows that online petitions can persist in gathering signatures and garner high signature totals even when a large proportion of those who are asked to sign don't sign or forward information about the action to anyone else. Given that this is true, it is possible to have both flash-style activism and varying levels of activity by any given potential participant. If potential participants have time one day and not the next, mobilizations can go forward as long as some people have some time each day.

Organizers' creation of opportunities to engage in e-tactics contributes to the ephemeral, sporadic, and episodic character of some Web activism. There have never before been opportunities to set up the bedrock of a petition campaign in minutes and then spend just another hour raising awareness through other online tools. Organizers' careers traditionally culminated in organizing opportunities for others to take action; now, your afternoon can culminate in the creation of an e-tactic. In chapter 7, we showed that lone individuals and drastically small teams could produce e-tactics quickly, with relative ease. We also demonstrated that these same organizers were unconstrained by the concerns of traditional social movement organizers, leading them to behave differently. For instance, these new organizers sometimes organize around nontraditional topics, target less traditional actors in their campaigns, and are concerned about issues such as privacy that have not concerned social movement organizers in the past. Moreover, in chapter 5, we showed that if you compare sites produced by SMOs to those that are not, there are no real differences in the e-tactics that can be produced. There are few barriers, in other words, to these new organizers creating protest according to their own expectations.

If you string out the arguments over time, you can see other likely impacts, such as protest actions on specific issues or causes becoming more sporadic, with less evidence of continued concern for the cause remaining between mobilizations. Since protest is no longer so dependent on SMOs and long-term activists, there are often extremely low start-up costs for creating campaigns. Further, there are low recurring costs and low investments that must be protected. This means that there is potentially less reason for abeyance to occur.

In addition, since the central tools needed to create e-tactics are usually software routines and databases, not the knowledge inside long-term activists' minds, e-tactic organizing is easy to shut off and restart later, unlike traditional organizing. Earl and Schussman (2001, 2003) assert that traditional abeyances structures (Taylor 1989) may be replaced by digital abeyance structures. Instead of SMOs, flash drives might hold the organizing blueprints (through archived Web pages and software) that allow online protest actions to be remounted in the future. It is clear in the data examined here that starting a second petition is no harder years after a first one than it would be the next day. In such a scenario, one might ask whether abeyance would provide any return to organizers or social movements. In other words, why not just shut off a movement and turn it back on later? Why not organize around something that is short term? Why not organize whenever the time seems right and not organize when it doesn't seem so? Without social movement activists and organizations to support, there can be real on and off switches that perhaps have fewer repercussions to a campaign's ability to mobilize.

If these arguments hold up across time, ephemeral protest will not be an isolated boundary case lurking between the studies of collective behavior and social movements. Rather, ephemeral protest will be an increasingly important exception that scholars are forced to deal with. We contend that protest (i.e., the use of tactics) will become more central to the study of contention, and enduring social movements will be forced to share the academic stage. That is, where tactics have always been attached to long-term movements, we think they can now be attached to short-term campaigns. This means that to really understand the use of tactics, we will have to think of ourselves as scholars of protest rather than as scholars of social movements.

Another way to think about the same trends is to understand what is being variablized. We argue that the temporal length of collective action campaigns has been a relative constant set to "long," but innovative uses of Web technologies can allow length to become a variable. So while we hope that we have effectively shown that despite their brevity, shorter campaigns can usually be understood using social movement concepts, we hold it is also true that the consideration of these shorter campaigns in social movement research can provide that literature with useful variation in return.

Most specifically, really trying to understand the ephemeral, sporadic, episodic, or enduring nature of contention will force social movement scholars to determine whether there are meaningful conceptual and theoretical differences between protest, contention, and social movements. If social movement scholars want to continue to think of social movements as long, enduring quests, they will need to also consider protest that occurs outside of social movements. And they will need to recognize whether and how their theoretical tool kit is limited to describing longer-duration engagements. Moreover, if enough ephemeral protest happens over time, we would not be surprised if the same scholars who think of themselves as students of social movements today consider themselves students of protest in a decade.

Challenges and Challengers without Movements

Social movements have been considered not just enduring contests over power but specifically enduring contests over *political* power—in other words, social movements are about "important" issues. Historically, this has been the case; social movements are about civil rights, human rights, local political decisions, and economic fortunes, among other weighty issues. There is good reason why social movements have been about this kind of weighty issue: they have been expensive to create and grow, leading people to only attempt to create (and likely only succeed in creating) a movement when the stakes are high enough to justify the costs. But when the costs are much lower, can the stakes be lower, too? Or can they at least be personally felt stakes—committed fans, after all, consider their issues weighty—as opposed to ubiquitously political? Another way to ask this question is to ask whether tactics that have social movement heritages can now be used to address a much wider array of goals. The answer from chapter 7 is clearly yes.

Further, these efforts don't require SMOs, as chapter 5 demonstrated. And since participants have lower costs as well, and hence less need for close identification with a movement, there is less pressure from the participant side for only big stakes, traditional political organizing.

To recap, the low cost of starting and organizing online protest actions (and participating in them) makes organizing collective action around entirely new issues (sometimes less political and sometimes even fairly idiosyncratic personal issues) far more likely. Now that online protest is cheap, individuals may find it worth the meager investment to create protest actions even when protest is not connected, nor intended to be so, to a larger movement. This means that the connection between contention and more enduring social causes will become a variable, not a shared common trait. What will be constant is the use of a protest form as a means of redress. Put differently, we are witnessing a decoupling of tactics and protest from social movements not just in the temporal sense that we discussed in the previous section but also in terms of the goals and scope of the issues that are being addressed.

In the language of repertoires, there was a strong linkage between tactical forms/specific protest actions and social movements in both the traditional and modern repertoires of contention. This is why social movement scholars have studied tactics. In the modern repertoire, tactics are in fact thought to be modular so that multiple movements could benefit from the same tactical form (e.g., petitions have been used by a broad range of movements, as have rallies). But social movement scholars did not expect that people outside of enduring social movements, indeed even outside of politics as commonly understood, would use protest tactics. Modular stopped at the boundaries of social movements. Online *Star Trek* and *Felicity* fans don't stop at—or maybe even recognize—those boundaries, however. In essence, we are arguing that the modularity of tactics that began in the modern repertoire has become so extreme that tactics and protest events in the digital repertoire can, and frequently are, deployed absent a relationship to a larger protest movement.

What Does a New Repertoire Offer to Social Movement Studies?

Up until now, protest, contention, and social movements have been almost equivalent terms. If one were to try to extract some subtle differences, it is possible to say that protest tactics are the forms used to enact or execute protest/contention, and protest/contention is always subsumed by larger social movements. But these are subtle and not well-enforced distinctions, in contrast to the close policing in other subareas of terms that seem related in common parlance yet come to carry specifically different technical meanings. For instance, while STS and Internet studies scholars both like to make a clear distinction between the Internet and the Web, it is unlikely that many nonexperts make such a distinction when referring to digital technologies.

The new digital repertoire of contention, though, challenges this casualness in terminology—it threatens the conflation of protest, contention, and social movements—because suddenly these terms could refer to empirically divergent phenomena. We think that e-tactics, particularly if they persist and/or grow, offer an opportunity to rethink whether there are useful distinctions between these terms and can lead to a productive widening of the field. As we mentioned earlier, we imagine that if these trends continue, instead of social movements being the top-level concept, protest might become the more inclusive term. We use protest here to refer to the use of contentious tactics, which we have shown may or may not be related to larger movements, and may or may not have any temporal longevity. In this sense, social movements as classically understood—enduring, unconventional political contests—would become a special (and quite important) case of protest. But protest itself would not necessarily need to be enduring or political. Were social movement scholars (read: protest scholars) to reorient their thinking in this way, we think a bounty of theoretically useful variation is to be had.

Let's peel back the onion. At the most basic level, the changes we are discussing allow students of protest to examine in a deep and nuanced way how costs matter. Costs have always been relatively high—for both participants and organizers—and now they can vary widely depending on how online tools are used. This affects "downstream" theoretical concepts, which have presumably mattered previously because of high costs. For instance, abeyance, collective identity, and biographical availability might have markedly different relationships to low-cost forms of protest when compared to traditional higher-cost forms. Likewise, copresence has always been a constant of prior repertoires of contention, but now when Web tools are well leveraged, physical copresence is not a necessity for participants or organizers, and collectivity isn't even a necessity anymore for organizers. This, too, is likely to affect downstream concepts such as collective identity and solidarity.

We have shown that the duration of protest and the continuity of contention can vary widely—from short campaigns, to episodic or recurring efforts, to long, enduring social causes. Using this variation to understand how and why duration matters to theoretical processes is a promising opportunity for social movement scholars, whether or not they are interested in Web dynamics. For example, are there certain kinds of efforts that are actually most successfully handled through flash activism? We suspect that there are; attempts to stop a proposal, say, are quite likely to benefit from swift and substantial action. On the other hand, efforts to change deeply embedded traditions and beliefs are probably not going to be advanced well through short, e-tactic campaigns. In this case, instead of assuming that enduring movements are always superior at achieving success, we can build an explanation that uses an interaction between the type of goal and the type of campaign to explain success.

Similarly, tactics themselves have always been bundled deep in the heart of social movements, but now protest can stand outside of larger movements, both temporally and politically. Whether a social movement scholar is interested in the Web or not, the variation that can be observed in how tightly or loosely connected a protest effort is to a larger movement opens new doors. For instance, it is likely that connection to a larger movement will remain important when the costs of participation are high. One might expect, for example, that if there is a large amount of repression directed at participants in a given protest, it will require the infrastructure of a social movement to nurture and maintain opposition in the face of such high costs. On the other hand, whether a large movement is connected to the cause may be rather epiphenomenal to people who are engaging in low-cost efforts. When the cause is nonpolitical, such as efforts to revive a canceled television show, there is probably little expectation that a movement might exist.

This brings us to another critical point. As Earl and Kimport (2009) pointed out in their examination of fan activism, social movement scholars have not previously enjoyed the opportunity to compare politically inflected protest to nonpolitically oriented protest. It is literally an open empirical question whether the theoretical dynamics differ at all. In other words, scholars have yet to even consider whether the political nature of protesters' goals matters to the underlying dynamics of mobilization and organizing. So whether or not scholars are interested in the Web, they should be interested in the variation that the Web offers.

To summarize our position, we argue that thinking about a digital repertoire of contention can reframe how we understand social movement activity and expand traditional definitions of protest, helping scholars answer questions about how, when, and where contention takes place. Further, instead of defining away the empirical and theoretical puzzles that Web activism offers social movement research, we maintain that scholars need to create or modify existing theoretical lenses for understanding what collective action means when efforts can be collectivized outside of conventional boundaries (Earl and Schussman 2001). Such a theoretical shift would likely affect such elemental issues as the analytic definition of collective action, which is the bedrock of what social movements, collective behavior, and collective action scholars study. Such theoretical shifts are also likely to trickle down to affect issues of operationalization and measurement, like how scholars can measure the size of mobilizations when people do not have to be physically copresent in time and space to participate.

What Does a New Repertoire Offer to Internet Studies?

We have had much to say throughout the book about what distinctions between supersize and theory 2.0 accounts along with what leveraged affordances theory can do for social movement scholarship. Yet we also think this approach has much to offer those interested primarily in the Web or ICTs more broadly for whom Web protest is just another case of online phenomena. Our assertions are fundamentally about pushing on what is unique about a technology that people can recognize and take advantage of (or fail to). That is, we are arguing for theoretical precision in understanding how and why technologies matter, and for considering the diverse ways in which people use technologies as fundamental to any explanation. We are arguing that technologies never just do one thing, or perhaps more appropriately, that technologies themselves never *do* anything. Technologies offer opportunities for people to do new things as well as to do old things in new ways, and the mix of uses that they are put toward typically heterogeneously combines the mundane with the ingenious.

In our approach, identifying truly meaningful affordances of a technology and understanding how they can be variously leveraged is critically important and difficult. When we opened our discussion of affordances we noted that while many people see the affordance of a door as opening to allow passage, it may well be that the most significant affordance that a door offers is its ability to be shut in order to forestall passage. Even simple technologies have multiple affordances, and learning to spot which ones might affect social processes is no easy task. Further, once an affordance is identified, coming to understand how that affordance can be leveraged, particularly with complex technologies like ICTs, is not a walk in the park. Scholars interested in technology must appreciate the diversity of uses that it can be put to, which will inevitably include poor as well as exceptional leveraging.

This point has a nonobvious corollary: Internet studies needs to study mundane uses of technology as much as it needs to study "revolutionary" ones. All too often, research related to technology heralds a well-known and exemplary case. How many studies are there that mention Wikipedia? How many studies of Web activism invoke MoveOn? Five years from now, if not already, how many studies will discuss Facebook? While we agree that studying such well-known success cases is important, they are not as helpful without contrast cases that are less successful. Put differently, it's hard to pinpoint what makes Wikipedia, MoveOn, or Facebook special without comparing those sites to less extraordinary ones.

Our work is also a call to deeply embed the effects of leveraging technological affordances into existing theory. We would no more advocate a theory that claims technology does something directly than we would advocate one that says new technology makes older theory useless. As we stated in chapter 2, we are not for throwing babies out with the bathwater. Rather, we encourage scholars to really unpack the theoretical nuts and bolts of phenomena that predate their technology of interest, and come to deeply understand how various uses of a technology could reshape that process within the confines of the known system. To illustrate, costs are not new to social movement scholars. They were lurking in social movement theory like air—hard to see, but all around us. We did not invent the importance of costs. Instead, we recognized that costs could become variable, and that when you trace the effects of variable costs through a set of complex social processes, that variation could produce new sets of empirical relationships and variations on known theoretical processes.

If scholars interested in technology don't choose such a path, they virtually ensure that technologically inflected theory and phenomena will remain exoticized or devalued by other scholars. Social movement scholars, like other scholars, are not likely to be willing to cast aside their traditions and practical career commitments if they don't feel that core social movement concerns are being engaged and addressed. Thus, we think that theoretically and practically, scholarship that deeply embeds technologically inflected insights into preexisting theories will be the most successful.

9   Conclusion

When we first embarked on our study of e-tactics, we were motivated by the theoretical opportunities that such an empirical study could yield, but we didn't realize just how quickly e-tactics would become a familiar part of everyday life. Judging from discussion of e-tactics in popular accounts, the set of e-tactics that we analyze in this book may be just the tip of the iceberg.

Since our initial data collection, mainstream stories of e-tactics have become even more commonplace, suggesting that e-tactics are an increasingly recognized means of claims making. For instance, the New York City Mayor's Office of Theater, Film, and Broadcasting proposed new regulations in summer 2007 that would govern filming within the city (see also Earl 2010). The proposed regulations were to require a permit and a substantial insurance policy for teams of two or more people engaged in filming for more than thirty minutes, including the setup and takedown of equipment. For larger teams—five or more people—permits and insurance would be required for only ten minutes of filming. Both the requirement to gain a permit in advance and the money needed to get the required $1,000,000 insurance policy would have effectively put a stop to a wide array of filming, from amateur to news, in New York City.

The mayor's administration released the rules with little lead time. Filmmakers and photographers—both amateur and professional—were aghast at the proposed regulations, and they sprung into action, forming a group called Picture New York that created and managed an online petition. In less than two weeks, the petition gathered over thirty-five thousand signatures. Many were from amateur and professional photographers, yet some were from individuals who were not photographers but were worried about freedom of expression and the future of art in the city. Other motivations were undoubtedly also at work. Some signers were famous, and some were unknown. But they all signed on and did so quite quickly.

The surge of action was enough to dissuade the Mayor's Office. The city withdrew its proposal and revised the rules. The petition went away; the flood was over. In its wake, though, was a Mayor's Office stunned and overwhelmed by the quick mobilization. Were it not for the ease, low cost, and speed of online petitioning, the outcome might have been much different.

While the evidence that we discussed in this book was U.S. based, e-tactics now appear to be proliferating globally as well. Earl and Schussman (2008) report evidence of global usage in their analysis of PetitionOnline. Anecdotal evidence suggests that these trends are continuing. For example, in early October 2009 on a late-night talk show, the Italian prime minister Silvio Berlusconi told Rosy Bindi, a foreign minister of the opposition party, that she was more beautiful than intelligent (Associated Press 2009). His comment ignited outrage, particularly among Italian women, who saw his statement as part of a larger pattern of sexist behavior. Many channeled this anger into action: three Italian intellectuals wrote an online petition demanding that the prime minister's offensive actions be stopped, and within just weeks, over a hundred thousand people had signed it. News outlets around the world picked up the story, including the *New York Times*, *Washington Post*, and *Los Angeles Times*. In this instance, organizers and participants turned to an e-tactic as a quick and effective (judging by the press it received) means to register a grievance.

Scholars aren't just studying e-tactics, they are using them too. In summer and fall 2009, for example, faculty, students, and staff at the University of California responded online to ever-deeper budget cuts to higher education. Spread across the geographically large state of California, members of the University of California turned to the Web to express their concerns about dramatic cuts to the university, including reductions to faculty and staff salaries. Various faculty, staff, and students called for a coordinated opposition to the budget changes over email. Someone started a blog about alternative ways of handling budget reductions, and many people contributed to it. And just as have many claims makers before them, two faculty members organized a petition on PetitionOnline to protest the University of California's budgetary decisions. Soon, over twenty-five hundred supporters had signed it, including people from each of the University of California's ten campuses. Simply put, opponents of the planned budget cuts used an e-tactic to bridge their geographic distances and register their collective dissent.

Similarly, concerned scholars and their allies leaped into action by creating a series of e-tactics when Senator Tom Coburn of Oklahoma proposed that the National Science Foundation stop funding grants in political science in fall 2009. On a warehouse site, opponents of the amendment wrote an online petition to senators, asking that they block the amendment. The petition quickly gathered signatures, nearing four thousand in less than a month. That wasn't all, though. After participants signed the petition, they were given the opportunity to send a personal email to their senators through the warehouse site and, for a fee, a printed letter as well. The claim in this example likely resonates with many academics who know the challenges and importance of research funding, and demonstrates that e-tactics can be scholars' go-to method of expressing opposition.

The e-tactics deployed in opposition to the Coburn amendment point to another marker of the increasing prominence of e-tactics in claims making: the emergence of new warehouse sites. The petition, email campaign, and letter-writing campaign supporting National Science Foundation funding for political science were housed on Petition2Congress, a warehouse site that didn't exist in 2004 when we initially collected our data. In November 2009, the site had 202 active petitions. Other new warehouse sites have also popped up, highlighting the vibrancy of the warehouse sector wherein e-tactics are available off-the-rack for interested organizers.

A more recent look at some of the warehouse sites that were around during our data collection further illustrates how dynamic the warehouse sector is. Along with evidence of new warehouse sites, we also find that some of the warehouse sites in our sample are no longer active. Seven of the fifteen that we studied are gone from the Web. At the same time, some of the warehouse sites that we examined have grown significantly in the years since we gathered our data. For example, when we coded ThePetitionSite in March 2004, it hosted 750 petitions. By September 2008, it hosted 3,455 petitions—an increase of over 450 percent. During that same period, PetitionOnline grew by over 10,000 petitions, hosting 48,700 e-tactics four and a half years after we took our sample.

Not only is there clear evidence that e-tactics are being used by organizers of protest, it appears that e-tactics are increasingly being recognized by their targets as a place of legitimate claims making. On June 12, 2009, PetitionOnline was attacked by a sophisticated botnet conducting a distributed denial-of-service attack. As with all denial-of-service attacks, the attackers made repeated requests to the PetitionOnline servers, ultimately overwhelming their ability to produce pages on the site and forcing the site to go offline. The scope of the attack was large—over 350,000 unique IP addresses targeted PetitionOnline servers in one three-minute period;

over a fifteen-minute interval, PetitionOnline servers received 2.5 million requests from a massive number of IP addresses. Despite the site's expansive hosting servers and ability to service hundreds of thousands of requests every day, it was unable to handle the increased volume of server requests. The site went down as a result and PetitionOnline was unavailable to any site visitor.

The attack continued unabated, and despite attempts by Petition Online's security firm to stem the flood of traffic, the site remained continuously inaccessible until June 16, when countermeasures allowed sporadic access to it. Consistent access to the site was not restored until June 18, when the security provider for the site was able to filter out many bad requests. The attack did not actually subside, though, until mid-July (approximately five weeks after it began); the security company had to keep up countermeasures the entire time lest the site become unavailable again.

Thinking about PetitionOnline as an online petition warehouse site, this means that potential participants were unable to sign any of the over forty-eight thousand petitions on the site and organizers were unable to create new online petitions. The site administrator estimated that the site missed between thirty and fifty thousand signatures each day that it was down, noting that the site receives a couple million visitors every month. An active arena of protest was effectively wiped out for several days.

As a result of the site going down, the petition creators seemed to move to other petition warehouse sites, with some sites seeing a marked increase in petition creation. PetitionOnline, on the other hand, saw its Alexa rating drop (Alexa is a rating service that gives a rough measure of online popularity). PetitionOnline at its peak had neared the top-thousand-sites mark and was regularly within the top five thousand sites that Alexa ranks. But after the denial-of-service action, PetitionOnline slipped out of the top five thousand, with June creating a notable pock on an otherwise-stellar record. At the end of 2009, it was still struggling to regain its preattack footing.

Moreover, the owner of PetitionOnline had no way of identifying the source of the attack. The attack was distributed across multiple computers, and it is likely that many of those computer owners were unaware that their machine had been co-opted for this attack. It has been reported that Iran and North Korea were probably responsible for denial-of-service attacks in the United States that took place in June through late summer of that year, but PetitionOnline is not one of the sites mentioned in reports, and the Federal Bureau of Investigation has been unable to determine the origin of the attack. While it is nearly impossible to know who perpetrated the denial-of-service attack against PetitionOnline and harder still to determine their motives, what is clear is that a sophisticated attack employing at least 350,000 machines at various points was used to suppress dissent by disabling the messenger. At a minimum, this suggests that the attackers perceived the use of e-tactics to be threatening. Through the attack, protest was silenced, along with all the other claims being made on the site.

While the skeptic that we introduced in chapter 4 may have been unconvinced that PetitionOnline or e-tactics more generally matter, clearly someone considered PetitionOnline important enough to attack. The size, duration, and scope of the attack were quite significant, and none of the financial motives common to hacking attacks were evident. This leaves the likely possibility that at least some people would like to see e-tactics matter less, or at least be less available. Across the examples that we just discussed, e-tactics mattered to the New York City's Mayor's Office, the media in Italy (if not to Berlusconi himself), and academics in California as a means of expressing opposition to actual and proposed funding cuts.

Contributions to Scholarship on Technology and Protest

At the advent of what we know as social movement studies, no one could have predicted how the rise of the Web would impact the process of social change. Actually, nobody could have even reasonably predicted the rise of technologies we now use every day. Can you imagine explaining to people in the 1960s that some day they would be able to carry their phone with them around the world? Or to someone in the 1970s that in the beginning of the twenty-first century, people would be able to watch a television show on a small handheld device that they could take with them wherever they go? And given these conceptual challenges, we can be sure that nobody could have predicted exactly how people would use these technologies.[1]

Yet while scholars can't predict in advance how technology will change and, in turn, how people will use technology, we nonetheless have a responsibility to analyze these uses. As anecdotal accounts of e-tactics abound—of reading about a boycott on your favorite blog, signing a petition for a cause that you believe in, the Web as "changing everything," or e-tactics simply not mattering as much as face-to-face action—social scientists can bring empirical precision to these stories and contextualize what they mean in a changing social world.

As we have suggested throughout the book, e-tactics do not arise in a vacuum. Their form is influenced by what the Web affords, how well organizers and participants leverage those affordances, and even organizers' and participants' offline experiences, both with social movements and in other fields. And so what we can say about e-tactics also has some intriguing consequences for what we can say about protest more generally and about the Web.

Constants No More

We have argued that the Web affords the possibilities of low-cost participation in and production of protest as well as freeing organizers and participants from the demands of copresence. These are pretty dramatic potentialities in light of historical understandings by both scholars and activists alike of how protest was done. Organizers against apartheid in South Africa in the 1980s assumed coordinated resistance would be expensive, and participants were at least tacitly aware of the personal costs that they could accrue by participating. Likewise, people concerned with the global image of African American males who chose to hold the Million Man March in 1995 did not imagine that such a feat could take place without the coordinated organization of many and the physical togetherness of the men who marched.

In the age of the Web, organizers and participants don't always have to make these assumptions. People who object to governmental policies and actions like the war in Iraq have organized petitions, letter-writing campaigns, email campaigns, and boycotts on the Web in just minutes, at little time and pecuniary cost. Supporters of these claims have logged on to participate in these online actions at little or even no marginal cost. Similarly, those opposed to the portrayal of different identity groups in the media, for example, have taken action into their own hands, sole authoring e-tactics or participating from the comfort of their own home without ever seeing another participant. No one had to worry about the costs of these actions because they were so low. And there were no expectations that many had to come together to organize or complete these actions since the Web facilitated both organization and participation without copresence. In other words, assumptions that were fundamental to protest without the Web could be less relevant to online protest.

Another way of saying this is that things that have always been assumed to be constant are actually variable. It's not that costs don't matter to protest; clearly costs continue to matter very much for many offline actions. And it's not that collective organizing and physical copresence don't matter for protest; there are many protest actions that are infeasible without copresence. But we can see that costs and copresence are less of a concern for participants in an online petition than in, say, civil disobedience.

Conceptualizing costs and copresence as variables rather than constants has important implications for social movement scholarship. First, it pushes social movement scholars to be more sensitive to technology. As we have noted throughout, some scholars insist that the Web has not altered the process of social change, having either no impact or only a supersizing one on protest. Going even further, our work is a call for social movement scholars to really engage deeply with research on technology and society so that theoretical approaches make sense to both experts on technology and on social movements. When social movement scholars fail to think deeply about the technology involved in their research, and fail to engage existing work on technology and society, they will almost inevitably build overly thin theories.

Likewise, rather than considering Web protest as simply business as usual in a different arena, social movement scholars must attend to how people's uses of technology change the dynamics of protest. For instance, in earlier chapters we noted the difficulty of building and maintaining collective identity online, even as a significant amount of protest is taking place online. The possibility of mobilization without a collective identity pushes scholars to rethink the centrality of collective identity for protest that happens online and distinguishes the dynamics of online protest from those of offline protest.

Our findings have implications even for social movement scholars who are not interested in technology because our approach shows that variation in key theoretical concepts is possible. For example, we have suggested in earlier chapters that when protest is easy, the free-rider dilemma becomes less salient for explaining participation. The possibility that the bar for participation is lowered for certain kinds of protest has important consequences for the dynamics of protest, calling for a reconceptualization of the role of selective incentives and even resources in mobilization, among other things. From this starting point, we might now ask what happens to protest broadly speaking when the costs can vary.

Similarly, the rise of the use of social movement practices for nonpolitical causes calls for a reframing of the boundaries historically drawn around protest. We might ask whether the dynamics of protest are the same for explicitly political and nonpolitical issues: Is there a meaningful difference in how protest is organized and who participates when the claim falls outside politics instead of within it?

We also see important implications of our work for research in the field of Internet studies. By connecting questions about Web affordances to literature that predates the Internet, our arguments can help contextualize work in Internet studies in theories from other fields. As a relatively new discipline of study, research on the effects of Web-based technologies sometimes risks reinventing the wheel because the relationship between online phenomena and offline behaviors is not always clear. By building bridges between dynamics of protest on the Web and offline, scholars in the field of Internet studies can collaborate with other fields to explain how uses of technology can and do change social phenomena. In effect, it weaves the study of technology into other areas of research.

A Focus on Uses and Affordances

The relevance of these findings to scholars across multiple disciplines underscores the importance of a leveraged affordances approach to studies of protest on the Web. By attending to the affordances of the Web, we are able to articulate how uses of the Web can lead to *both* supersize and theory 2.0 effects. In some e-tactics that we've discussed, for instance, the affordances of the Web are leveraged to increase the volume of petition signers or letter senders, yielding cases of online activism that look like supersized versions of offline activism. Lower costs for organizing and participating in online actions along with the absence of the requirement of copresence can make it easier to get large volumes of people involved in, say, an email campaign.

In other e-tactics that we analyze, the affordances of the Web are leveraged to actually change the processes of organizing or participating in protest, calling for a theory 2.0 understanding of online protest. Those same low costs that may enable organizers to secure higher volumes of participants may also enable people to organize around nonpolitical causes, which is something that scholars have little to say about as yet. And the ability to use the Web for protest without copresent participants or organizers allows people without a background in social movements to become organizers of protest, bringing with them their own expectations of how action on the Web should take place. These examples require a new generation of social movement theory.

We hold that this variation in e-tactics themselves mirrors the variation in scholars' findings about the impact of uses of the Web on protest.

E-tactics can do both: they can supersize protest and they can call for theory 2.0. More important, we contend that this variation is caused by the extent to which an e-tactic leverages the affordances of the Web.

In other words, we can understand the heterogeneity of findings on the impact of uses of the Web on protest by thinking more globally about leveraged affordances. By attending to variation in how those affordances are leveraged, we are able to bring both supersize and theory 2.0 findings into relief. We can see them on a continuum of uses of the Web, rather than as contradictory findings. In essence, the leveraged affordances approach brings together disparate findings on online activism, supporting both work that has found supersize effects and research that argues for the need for theory 2.0. Better still, by focusing on uses of the Web, the leveraged affordances approach is able to explain why some studies are more likely to find supersize than theory 2.0 effects and vice versa.

Further, it is not just that the causes of the changes we are pointing to are common—the leveraging of key affordances—but also that the consequences of these changes add up to a potential change in the repertoire of contention. In the new digital repertoire of contention, coordinated collective action, not copresence, is the common characteristic that binds tactics. The duration of protest can also vary substantially, marking a separation between protest and more enduring social movements. Thus, rather than tactics sharing a connection to social movements, they now only share a connection to specific instances of contention. Finally, as nonpolitical protest has emerged, the connection between tactics and political goals has been fractured. Instead, hypermodularity is a common feature of tactics, allowing their use in areas far removed from traditional protest causes.

Indeed, it is the leveraged affordances approach that allows the study of e-tactics to be understood in the social movement literature and bridges Internet studies to other fields. Centrally, we are studying people's *uses* of the Web for protest, just as other scholars of protest focus on what people are doing. And through this process of emphasizing the relationship of findings on social phenomena on the Web to existing offline theories, we trace a path for Internet studies to build relationships to existing theories in other disciplines as well.

What Comes Next?
In this book, we've thought through how uses of the Web can change the processes of claims making by looking specifically at e-tactics. As we introduced them in chapter 3, each of these e-tactical forms has an offline

progenitor and a long offline legacy, although each is also decidedly an online tactical form. Our analysis has aimed to articulate how common assumptions developed from the study of offline protest must be revised and expanded to account for uses of the Web. And we've gone so far as to suggest the dawning of a new digital repertoire of contention that is explicitly distinguished from repertoires grounded in only offline protest.

Moving forward, though, we expect that the story won't be so linear. Although we describe the migration of offline tactics on to the Web, the increasing blurring between off- and online life leads us to anticipate seeing more occasions where uses of the Web for protest "speak back" to offline protest. For instance, picking up on the discussion of the birth of private collective actions in chapter 7, we expect that privacy concerns about political action will become increasingly salient offline as well as online. The recent controversy about the privacy of signatures on petitions to qualify ballot measures in several states offers some support for our expectation.

In 2009 in Washington State, gay rights supporters requested the names of petition signers who qualified a referendum for a vote that would roll back the state's expansion of domestic partnership benefits. They claimed that the public disclosure of the names was important to prevent fraud, but also acknowledged that making the names public might directly or indirectly put pressure on signers for their position. In a *New York Times* article on the topic, advocates of making the signatures public explained that it could facilitate conversations between those with opposing viewpoints (Yardley 2009). The Washington secretary of state agreed that the names could be released, noting that public records law does not prevent it and that the state has released signers' names in the past.

This push to release the names, however, met with stiff resistance. Opponents argued that releasing the names would infringe on First Amendment rights to free speech and expressed concerns that signers could be subject to intimidation. In the court battle that ensued, a lower court first ruled that the names should not be released. On appeal to the Ninth Circuit, that decision was overturned and the secretary of state was ordered to disclose the names. Initially, the U.S. Supreme Court stayed the Ninth Circuit's decision and let the ruling stand that prevented the names' release; but ultimately the Court ruled 8–1 to require the signers' names to be made public.

Since petition signers' names have been disclosed before, it is a bit of a puzzle why they should be kept private now. Some of the solution to that puzzle comes by way of current uses of the Web. A strong proponent of releasing the names was the Web site KnowThyNeighbor.org, which has an explicitly activist mission, aiming to draw attention to anti–gay rights initiatives. The site boasts of altering the petitioning process by making signers' names public and easily accessible (KnowThyNeighbor.org 2009). With the Web, in other words, those names are not just publicly available, they are quickly, easily, and cheaply available. People concerned about fraud, hoping to have a "difficult conversation" with someone with an opposing viewpoint, or even intending to intimidate someone who signed the petition can get the names of signers with little to no effort. Thanks to the cost affordance of the Web, they don't need to spend the time traveling to the secretary of state's office or pay a fee to get the names. And because the Web is global, they don't even need to be in Washington State. For both proponents and opponents of releasing the names, it was important that anyone and everyone could access those names once they were released.

We believe that the expectation of privacy on the Web—and concerns over how easily privacy can be undone on the Web—has heightened people's expectation of privacy offline. The concern over privacy in protest, we have argued, is a relatively new phenomenon and one that is linked to uses of the Web. These online experiences have encouraged people to be concerned about their privacy and this concern, as in the example above, has migrated back offline into new claims for the privacy of offline actions. We might think of this as spillover from online actions to offline ones.

In this way, it is increasingly difficult to think of offline action as simply the progenitor of online action. We anticipate that the uses of online action and expectations about the dynamics of protest online cannot help but affect offline action. Whether in subtle ways such as the increased expectation of privacy for offline political action or in a yet-unseen more dramatic way, the uses and expectations of online action will trickle into the uses and expectations of offline action. The reverse is also true. As offline tactics continue to innovate, e-tactics will be affected.

Continuing Innovation through New Uses of the Web

We also expect further innovations in online protest, in ways that both cite a history of offline action and are entirely novel. As some of the examples that we opened the chapter with suggest, there are contemporary uses of e-tactics that we did not find in our sample. The Coburn amend-ment protest, for instance, combined three e-tactics on behalf of a single claim. Compared to our findings in chapter 5 about how frequently sites contained just a single e-tactical form, the three-form setup was an innovation. That these three e-tactics were part of a warehouse site is especially different; all of the warehouse sites in our sample specialized in a single e-tactical form—never three.

The petition protesting statements by Berlusconi was also a multiple e-tactic protest of sorts. In addition to signing the petition, participants were encouraged to send in a photo of themselves, according to the Associated Press (2009), "with the words 'offended by the premier' or 'not at your disposal' or similar statements written on them." Distinct from a petition of signatures, these photographs constitute a photo petition. Similarly, in 2009 MoveOn called for Toyota owners to print a sign saying, "Toyota: Stop Opposing Clean Energy. Quit the Chamber of Commerce." Participants were asked to write their names and the model of the Toyota that they owned on the sign, and then take a photo of themselves. The photos were collected by MoveOn, which then transmitted them to Toyota. How does this e-tactical form differ from others that we have discussed? Does producing the photo increase the costs of participation? Do photographs simulate the feeling of physical copresence in ways that letters and words cannot? Although we did not come across any photo petitions in our sample, we believe that the initial tools to analyze this e-tactical form lie in a leveraged affordances approach.

Some contemporary online actions have even utilized video and sound, such as a video in 2009 by the Courage Campaign advocating that California's constitutional amendment against same-sex marriage be overturned. In the weeks leading up to a decision by the California Supreme Court on the fate of the amendment and the same-sex marriages that had already taken place, the Courage Campaign collected photographs of lesbian and gay couples, their families, and their allies holding signs asking the court not to divorce same-sex couples. The photographs were made into a video slide show and set to music. This sort of innovation could usefully be analyzed by drawing on work on the role of music in (offline) protest (e.g., Eyerman and Jamison 1998). We might ask how the use of music in online protest leverages the affordances of the Web and how this online protest differs from music-associated offline protest. Essentially, these cases provide even further variation in how the affordances of the Web can be leveraged for protest.

Theory 2.0 for Web 2.0

We also expect that social networking sites like Facebook will encourage new uses and dynamics of online protest. With the ability of social networking sites to connect and maintain social relationships as well as telegraph action immediately, these sites might, for one, find a way to more clearly represent collective participation, alerting members of a network when their friend participated in an action. And they might be able to produce and nurture collective identity in ways that the e-tactics we studied here both cannot and probably don't need to do. So when that friend participates in an action, others might see themselves as likely participants because of things they share in common with that friend. Or other members of the network who also participated might now feel a new sense of we-ness based on their network membership and participation. Networks could even be created around specific actions, linking people virtually rather than physically through shared space. We already see something like this on Facebook, where members can "join" groups for specific causes. Social networking sites may also take protest in directions that we do not anticipate, although we believe the leveraged affordances approach gives us the tools to unpack and understand these uses as they arise.

There are likely some supersize effects from social networking sites as well. Much of the rapid participation in the petition against Berlusconi was attributed to the use of social networking sites to popularize the petition (Adnkronos International 2009). And the always-on, mass communication, viral nature of many social networking sites means that information can travel fast.

In closing, just as there has been significant, innovative protest in the past, so too do we anticipate that online activism will be rich terrain for the study of protest. Through our focused examination of four e-tactical forms, we have argued for the importance of new theories about the dynamics of online activism that more broadly speak to the uses of the Web for protest. The expanding online protest sector—with lone-wolf organizers alongside SMOs, political causes trumpeted next to nonpolitical claims, and different and often-lower barriers to entry—promises to be a rich and exciting area for research.

Methodological Appendix

The data used in this study were collected using an innovative method that breaks important new ground in the study of Web protest and holds significant promise for Internet studies more broadly. As detailed below, for this study we generated quasi-random samples of Web sites hosting or linking to four kinds of e-tactics: online petitions, online boycotts, and online letter-writing and email campaigns. The samples were then content coded to produce population-level estimates of characteristics of the four kinds of e-tactics.[1] In developing a procedure to do so, this method overcomes challenges that have beset Web researchers and represents a major advance in Web research that has implications far beyond social movement research, given the ability of this method to be applied to a range of different topics (Earl 2006b; Earl and Kimport 2008, 2009).

The following sections outline existing challenges to research on the Web and how our method addresses them, the process that was used to develop random samples of the e-tactics on which we focus along with important distinctions between warehouse and nonwarehouse sites, our sampling techniques, and an overview of the content coding of the samples (as introduced in chapter 3). This more technically specific appendix is designed to give the methodologically sophisticated reader insight into the strengths of this method and its appropriateness for the research questions at hand.

Overcoming Existing Challenges in Web Research

Historically, researchers interested in populations and/or probabilistic samples of Web content have faced two central difficulties. First, there is no single population list of Web sites and/or Web pages, let alone population lists of Web pages featuring protest. Uniform resource locators (URLs) are not registered with a central authority, and domain registration records do not provide data on the content of sites and also contain inaccuracies.[2] Second, URLs do not have a standard enough format or underlying patterning to allow researchers to randomly generate valid Web addresses (e.g., as random digital dialing did for phone surveys).[3] And even if this were possible, researchers would still have no information on the content of URLs to develop more targeted populations from which to sample. Instead, the technical architecture of the Web requires that URLs are advertised by their owners (e.g., through emails or links from high-profile sites), identified by following links from known sites, or retrieved through search or Web site directories. Search engines are created either by allowing URL owners to register their URLs or by indexing the results of large Web crawlers, which follow links from one Web page to another in order to produce a catalog of searchable Web pages.

Without the ability to produce or develop a population list of URLs, Web researchers have been confined to methods of study that do not depend on random sampling procedures, and as a consequence, have potentially limited generalizability. For the most part, research has been restricted to the study of specific movement Web sites or larger sets of sites connected to these seed sites. In either case, the movement Web sites are usually located by examining: popular movement Web sites (e.g., studying MoveOn); the online presence of organizations that predate the pervasive use of the Web in the United States (e.g., studying the National Organization for Women's Web site); or sites tightly connected to a popular or iconic Web site through hyperlinks, and then conceptualizing those sites as a community (e.g., research on sets of right-wing Web sites). While certainly valid and productive choices for some research questions, each of these methods has serious hazards when the goal is to build a vision of e-tactics or Web protest generally. For instance, popular Web sites likely vary from unpopular sites in theoretically significant ways that are not evident when only popular sites are studied. Likewise, as Paul DiMaggio and his colleagues (2001) assert, organizations that predate pervasive Internet usage systematically use the technology in different ways than organizations and actors that postdate the pervasive use of the Internet. Further, when looking at only tightly clustered sites, it is problematic to assume the nonexistence of rival sites that have explicitly chosen not to share links; such research approaches risk missing pockets of important sites. Finally, studying organizations or movements through case studies misses critical findings—such as those explored in chapters 5 and 7—about the nature of Web protest as conceptualized distinctly from social movements and SMOs.

Moreover, aside from how cases are selected and the effect that might have on findings, there are larger issues about the ability of case studies to be used to describe broader trends beyond the cases studied. Without population-level data on Web activism, the rich findings from existing case study research lack empirically based contextualization. And with only these limited angles on the use of the Web for protest, scholars lack insight into how to determine what might or might not be generalizable as well as scope conditions for any generalizations. To fully understand this burgeoning area, scholars need *both* in-depth case studies and broader empirical population data.

Producing Population-Level, Generalizable Data on the Web

This project overcomes these significant obstacles to population-level, generalizable data on the Web by harnessing the capacity of large search engines—in this study, Google—to produce a scalable algorithm for creating best approximations of populations of *reachable* Web sites hosting or linking to petitions, boycotts, and letter-writing and email campaigns. These populations can be randomly sampled when the populations are large, producing data that are generalizable.

In this study, Google was selected as the basis for generating populations of Web sites featuring the kinds of e-tactics that we study because it is the world's most extensive, searchable, and publicly accessible database of URLs (Jarboe 2003; Sullivan 2007). Although Google does not contain all URLs for all Web pages on all domains, it does represent the most extensive catalog of Web sites available.

It is worth noting that Google is language specific; in the U.S.-based version of Google, English-language queries generally generate English-language results. In this study, we used a Simple Object Access Protocol–Application Program Interface (SOAP-API), discussed in more detail below, to query Google, which limited search results to U.S. domains (i.e., domains without country markers) and English-language sites. These restrictions are not inherently necessary in the search process but were instead necessary given the resource constraints on coding.

Importantly, search engines generally and Google specifically find Web content in ways that mimic the processes by which Web site visitors identify Web sites. To find a specific Web page without knowing its address, users follow one of two procedures. One is to query a searchable index of Web sites, like Google. The second is to follow links from a known site, which Googlebot, Google's Web crawler, already does as it identifies new sites by traversing links from already-identified sites (for a fuller

discussion, see <http://www.google.com/support/webmasters/bin/answer
.py?hl=en&answer=70897>; see also Hindman, Tsioutsiouliklis, and
Johnson 2004). This means that Google is most likely to find sites that are
linked to other sites, but unlikely to find structurally isolated sites. Thus,
not only does Google offer the most extensive, publicly available, searchable catalog of Web pages, it also captures the pages most likely to be
identified by users. This suggests that to the extent that Google does not
itself represent a population of Web pages, results from properly conducted
and concatenated searches can represent the best approximation of a
population of *reachable* Web sites. In other words, we can create a population of Web sites at risk of being found by Web users' searches for particular
topics on U.S. and English-language sites.[4]

Conducting Google Searches to Develop Populations of Reachable Sites

Before describing the data collection process, we first discuss the broad
contours in the distribution of e-tactics that the populations and samples
will enumerate. In this case, this involved initial, informal investigations
into Web sites that host or link to petitions, boycotts, and letter-writing
and e-mail campaigns. Based on these preliminary findings on the structure of e-tactics, we deployed a Google SOAP-API to produce five distinct
populations of Web sites: one for each focal e-tactic, and one for the separate category of warehouse sites.

Locating the Featured E-tactics on the Web

Investigations conducted in preparation for this research showed that
e-tactics (i.e., specific petitions, etc.) tend to be housed within larger Web
sites, rather than being "free floating" throughout the Web. That is, e-
tactics tended to be on Web pages along with other content. Alternatively,
when e-tactics were on stand-alone Web pages, these pages were nonetheless only one page on a larger Web site/domain. The data collection
strategy was therefore designed to identify the larger sites on which
e-tactics resided and capture e-tactics through those larger sites. This
allowed us to discuss larger Web sites, or by changing the unit of analysis,
specific e-tactics housed on those larger sites. In the end, two different
units of analysis are available for investigation: data on sites and data on
e-tactics.

Exploratory analyses also indicated that e-tactics could be found on two
different types of Web sites. First, some large Web sites specialized in a
particular e-tactic; we label these warehouse sites since they served as

clearinghouses for actions such as petitions (e.g., PetitionOnline.com). The remaining Web sites, our second category, did not explicitly specialize by e-tactic and did not serve as large-scale repositories for online actions, so we label these nonwarehouse sites (e.g., amnestyusa.org). While it is the case that many nonwarehouse sites were focused on particular causes, there were also ones that included content on a wide range of topics, making it problematic to classify them as cause focused. For more discussion of the differences between these types of sites, see chapter 3.

Our initial investigations revealed that a small minority of warehouse sites were up to orders of magnitude larger than most nonwarehouse sites. For example, PetitionOnline housed thousands of petitions. Yet in terms of the number of Web sites, as opposed to the number of e-tactics (e.g., the count of petitions), there were relatively few warehouse sites.

The data collection process was designed to take into account the distinction between warehouse and nonwarehouse sites (as reflected in figure A.1); failing to distinguish between these types of sites would have had negative repercussions. More important, because there were relatively few warehouse sites (ultimately only fifteen), it is likely that samples drawn from combined populations of warehouse and nonwarehouse sites would have sampled between zero to two warehouse sites. Further, because it was likely that warehouse sites differed from nonwarehouse ones in elemental ways, in order to compare warehouse and nonwarehouse sites it was necessary to gather data on all warehouse sites to have enough data for comparisons.

Using the Google SOAP-API to Identify Populations of Sites

For the reasons enumerated above, this study used Google to generate reachable populations of Web sites hosting or linking to the four protest e-tactics. Attending to the structure of Web sites, this study began by separately generating five reachable populations: a population of nonwarehouse sites that discussed petitions; a population of nonwarehouse sites that discussed letter-writing campaigns; a population of nonwarehouse sites that discussed email campaigns; a population of nonwarehouse sites that discussed boycotts; and a population of warehouse sites that discussed any of the four featured e-tactics.

The populations were produced using a Google SOAP-API, which initiates contact with Google, submits queries automatically, and saves the results returned from Google into a database.[5] The interface allowed "advanced" search options to be used in Google, which were set to exclude non-English pages, pages hosted on non-U.S. domains, and domains

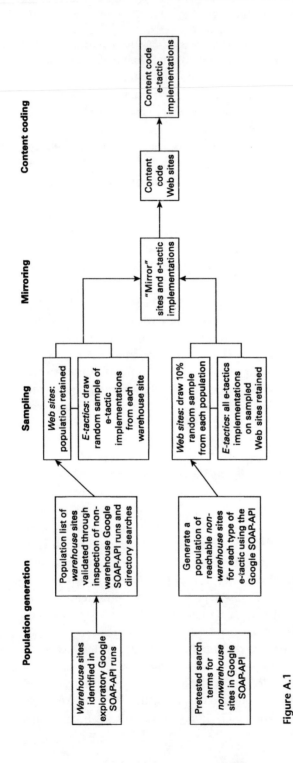

Figure A.1
Schematic of data collection process.

located and tracked as warehouse sites (see below for details). As noted above, these restrictions are not inherently necessary in the search process but instead were employed due to resource constraints.

The four nonwarehouse populations were generated using search terms pretested for breadth and depth prior to this study. Analyses of the pretest results also revealed many of the warehouse sites ultimately documented by this study. For each search term, Google limited the saved results from each query to the first one thousand results. In order to build much more extensive sets of unique URLs on petitions, boycotts, and letter-writing and email campaigns, we employed multiple search terms for each focal e-tactic; by varying the search terms and appending the results of consecutive searches to one another, this study attenuated the effects of Google's limitation on results after the thousandth-identified page because pages that were close to the thousandth result in one search were likely to be pulled into the first thousand results across at least one other search. Given that, only very weak matches were entirely missed because they failed to be in the first thousand results of any of numerous searches. To validate this, nonautomated draws from search results beyond the thousandth result were inspected; those inspections confirmed that only a negligible number of URLs after the thousandth cutoff were of interest to the study.

To further mitigate against any sampling bias that Google may have produced, the concatenation of results, and any sampling from those results, excluded any information on the "page rank" of the result (except with respect to the limitation regarding results after the thousandth result). This was crucial because a potential drawback to Google is that the ranking (i.e., order) of search results can be manipulated. Yet this manipulation is generally done in the hopes of securing a high rank, such as the first listed Web site in a set of results or a result on the first page of listed results. Such manipulation is not thought to be used to push a site from the thousandth to the nine hundredth result.

The results from all nonwarehouse runs of the SOAP-API for each e-tactic were concatenated (e.g., one concatenation for petitions, one for boycotts, etc.). When a Web site appeared more than forty times in the concatenated search results, it was examined to determine if it was a warehouse site. If it was a warehouse site, the SOAP-API was programmed to exclude it from all Google queries used to create the nonwarehouse samples, nonwarehouse queries were rerun where necessary, and the site was moved to the warehouse population. If the site was not a warehouse site, or appeared less than forty times (so that it was not examined to determine if it was a warehouse site or not), it was concatenated along with the other

results into the appropriate nonwarehouse population (e.g., petition population). After the SOAP-API searches were completed, the exhaustiveness
of the list of fifteen warehouse sites was validated using comparisons with
news articles and online directory services. We conducted this validation
because of the extremely small size of the population list.

To remove redundant or inapplicable URLs, concatenated search results
were cleaned to remove duplicates and Web sites that were obviously news
sites likely to be reporting on, but not hosting or linking to, an e-tactic
(e.g., cnn.com, latimes.com, etc.).

The Google searches for the data presented here were run in March
2004. Table A.1 reports the number of search strings and raw counts of
URLs identified using this process. The fourth column of the table contains
counts of the URLs that remained after the removal of obvious news and
media sites.

Sampling and Mirroring of Populations of Reachable Sites

As introduced above, this project employs two units of analysis, gathering
data on both Web sites and e-tactics. As summarized in figure A.1, using
the Google SOAP-API, search terms designed to capture implementations
of e-tactics were used to create lists of relevant Web sites. The Web sites,
in turn, provided access to e-tactics. In the four nonwarehouse populations, the list of Web sites was so large that sampling was required, and
in the warehouse population, the volume of e-tactics for many of the
sites was so large that sampling was required. The following sections
detail the sampling procedures for Web sites and e-tactics, respectively, as
well as the mirroring process by which local copies of the Web pages
were saved.

Sampling of Sites

As reported in table A.1, the populations of nonwarehouse sites resulting
from concatenating the Google results were so large that sampling was
required. The four nonwarehouse populations were randomly sampled,
using a 10 percent sampling rate. In contrast, only fifteen warehouse sites
were located, constituting the complete population of warehouse sites.
Because of the small N, warehouse sites were not sampled.

Sampling of E-tactics

While there were far fewer warehouse sites than nonwarehouse ones identified, warehouse sites often housed far more e-tactics than nonwarehouse

Table A.1

Population and Sample Values for Nonwarehouse Sites

	Search strings (N)	URLs identified from searches (N)	Unique URLs from searches (N)*	URLs that did not include news or media domains (N)	URLs included in 10% sample (N)	Missing or irrelevant sites in sample (%)	URLs in sample that did not have a unique author (%, e.g., listserv archives)	URLs in sample that were news or historical reports (%)	URLs in sample with appeal but no specific means of participating in action (%)	URLs in sample hosting e-tactic (%)	URLs in sample linking to e-tactic (%)
Petitions	16	15,979	10,551	8,673	868	17	13	57	2	8	3
Letter-writing campaigns	20	19,993	8,387	7,338	734	48	7	33	2	8	1
Email campaigns	16	15,988	8,183	6,762	677	85	5	4	1	5	.3
Boycotts	8	7,994	6,745	5,210	521	17	8	68	0	7	0

*In addition to excluding duplicated URLs, the unique URLs value also excludes URLs whose syntax was improper and therefore were unreachable, URLs that were clearly hosted on non-U.S. servers (based on their URL), and government URLs. Reported percentages may not sum to 100% because of rounding error.

sites and far more e-tactics than could be feasibly coded. Thus, the e-tactics from warehouse sites were sampled based on the relative size of the site (effectively "oversampling" e-tactics from the smaller sites): 10 percent of the e-tactics on the largest sites were sampled, 50 percent of the e-tactics were sampled on moderately sized warehouse sites, and 100 percent of the e-tactics were sampled (i.e., the population) on the smallest warehouse sites. In order to capture a list of protest actions similar to those captured for nonwarehouse sites, Google searches using the same SOAP-API as discussed above were run for each warehouse site, but those queries restricted the results to URLs from the warehouse domain. For instance, a query was submitted using the Google SOAP-API requesting all results for petitions on PetitionOnline's domain. The results from those returns were then used as the list from which sampling was completed. The differential sampling rates allowed the project to collect enough data on e-tactics from each warehouse site that an understanding of the "character" of each distinct warehouse site could be developed. In the analyses used in this book, a weighting scheme is employed to eliminate any artifacts of this differential sampling rate.

Because so few e-tactics were found on nonwarehouse sites, no sampling of e-tactics was necessary for nonwarehouse sites. That is, all e-tactics found on nonwarehouse sites were retained in the study and coded. The only exceptions to the 100 percent rule were archives of old e-tactics and "hidden" e-tactics where the existence of the action on the site was not evident from either the site's main page or the URL identified by the Google SOAP-API. Both archived and hidden e-tactics were excluded since they were not considered reachable, active e-tactics.

Understood across the entire process represented in figure A.1, the study used a two-pronged sampling scheme: warehouse sites were not sampled, but e-tactics on those sites were sampled at varying rates depending on the size of the site; nonwarehouse sites were sampled at a 10 percent rate, but all e-tactics on sampled sites were included in the study.

Mirroring Sampled Web Sites and E-tactics

As shown in figure A.1, the next step in the process was to mirror (i.e., download and save into local files for archiving and later examination) the population of warehouse sites and the four random samples of nonwarehouse sites. Mirroring was completed using Windows batch files and WGet, a freely available mirroring program. The mirroring process honored robot exclusions posted to servers' robots.txt files and also included, as a courtesy, thirty-second delays between requests to the same server to reduce the bandwidth required for mirroring. Mirroring took place across four weeks in March and April 2004, during which tens of thousands of pages were mirrored.

Content Coding of Web sites and E-tactics

Content coding of Web sites took place in three stages. First, all URLs in the five samples were evaluated for their relevance to the research questions at hand (i.e., did they contain or directly link to at least one e-tactic). Second, Web sites assessed as relevant to the study were then further analyzed using quantitative content coding. Third, e-tactics hosted on or linked to from these sites—or in the case of several of the warehouse sites, a sample thereof—were quantitatively content coded for the data discussed below.

Intercoder reliability tests were conducted frequently during the initial phase of coding and were conducted twice during the detail-coding phase. Test results revealed high levels of consistency between coders, although a few particular items were inconsistent and were thus excluded from analysis. As well, when the data collection process was complete, all data sets were programmatically checked for unallowable values, logically inconsistent relationships between different variables' values, and other sources of error.

Assessing Samples for Sites Hosting or Linking to E-tactics

The first step in coding was to identify a home page for each URL in the sample. We define a home page as the highest-order domain (and corresponding URL) with a unique author or group of authors, where authorship is based on individual or organizational capacities to publish, remove, and/or edit material. For instance, Jennifer Earl controls a number of specific Web pages, including <http://www.soc.ucsb.edu/faculty/earl/recreq.html>. The home page for this URL would be identified as <http://www.soc.ucsb.edu/faculty/earl/index.html>, and any materials nested within the domain or subdomains of <www.soc.ucsb.edu/faculty/earl/> would be considered part of the Web site. We have used this authorship requirement because identifying <www.soc.ucsb.edu> or <www.ucsb.edu> as the home page would clearly misunderstand the boundaries of Earl's Web site. Web sites such as bulletin boards or listservs that allow any member to post content, and therefore lack a unique author or set of authors, were excluded from further analysis (counts of this type of site are listed in the seventh column of table A.1).

Next, in order to eliminate sites that did not host or link to e-tactics, content coders assessed whether the site hosted one of the four featured e-tactics (for nonwarehouse sites, the second to last column of table A.1), or had a direct link to a site on another domain that hosted one of the four featured e-tactics (for nonwarehouse sites, the last column of table A.1). Coders were instructed to label the site as fitting into one of the categories listed in the last six columns of table A.1. For the purposes of this table, when a site hosted and linked to a focal e-tactic, it is counted in the hosting column. The e-tactic was hosted if the site contained enough information to allow visitors to participate. Coders coded the site as linking to the e-tactic, instead of hosting it, if necessary elements (i.e., contact addresses in a letter-writing campaign) were located on a different domain from the coded site. To qualify for the linking category, the link had to directly connect surfers to the protest implementation, not to a general information page of another Web site that may or may not have hosted such an e-tactic. For instance, if a link advertising a human rights petition actually sent surfers to the general Amnesty International home page, instead of directly to the petition page, that link was not coded because the link did not directly connect to an opportunity to participate. Some sites were coded as "linking directly" rather than hosting although they housed information on the e-tactic because they contained such cursory discussions of the action that users would have to follow the outbound link in order to participate. Table A.1 shows the results from this preliminary coding for nonwarehouse sites. All fifteen warehouse sites either hosted or directly linked to an e-tactic.

Since the study was interested in actual e-tactics, as opposed to general discussions about e-tactics, sites not coded as hosting or directly linking to one of the four featured e-tactics were eliminated from the study.[6] This means that sites that encouraged participation in offline (i.e., street) protest events, but did not discuss any of the four featured e-tactics, were not coded further. Similarly, if a site discussed Web protest using only protest forms *other* than the featured e-tactics, the site would not be coded. Finally, sites that contained only general calls to action (e.g., "Take action now!"), but failed to provide or link to a means to participate were not coded further (see column nine of table A.1).

In all, depending on the type of e-tactic examined, between approximately 8–12 percent of the original 10 percent sample of nonwarehouse sites met these requirements and were thus retained in the study; 100 percent of warehouse sites met these requirements and were retained in the study. In raw counts, 169 nonwarehouse sites and all 15 warehouse sites were retained.

Content Coding of Sites Hosting or Linking to E-tactics

These 184 remaining sites were then coded further using quantitative content coding to capture key features of and variation across the Web sites. For each site, the various causes, up to 4, that were discussed on the site were coded. In total, sites were assessed for the presence of 168 different causes and then further coded for their position (for, against, or neutral) on the issue. Further variation in sites' positions on specific causes was captured through a text field where coders could elaborate on any nuances of a site's position. Taken together, the collection of sites was impressively diverse. These Web sites covered a broad range of issues, from traditional protest issues such as antiwar protests opposing the U.S. invasion and occupation of Iraq, to far less traditional protest topics such as advocacy on behalf of a favorite television show.

Sites were further coded to determine whether they were politically focused. They were considered to have politically focused content if they challenged decisions, actions, or policies of an institutional authority or a person perceived to be a representative of a political cause (for more on this definition, see Snow, Soule, and Kriesi 2004). If the site was not politically focused, coders elaborated on the specific nature of its focus.

Coders also assessed sites for affiliation with social movements and the mention of specific SMOs. That is, they evaluated whether the site contained specific language of affiliation with one or more social movements, and named organizations with physical offices and a history of advocacy activity (i.e., SMOs).

Finally, coders counted the number of offline, hosted online, and linked to online tactical forms (up to four each) along with their respective quantities of implementations (i.e., counts for individual tactical forms). Offline forms included actions such as rallies, marches, and vigils. Online forms included the four focal e-tactics as well as faxes, denial-of-service attacks, and hacktivism. Coders were also able to enter a form of "other" that was further specified in a notes field. Among the e-tactics, e-tactics were considered *internal* to a site when they were hosted on the site itself, whereas e-tactics reached via links to external domains—that is, e-tactics hosted on a different domain—were considered *external* to the site.

Content Coding of E-tactics on Web Sites

The ultimate goal of the study was to generate random samples of the four focal e-tactics and content code those actions so that generalizable data on such e-tactics would be available. Thus, at this point, the final coding mechanism treated e-tactics, not Web sites, as the unit of analysis so that data on the e-tactics themselves were coded. Because such an unexpectedly large number of fax campaigns were hosted on and/or linked to by sites in our samples, and they represent a variation on the letter-writing campaign, we detail coded information on individual fax campaigns and report on these findings in the book. Still, we remind the reader to interpret these findings with caution since we did not produce an independent sample of fax campaigns; the fax campaigns we report on were found co-occurring with at least one of the four featured e-tactics. The counts of other tactical forms, off- and online, were made at the Web site level. In all, 153 petitions, 212 letter-writing campaigns, 152 email campaigns, 82 boycotts, and 149 fax campaigns were coded from nonwarehouse sites, for a total of 748 e-tactics.[7] From the 15 warehouse sites, 287 petitions, 12 letter-writing campaigns, 10 email campaigns, 49 boycotts, and 4 fax campaigns were coded for a total of 362 e-tactics. These e-tactics were detail coded for the following data.

First, up to four unique claim-target combinations could be assigned, using the same set of claims and position-evaluation codes as applied to Web sites (i.e., 168 cause codes and 3 positions—for, against, or neutral—on each), and matching the claim with information on a target. For each claim-target combination, coders specified the type of entity that the e-tactic targeted for that claim: government, quasi-government, private, or other for not elsewhere classified individuals and groups. Government targets included the legislative, judicial, and executive branches of the state, government agencies (such as the Food and Drug Administration or the Internal Revenue Service), foreign governments or embassies, law enforcement, and tribal governments. Quasi-government entities included organizations affiliated with the state yet officially independent of any specific administration, such as the United Nations. Private targets included businesses, political organizations, religious organizations, social movements or SMOs, educational institutions, and labor unions. If the target was an ambiguous group, such as "the world academic community," a category of "other" was used. Targets were further coded for their level; coders assessed whether the target was local, state level, regional, national, a foreign entity, relations between the United States and a foreign entity, or other. Because each e-tactic could be associated with up to 4 claim-target combinations, a given implementation could be coded to target government, quasi-government, *and* private entities, multiple levels of government, and/or multiple branches within government.

E-tactics were also coded to determine whether an institutional authority was targeted (as discussed earlier in this appendix). If the e-tactic was judged to not target an institutional authority, coders elaborated on the specific nature of the target.

Coders also evaluated the mechanism of participation in these e-tactics, identifying variation in the automation of participation and the extent to which participation took place in virtual space. E-tactics were described as automated when users only had to furnish personal information such as their name and email address to participate. For example, an online petition that could be signed by simply typing one's name into a field on the page was considered to have automated participation. Participation was coded as semiautomated when the site partially completed the action yet the user had to perform additional tasks, as in the case of a prewritten letter that a site would populate with information supplied by a user, but that the user nonetheless still had to print and mail. Lastly, participation was considered manual when it was entirely completed by the user, such as in a call for an email campaign where only the target's email address was listed, requiring the user to compose and send an email entirely independently.

To code the extent to which participation took place virtually, coders determined to what extent a connection to the Web was required to participate in the action. Actions were categorized into one of three options. E-tactics were considered entirely online when a connection to the Web was required for all aspects of participation, such as with an email action. They were coded as mostly online if a Web connection was required for most, but not all, aspects of participation. For example, a letter formatted online by the site for the user that the user must print and mail offline would be considered mostly online. And actions were considered mostly offline if the bulk of participation took place without need for a connection to the Web, such as with a letter-writing campaign in which the user must compose and send a letter offline, with the target's address and talking points provided on the Web site. All e-tactics were considered to have some online component to their participation since without access to the Web, users would not be aware of the specific e-tactic action, let alone able to participate.

Data Analyses

Data were analyzed using Stata 9 SE. For observations from warehouse sites, weighting was necessary to adjust for the varying sampling rates; "p weights" were used.

Additional Data

We captured the email addresses as available of the site administrators, owners, and/or operators of all Web sites in the sample as well as those for Web sites hosting or linking to e-tactics that were gathered in a supplemental cross-sectional sample. Overall, we were able to find a contact for 147 sites between the two samples. We solicited these site contacts for an interview. Thirty-eight of them agreed to an interview. The interviews were open-ended and conducted over the phone. They were conducted in early 2006 and lasted between thirty minutes and an hour and forty-five minutes—averaging just under an hour. The interviews were transcribed and analyzed to supplement aggregate findings on the sites and e-tactics in our sample, but where applicable, were not associated with the specific sites that the respondents worked on. Because of the low response rate, it is important to underscore that the interview sample is not representative.

Notes

Chapter 1

1. This figure is according to the organizers (Urbina 2007). Other sources put the number at tens of thousands. Police records show that UFPJ applied for a permit for fifty thousand (Howell 2007).

2. Although scholars of social movements may be more familiar with research on "Internet activism," we follow the standard nomenclature of Internet studies scholars by referring to the "Web" more specifically to describe the particular information and communication technology (ICT) in our study—the World Wide Web—and to clarify that our analysis does not also encompass other ways the Internet can be used for protest (e.g., instant messaging).

3. The site first announced the planned event in November 2006, following the midterm congressional elections. UFPJ had initially called for an antiwar march on Washington to coincide with the fourth anniversary of the war, in March 2007, but amended this call and moved the date to January in the week following the 2006 elections.

4. While the effectiveness of such online actions in garnering social change is indeterminate right now as compared to the impact of a person's presence at a march or rally (recalling that social movement scholars often cannot conclusively demonstrate the effects of prior protest cycles on policy and certainly cannot indicate whether each additional person at a rally makes a marginal difference to the impact), millions of people engage in this kind of action online annually.

5. For ease of reading, we use several terms interchangeably to refer to, respectively, tactical forms (aka protest forms or kinds of e-tactics) and individual actions (aka individual e-tactics). The former, tactical forms, refers to established types of collective action (e.g., petitioning or holding a rally), while the latter specifies particular deployments of an e-tactical form (e.g., a petition).

6. Changes to the repertoire may also include the addition of entirely new tactical forms—such as denial-of-service actions (Wray 1999). Denial-of-service actions

occur when a large number of computers make frequent and repetitive requests to a Web server, thereby overloading the server and rendering it inoperable.

Chapter 2

1. As also defined in the glossary, hacktivism is the use of hacking-related techniques to disrupt an opponent's or target's Web site.

2. Joanna McGenere and Wayne Ho (2000) provide a brief review of the uses of the term inside and outside HCI. The debate over the term between Ian Hutchby (2001, 2003) and Brian Rappert (2003) suggests how varied its usage and understanding have become in STS and the sociology of technology.

3. Hutchby (2001, 442) describes constructivist concerns for the development of technologies in this way: "While there are a range of (often fiercely competitive) theoretical perspectives involved in this consensus [against technological determinism], they all begin from the viewpoint that precisely what the characteristics of technologies are, as well as their relationship with social structures, are both socially constructed: the outcome of a whole range of social factors and processes."

4. Wellman and his colleagues (2003) also discuss the social affordances of the Internet, claiming that technological changes lead to social affordances, but they do not precisely define the term social affordance.

Chapter 3

1. It is critical to note, though, that while we will present data on fax campaigns, we did not draw an independent sample of faxes. So strictly speaking, what we can say about faxes is limited to the population of faxes that co-occur with online petitions, boycotts, and/or letter-writing and/or email campaigns.

2. Case 2101752. To refer to the original archived data, we use unique case identifiers. The sites are identified using a seven-digit number formatted to identify the e-tactic form sample that the site was found in (the initial digit) and its placement in the initial concatenation of Google searches. The tactics are identified with a nine- or ten-digit number containing the full site identifier, followed by an underscore and a unique two- to four-digit number. From here forward, when we refer to a specific case, we will list the case number in a footnote.

3. Case 1102479.

4. To read the graph, first start by looking at the axes. The vertical Y axis illustrates the percentage of sites that only hosted an e-tactic. Meanwhile, the horizontal X axis shows the percentage of sites linking to e-tactics to the right, and both hosting and linking to the left. Nonwarehouse sites are depicted on the top half of the graphic and warehouse sites are portrayed on the bottom. You can see that the

shaded areas in all of the graphic's quadrants have been represented along the respective axes based on our findings.

5. Case 3103234_976.

6. Readers need to be aware that while we report on fax campaigns that we observed, because we did not independently sample for them, our findings related to faxes are far more speculative than for other e-tactical forms.

7. If one weights the data to correct for the oversampling of e-tactics on smaller warehouse sites, the relative frequencies change somewhat: in weighted data, petitions constitute 88 percent of the e-tactics, boycotts make up 8 percent, and letter-writing, email, and fax campaigns each make up about 1 percent.

8. Case 6400997_157.

9. Case 4102258_983.

10. Case 4102526_27.

11. Case 2103726.

Chapter 4

1. Zald and Roberta Ash [Garner] (1966) had already started to theorize about SMOs along with the determinants of organization growth, maintenance, and decline, but McCarthy and Zald (1973, 1977) are largely considered the "founders" of resource mobilization.

2. Save for 1 percent of nonwarehouse letter-writing campaigns, there were few instances of nonwarehouse e-tactics with mostly online participation. For warehouse e-tactics, less than 1 percent of the petitions and just 5 percent of the letter-writing campaigns fell into the mostly online participation category. The surprisingly low quantity of e-tactics that required mostly online participation (i.e., where a significant portion, but not all, of the participation required an Internet connection, versus entirely online or mostly offline participation) suggests an all-or-nothing approach to virtual participation in which e-tactics were either completely or barely virtual. Speculating on why this might be the case is difficult with so few examples, however, so we restrict ourselves to pointing out this pattern and leave it to future research to investigate why it might be so.

3. Case 3105074_771.

4. Case 3100179_325.

5. Case 2103136_542.

6. Case 7900056.

7. Case 7900056_1087.

8. Case 7800022.

9. Case 1106949_358.

10. Case 7600115_263.

11. Case 2101510_951.

12. Case 1101062_334.

13. Case 2101738_399.

14. Case 2100972_394.

15. Case 2103428_551.

16. Cases 6400997_144, 6500872_244, and 6100790_54, respectively.

17. Case 7600115_273.

18. Case 4101705_11.

19. Case 7900056_1091.

20. Case 3105074_774.

21. Case 7600115_264.

22. Case 2100198_947.

23. Case 2103136_539.

24. Because so few nonwarehouse sites reported participation, this mean is based on only twenty-two e-tactics. Additionally, it does not include one nonwarehouse, semiautomated petition that garnered substantial participation, which we regard as an outlier.

25. This mean is computed from the 257 entirely online warehouse e-tactics that reported participation. And perhaps this variation in participation, compared to the lack of it across nonwarehouse e-tactics, is because warehouse e-tactics reported participation more often, thereby allowing us to observe variation in participation, not because nonwarehouse e-tactics did not have variation in their participation rates.

26. N = 3 because the nonwarehouse, semiautomated outlier with 350,000 reported participants is discarded from this figure.

Chapter 5

1. As we discuss below, Earl and Schussman (2003, 165) make a similar argument about e-movements: "Tarrow's advocacy for a distinction between the concepts of organizing and organizations suggests the possibility that formal, or even

informal, organizations may not be absolutely necessary building blocks for e-movements."

2. Our data distinguish SMOs from other types of organizations, such as businesses, social groups, and professional associations. SMOs have a cause-oriented mission while other organizations do not. This means that actions we describe as non-SMO ones are not solely generated by lone individuals, although most are. We discuss the constitution of organizing teams more fully in chapter 7.

3. Cases 1106738, 1106738_871, and 1106738_870, respectively.

4. Case 3105173.

5. Case 1107538.

6. Case 3102644.

7. We are using a standard $p < .05$ level for significance. If we were to loosen our requirements, however, the values for petitions and letter-writing campaigns would be significantly different for SMO and non-SMO sites at the 0.10 level.

8. Cases 2104910, 3100996, and 1103001, respectively.

9. Case 1104936_352.

10. Cases 2101752 and 2102801, respectively.

11. Case 4102470.

12. Case 1107834.

13. Case 4101864.

14. Case 1108599.

15. Case 2103726.

16. Case 1107686.

17. Case 2100198_947.

18. Case 1102419_817.

19. Case 2103339.

20. Case 2104702.

21. Case 4103719.

22. The non-SMO average was calculated after dropping one outlier case with an e-tactic volume that was nearly twenty times greater than any other non-SMO site in the sample. The difference between SMO and non-SMO sites was not significant when this outlier was included; once the outlier was dropped, this difference was significant at the 0.01 level.

23. Case 2101738.

24. Case 1107686.

25. Case 1102479.

26. Cases 1106194, 2100198, and 3102913, respectively.

27. Case 1103553.

28. Case 2100527.

29. Case 2105437_700.

30. Case 2105216_673.

Chapter 6

1. Case 1103482_342.

2. Case 1106738_869.

3. Case 6400997_151.

4. Case 1100986_808.

5. Case 1101542_801.

6. Case 1100624_332.

7. Case 6100790_96.

8. Case 1104936_351.

9. Case 3102270_744.

10. Case 2107045_966.

11. Case 1106194_839.

12. Cases 7900056_1091 and 7900056_1090, respectively.

13. Cases 7900056_1105 (Boeing) and 7900056_1107 (Cadbury).

14. Case 7900056_1089.

15. Case 6700001_292.

16. Case 6100790_49.

17. Case 6100790_66.

18. Case 6600000_931.

19. Case 6400997_171.

20. Case 6100790_129.

21. Case 7300107_313.

22. Case 3102270_750.

23. Case 6100790_68.

24. Case 7200002_306.

25. Case 1104328_366.

26. Case 1102352_804.

27. Case 6100790_94.

28. Case 1107414_365.

29. Cases 1100986_807 and 1100986_808, respectively.

30. Case 1106949_358.

31. Case 6400997_138.

32. Case 4104544_319.

33. Case 6100790_36.

34. Case 6100790_123.

35. Case 1107414_365.

36. Case 4101705.

37. These are weighted percentages based on a sampling strategy employed to code large warehouse sites. For more detail on our sampling, see the methodological appendix.

38. Cases 6500872_237 and 6500872_230, respectively.

39. Cases 3103234_975 and 2101181_949, respectively.

40. Case 1107318_877.

41. Cases 1105454_354 and 1102022_337, respectively.

42. Cases 7600115_273 and 7600115_274, respectively.

43. Case 6200024_134.

44. Cases 1100060_331 and 1100624_332, respectively.

45. Case 2101605_398.

Chapter 7

1. It is important to note that Shirky's organizers are not the same people we label organizers. His organizers are major Web site owner/operators like Flickr, Facebook,

Wikipedia, and so on. Instead of thinking about how participation-related power laws can benefit the organizers of Web sites as Shirky does (for a clear expression of this, see Shirky 2008, chapter 10), we want to think about how organizing itself might be able to successfully follow a power law online where the most active organizer puts in twice the effort as the second most active organizer and puts in three times the effort as the third most active organizer, and so forth.

2. Interview 4. See chapter 3 and the methodological appendix for a full discussion of the interview data. Interviews are numbered as references to original transcripts as unique case identifiers. From here forward, when we refer to a specific interview, we will list the interview number in a footnote.

3. Interview 29.

4. Interview 27.

5. Interview 5.

6. Interview 31.

7. Interview 2.

8. Interview 28.

9. Interview 1.

10. Case 2105398.

11. Case 3101690.

12. Interview 10.

13. Interview 15.

14. Interview 27.

15. Interview 31.

16. Interview 16.

17. Interview 11.

18. Interview 2.

19. Interview 29.

20. Interview 15.

21. Interview 1.

22. Interview 4.

23. Case 6400997_178.

24. The remaining thirteen e-tactics qualified as nonpolitical because they rewrote the historical relationship between grievance and collective action. Rather than

deploying collective action to address collective grievances as social movements have historically done, these e-tactics were premised on different combinations of individual and collective action and grievances. For an extended description of them, see Earl and Kimport 2009.

25. Cases 6400997_143 and 6400997_139, respectively.

26. Cases 6400997_172 and 6400997_208, respectively.

27. Case 6500872_240.

28. Case 6100790_83.

29. Case 6100790_91.

30. Case 6500872_250.

31. Case 7800022_1084.

32. Case 6700001_282.

33. Case 6400997.

34. Case 6500872.

35. Case 6500872_239.

36. Cases 7600115_271 and 7600115_270, respectively.

37. Case 6100790.

38. Case 6800002.

39. Case 6800002_256.

40. Case 7900056.

41. Case 2101181_950.

42. Case 2104612_944.

43. Case 1106738_870.

44. Case 1101062_334.

45. Case 2104612_826.

46. Case 1106194_838.

Chapter 9

1. This does not mean, however, that what we have described in this book is entirely new. Some scholars of new social movements might argue that online protest has some antecedents. For instance, Alberto Melucci (1980, 1985, 1989, 1994) argued

fervently against overinvesting analytically in SMOs. He contended that social movement scholars all too often considered social movements to be reducible without remainder to SMOs. Yet Melucci claimed that this missed much of the organizing that happened outside of SMOs and limited scholars' understanding of the scope of social movements. All that being said, new social movement scholars also focus on the importance of collective identity and the production of meaning; we have suggested that under some circumstances, collective identity might actually become less important to driving action.

Methodological Appendix

1. As we discuss later in the appendix, we also content coded fax campaigns that were found co-occurring with one of the four featured e-tactics.

2. Tim Jordan (2001) reports on top-level domain data, but data do not offer any insight into the content of domains.

3. Some scholars, such as those involved with the C5 project (Jevbratt 2004), have unsuccessfully attempted to use the underlying IP addresses associated with URLs, which are patterned, to create a population map of the Web.

4. We do not, however, attempt to mimic user behavior in focusing on the first ten returns from a search engine, given that research shows that the vast majority of users do not click through to more results, and even fewer click through at each subsequent results page.

5. The SOAP-API's Perl script was written by Alan Schussman.

6. As is evident from table A.1, the procedure captures a wide swath of different kinds of URLs discussing protest, which is excellent for projects wanting to collect data on any discussion of particular protest tactics. For the purposes of this project, however, the sample was not as efficient as would be desired since most sampled pages did not invite and allow participation. Future refinements in the technique should focus on increasing the efficiency of samples. Other projects using automated search and retrieval of Web pages have also faced problems with efficiency (Hindman, Tsioutsiouliklis, and Johnson 2004).

7. Four of these individual tactics appeared twice in our sample, as both hosted by a Web site in the sample and linked to by a different site in the sample. So as not to artificially inflate our findings on how e-tactics accomplish protest, these four actions are included in the full tactics data set only once, but in order to fully describe how sites vary, are included in all appropriate site data set counts of e-tactics.

Glossary

Affordance: The actions and/or characteristics of usage that a technology makes qualitatively easier or possible when compared to prior like technologies.

Collective action: Coordinated action by multiple participants toward a common goal.

E-mobilizations: The use of online tools to facilitate offline protest.

E-movements: Social movements that emerge and thrive online.

E-tactics: Discrete protest actions where participation occurs at least partially online. Examples include online petitions, boycotts, and letter and email campaigns.

ICT: Information and communication technology.

Internet: The hardware and set of protocols that underlie a global network of computers and subnetworks.

Hacktivism: Using hacking-related techniques for political ends. Examples include politically motivated denial-of-service actions or politically motivated Web site defacements.

Leveraging: Making strong use of, as in "To make strong use of an affordance is to leverage the affordance."

Mobilization: In social movement studies, it can refer to participation at the micro-level or more aggregate levels of participation and/or protest levels.

Repertoire of contention: Describes both the set of tactical forms from which social movement actors can choose at any given historical moment and the common characteristics shared by that set of tactics.

Server-side applications: Software or applications that reside on the Web server and are not necessarily directly observable to a site visitor, but that drive many interactive elements of a Web site.

Supersize: To change theoretical processes in scale only.

Theory 2.0: A set of model-changing approaches where technology usage can lead to changes in the underlying theoretical processes.

Uniform resource locator (URL): The address that one types into a browser to reach a specific Web site, as in <http://mitpress.mit.edu>.

Web, the: The set of Web pages and other texts, images, videos, or other digital artifacts that are located via URLs and hypertext. Often accessed through a Web browser.

Web activism: The entire set of ways for using the Web to promote, participate in, or organize activism.

References

Adnkronos International. 2009. "Italy: Over 95,000 Women Sign Anti-Berlusconi Petition." <http://www.adnkronos.com/AKI/English/Politics/?id=3.0.3893216607> (accessed November 3, 2009).

Amenta, Edwin, and Neal Caren. 2004. "The Legislative, Organizational, and Beneficiary Consequences of State-Oriented Challengers." In *The Blackwell Companion to Social Movements*, eds. David A. Snow, Sarah A. Soule, and Hanspeter Kriesi, 461–488. Oxford: Blackwell Publishing.

Anderson, B. 1983. *Imagined Communities*. New York: Verso.

Andrews, Kenneth T. 2001. "Social Movements and Policy Implementation: The Mississippi Civil Rights Movement and the War on Poverty, 1965 to 1971." *American Sociological Review* 66:71–95.

Arquilla, John, and David Ronfeldt. 2001. *Networks and Netwars: The Future of Terror, Crime, and Militancy*. Santa Monica: RAND.

Associated Press. 2009. "100,000 Women Say They're Offended by Berlusconi." *New York Times*, October 22. <http://www.nytimes.com/aponline/2009/10/22/world/AP-EU-Italy-Berlusconi.htm> (accessed November 3, 2009).

Ayers, Michael D. 2003. "Comparing Collective Identity in Online and Offline Feminist Activists." In *Cyberactivism: Online Activism in Theory and Practice*, eds. Martha McCaughey and Michael D. Ayers, 145–164. New York: Routledge.

Ayres, Jeffrey M. 1999. "From the Streets to the Internet: The Cyber-Diffusion of Contention." *Annals of the American Academy of Political and Social Science* 566:132–143.

Barber, Benjamin R. 1998. "Three Scenarios for the Future of Technology and Strong Democracy." *Political Science Quarterly* 113:573–589.

Barkan, Steven E. 1984. "Legal Control of the Southern Civil Rights Movement." *American Sociological Review* 49:552–565.

Benkler, Yochai. 2006. *The Wealth of Networks: How Social Production Transforms Markets and Freedom.* New Haven, CT: Yale University Press.

Bennett, Daniel, and Pam Fielding. 1999. *The Net Effect: How Cyberadvocacy Is Changing the Political Landscape.* Merrifield, VA: e-advocates Press.

Bennett, W. Lance. 2003a. "Communicating Global Activism: Strengths and Vulnerabilities of Networked Politics." *Information, Communication and Society* 6:143–168.

Bennett, W. Lance 2003b. "New Media Power: The Internet and Global Activism." In *Contesting Media Power*, eds. Nick Couldry and James Curran, 17–37. Lanham, MD: Rowman and Littlefield.

Bennett, W. Lance. 2004a. "Communicating Global Activism: Strengths and Vulnerabilities of Networked Politics." In *Cyberprotest: New Media, Citizens, and Social Movements*, eds. Wim van de Donk, Brian D. Loader, Paul G. Nixon, and Deiter Rucht, 123–146. New York: Routledge.

Bennett, W. Lance. 2004b. "Social Movements beyond Borders: Understanding Two Eras of Transnational Activism." In *Transnational Protest and Global Activism*, eds. Donatella della Porta and Sydney Tarrow, 203–226. Lanham, MD: Rowman and Littlefield.

Bijker, Wiebe E. 1995. *Of Bicycles, Bakelites, and Bulbs: Toward a Theory of Sociotechnical Change.* Cambridge, MA: MIT Press.

Bijker, Wiebe E., and Trevor J. Pinch. 2002. "SCOT Answers, Other Questions: A Reply to Nick Clayton." *Technology and Culture* 43:361–369.

Bimber, Bruce. 1998. "The Internet and Political Transformation: Populism, Community, and Accelerated Pluralism." *Polity* 31:133–160.

Bimber, Bruce. 2001. *Information and American Democracy: Technology in the Evolution of Political Power.* Cambridge: Cambridge University Press.

Bimber, Bruce. 2006. "How Information Shapes Political Institutions." In *Media Power in Politics*, ed. Dorris A. Graber. Washington, DC: CQ Press.

Bimber, Bruce, Andrew J. Flanagin, and Cynthia Stohl. 2005. "Reconceptualizing Collective Action in the Contemporary Media Environment." *Communication Theory* 15:365–388.

Bimber, Bruce, Cynthia Stohl, and Andrew J. Flanagin. 2008. "Technological Change and the Shifting Nature of Political Organization." In *Handbook of Internet Politics*, ed. Andrew Chadwick and Philip N. Howard, 72–85. New York: Routledge.

Boase, Jeffrey, and Barry Wellman. 2006. "Personal Relationships: On and Off the Internet." In *Cambridge Handbook of Personal Relations*, eds. Anita L. Vangelisti and Dan Perlman, 709–723. Cambridge: Cambridge University Press.

British Office of Communication. 2009. *Citizens' Digital Participation*. London: British Office of Communication.

Brown, M. Helen. 1989. "Organizing Activity in the Women's Movement: An Example of Distributed Leadership." *International Social Movement Research* 2:225–240.

Brunsting, Suzanne, and Tom Postmes. 2002. "Social Movement Participation in the Digital Age: Predicting Offline and Online Collective Action." *Small Group Research* 33:525–554.

Cardoso, Gustavo, and Pedro Pereira Neto. 2004. "Mass Media Driven Mobilization and Online Protest: ICTs and the Pro–East Timor Movement in Portugal." In *Cyberprotest: New Media, Citizens, and Social Movements*, eds. Wim van de Donk, Brian D. Loader, Paul G. Nixon, and Dieter Rucht, 129–144. New York: Routledge.

Carty, Victoria. 2002. "Technology and Counter-hegemonic Movements: The Case of Nike Corporation." *Social Movement Studies* 1:129–146.

Castells, Manuel. 1997. *The Power of Identity*. Malden, MA: Blackwell.

Clemens, Elisabeth S., and Debra C. Minkoff. 2004. "Beyond the Iron Law: Rethinking the Place of Organizations in Social Movement Research." In *The Blackwell Companion to Social Movements*, eds. David A. Snow, Sarah A. Soule, and Hanspeter Kriesi, 155–170. Oxford: Blackwell Publishing.

Cloward, Richard A., and Frances Fox Piven. 2001. "Disrupting Cyberspace: A New Frontier for Labor Activism?" *New Labour Forum* (Spring–Summer): 91–94.

Danitz, Tiffany, and Warren P. Strobel. 1999. "The Internet's Impact on Activism: the Case of Burma." *Studies in Conflict and Terrorism* 22:257–269.

Davenport, Christian. 2007. "State Repression and Political Order." *Annual Review of Political Science* 10:1–23.

Deibert, Ronald, John Palfrey, Rafal Rohozinski, and Jonathan Zittrain, eds. 2008. *Access Denied: The Practice and Policy of Global Internet Filtering*. Cambridge, MA: MIT Press.

Diani, Mario. 2000. "Social Movement Networks Virtual and Real." *Information, Communication and Society* 3:386–401.

DiMaggio, Paul, Eszter Hargittai, W. Russell Neuman, and John P. Robinson. 2001. "The Social Implications of the Internet." *Annual Review of Sociology* 27:307–336.

Downing, John D. H. 1989. "Computers for Political Change: PeaceNet and Public Data Access." *Journal of Communication* 39:154–162.

Dutton, William H., Ellen J. Helsper, and Monica M. Gerber. 2009. *The Internet in Britain*. Oxford: Oxford Internet Institute.

Eagleton-Pierce, Mathew. 2001. "The Internet and the Seattle WTO Protests." *Peace Review* 13:331–337.

Earl, Jennifer. 2000. "Methods, Movements, and Outcomes: Methodological Difficulties in the Study of Extra-Movement Outcomes." *Research in Social Movements, Conflicts and Change* 22:3–25.

Earl, Jennifer. 2004. "The Cultural Consequences of Social Movements." In *The Blackwell Companion to Social Movements*, eds. David A. Snow, Sarah A. Soule, and Hanspeter Kriesi, 508–530. Oxford: Blackwell Publishing.

Earl, Jennifer. 2006a. "Introduction: Repression and the Social Control of Protest." *Mobilization* 11:129–143.

Earl, Jennifer. 2006b. "Pursuing Social Change Online: The Use of Four Protest Tactics on the Internet." *Social Science Computer Review* 24:362–377.

Earl, Jennifer. 2007. "Leading Tasks in a Leaderless Movement: The Case of Strategic Voting." *American Behavioral Scientist* 50:1327–1349.

Earl, Jennifer. 2010. "Dynamics of Protest-Related Diffusion on the Web." *Information, Communication and Society* 13:209–225.

Earl, Jennifer, and Katrina Kimport. 2008. "The Targets of Online Protest: State and Private Targets of Four Online Protest Tactics." *Information, Communication and Society* 11:449–472.

Earl, Jennifer, and Katrina Kimport. 2009. "Movement Societies and Digital Protest: Fan Activism and Other Non-Political Protest Online." *Sociological Theory* 23:220–243.

Earl, Jennifer, Katrina Kimport, Greg Prieto, Carly Rush, and Kimberly Reynoso. (Forthcoming). "Changing the World One Webpage at a Time: Conceptualizing and Explaining 'Internet Activism.'" Forthcoming in *Mobilization*.

Earl, Jennifer, and Alan Schussman. 2003. "The New Site of Activism: On-Line Organizations, Movement Entrepreneurs, and the Changing Location of Social Movement Decision-Making." *Research in Social Movements, Conflicts and Change* 24:155–187.

Earl, Jennifer, and Alan Schussman. 2004. "Cease and Desist: Repression, Strategic Voting, and the 2000 Presidential Election." *Mobilization* 9:181–202.

Earl, Jennifer, and Alan Schussman. 2008. "Contesting Cultural Control: Youth Culture and Online Petitioning." In *Digital Media and Civic Engagement*, ed. W. Lance Bennett, 71–95. Cambridge, MA: MIT Press.

Earl, Jennifer, Sarah A. Soule, and John D. McCarthy. 2003. "Protests under Fire? Explaining Protest Policing." *American Sociological Review* 68:581–606.

Eichler, Margrit. 1977. "Leadership in Social Movements." *Sociological Inquiry* 47:99–107.

Eyerman, Ron, and Andrew Jamison. 1998. *Music and Social Movements: Mobilizing Traditions in the Twentieth Century.* Cambridge: Cambridge University Press.

Fandy, Mamoun. 1999. "CyberResistance: Saudi Opposition Between Globalization and Localization." *Comparative Studies in Society and History* 41:124–147.

Fantasia, Rick. 1988. *Cultures of Solidarity: Consciousness, Action, and Contemporary American Workers.* Berkeley: University of California Press.

Fisher, Dana, Kevin Stanley, David Berman, and Gina Neff. 2005. "How Do Organizations Matter? Mobilization and Support for Participants at Five Globalization Protests." *Social Problems* 52:102–121.

Flanagin, Andrew J., Cynthia Stohl, and Bruce Bimber. 2006. "Modeling the Structure of Collective Action." *Communication Monographs* 73:29–54.

Foot, Kirsten A., and Steven M. Schneider. 2002. "Online Action in Campaign 2000: An Exploratory Analysis of the U.S. Political Web Sphere." *Journal of Broadcasting and Electronic Media* 46:222–244.

Garner, Roberta. 1997. "Fifty Years of Social Movement Theory: An Interpretation." In *Social Movement Theory and Research: An Annotated Bibliographical Guide*, eds. Roberta Garner and John Tenuto, 1–58. Lanham, MD: Scarecrow Press.

Garrett, R. Kelly. 2006. "Protest in an Information Society: A Review of the Literature on Social Movement and New ICTs." *Information, Communication and Society* 9:202–224.

Garrett, R. Kelly, and Paul N. Edwards. 2007. "Revolutionary Secrets: Technology's Role in the South African Anti-Apartheid Movement." *Social Science Computer Review* 25:13–26.

Garrido, Maria, and Alexander Halavais. 2003. "Mapping Networks of Support for the Zapatista Movement: Applying Social-Networks Analysis to Study Contemporary Social Movements." In *Cyberactivism: Online Activism in Theory and Practice*, eds. Martha McCaughey and Michael D. Ayers, 165–184. New York: Routledge.

Garton, Laura, Caroline Haythornthwaite, and Barry Wellman. 1997. "Studying Online Social Networks." *Journal of Computer-Mediated Communication* 3 (1).

Gaver, William W. 1991. "Technology Affordances." *Conference on Human Factors in Computing Systems: Proceedings of the SIGCHI Conference on Human Factors in Computing Systems: Reaching through Technology*, 79–84.

Gerhards, Jurgen, and Dieter Rucht. 1992. "Mesomobilization: Organizing and Framing in Two Protest Campaigns in West Germany." *American Journal of Sociology* 98:555–595.

Gerlach, Luther P., and Virginia H. Hine. 1970. *People, Power, Change: Movements of Social Transformation.* New York: Bobbs-Merrill Company.

Gibson, James J. 1979. *The Ecological Approach to Visual Perception.* New York: Houghton Mifflin.

Gitlin, Todd. 1980. *The Whole World Is Watching: Mass Media in the Making and Unmaking of the New Left.* Berkeley: University of California Press.

Giugni, Marco G. 1998. "Was It Worth the Effort? The Outcomes and Consequences of Social Movements." *Annual Review of Sociology* 98:371–393.

Goodwin, Jeff, James M. Jasper, and Francesca Polletta. 2004. "Emotional Dimensions of Social Movements." In *The Blackwell Companion to Social Movements,* eds. David A. Snow, Sarah A. Soule, and Hanspeter Kriesi, 413–432. Oxford: Blackwell Publishing.

Graves, Lucas. 2007. "The Affordances of Blogging: A Case Study in Culture and Technological Effects." *Journal of Communication Inquiry* 31:331–346.

Gurak, Laura J. 1997. *Persuasion and Privacy in Cyberspace: The Online Protests over Lotus MarketPlace and the Clipper Chip.* New Haven, CT: Yale University Press.

Gurak, Laura J. 1999. "The Promise and the Peril of Social Action in Cyberspace." In *Communities in Cyberspace,* eds. Mark A. Smith and Peter Kollock, 243–263. London: Routledge.

Gurak, Laura J., and John Logie. 2003. "Internet Protests, from Text to Web." In *Cyberactivism: Online Activism and Theory and Practice,* eds. Martha McCaughey and Michael D. Ayers, 25–46. New York: Routledge.

Hartson, H. Rex. 2003. "Cognitive, Physical, Sensory, and Functional Affordances in Interaction Design." *Behaviour and Information Technology* 22:315–338.

Hasian, Marouf, Jr. 2001. "The Internet and the Human Genome." *Peace Review* 13:375–380.

Herda-Rapp, Ann. 1998. "The Power of Informal Leadership: Women Leaders in the Civil Rights Movement." *Sociological Focus* 31:341–355.

Hindman, Matthew, Kostas Tsioutsiouliklis, and Judy A. Johnson. 2004. "How and Why the Web Matters for Politics: An Empirical Examination of Link Structure within Online Political Communities."

Hirsch, Eric L. 1990. "Sacrifice for the Cause: Group Processes, Recruitment, and Commitment in a Student Social Movement." *American Sociological Review* 55:243–254.

Horton, Dave. 2004. "Local Environmentalism and the Internet." *Environmental Politics* 13:734–753.

Howell, Deborah. 2007. "Dissatisfaction on the Marches." *Washington Post*, B6, February 4.

Hutchby, Ian. 2001. "Technologies, Texts, and Affordances." *Sociology* 35:441–456.

Hutchby, Ian. 2003. "Affordances and the Analysis of Technological Mediated Interaction: A Response to Brian Rappert." *Sociology* 37:581–589.

Jarboe, Greg. 2003. "Can You Name the Top Ten Search Engines." <http://www.isedb.com/news/article/1108> (accessed April 15, 2005).

Jenkins, Henry. 1992. *Textual Poachers: Television Fans and Participatory Culture*. New York: Routledge.

Jenkins, J. Craig. 1983. "Resource Mobilization Theory and the Study of Social Movements." *Annual Review of Sociology* 9:527–553.

Jenkins, J. Craig, and Craig M. Eckhert. 1986. "Channeling Black Insurgency: Elite Patronage and Professional Social Movement Organizations in the Development of the Black Insurgency." *American Sociological Review* 51:812–829.

Jenkins, J. Craig, and Charles Perrow. 1977. "Insurgency of the Powerless: Farm Worker Movements (1946–1972)." *American Sociological Review* 42:249–268.

Jevbratt, Lisa. 2004. "Projects and Documentation." <http://www.jevbratt.com/projects.html> (accessed June 2, 2010).

Johnson, Norris R. 1987. "The Who Concert Stampede: An Empirical Assessment." *Social Problems* 34:362–373.

Johnston, Hank. 2005. "Talking the Walk: Speech Acts and Resistance in Authoritarian Regimes." In *Repression and Mobilization*, eds. Christian Davenport, Hank Johnston, and Carol Mueller, 108–137. Minneapolis: University of Minnesota Press.

Jordan, Tim. 2001. "Measuring the Internet: The Host Counts versus Business Plans." *Information, Communication and Society* 4:34–53.

Jordan, Tim, and Paul Taylor. 2004. *Hacktivism and Cyberwars: Rebels with a Cause*. New York: Routledge.

King Center. 2004. "The King Holiday: A Chronology." <http://www.thekingcenter.org/holiday/chronology.pdf> (accessed March 2007).

Klandermans, Bert. 1989. "Introduction." *International Social Movement Research* 2:215–224.

Klandermans, Bert. 2004. "The Demand and Supply of Participation: Social-Psychological Correlates of Participation in Social Movements." In *The Blackwell Companion to Social Movements*, eds. David A. Snow, Sarah A. Soule, and Hanspeter Kriesi, 360–379. Oxford: Blackwell Publishing.

Klandermans, Bert, and Dirk Oegema. 1987. "Potentials, Networks, Motivations, and Barriers: Steps towards Participation in Social Movements." *American Sociological Review* 52:519–531.

Klandermans, Bert, Jojanneke van der Toorn, and Jacquelien van Stekelenburg. 2008. "Embeddedness and Identity: How Immigrants Turn Grievances into Action." *American Sociological Review* 73:992–1012.

Klein, Hans. 2001. "Online Social Movements and Internet Governance." *Peace Review* 13:403–410.

KnowThyNeighbor.org. 2009. <http://knowthyneighbor.org/national/> (accessed November 3, 2009).

Kornhauser, William. 1959. *The Politics of Mass Society*. New York: Free Press.

Kriesi, Hanspeter. 1988. "Local Mobilization for the People's Petition of the Dutch Peace Movement." *International Social Movement Research* 1:41–82.

Kriesi, Hanspeter. 1989. "New Social Movements and the New Class in the Netherlands." *American Journal of Sociology* 94:1078–1116.

Lebert, Joanne. 2003. "Wiring Human Rights Activism: Amnesty International and the Challenges of Information and Communication Technologies." In *Cyberactivism: Online Activism in Theory and Practice*, eds. Martha McCaughey and Michael D. Ayers, 209–231. New York: Routledge.

Le Bon, Gustave. [1895] 1960. *The Crowd: A Study of the Popular Mind*. New York: Viking Press.

Leizerov, Sagi. 2000. "Privacy Advocacy Group versus Intel." *Social Science Computer Review* 18:461–483.

Liben-Nowell, David, and Jon Kleinberg. 2008. "Tracing Information Flow on a Global Scale Using Internet Chain-Letter Data." *Proceedings of the National Academy of Sciences of the United States of America* 105:4633–4638.

Lober, Douglas J. 1995. "Why Protest? Public Behavioral and Attitudinal Response to Siting a Waste Disposal Facility." *Policy Studies Journal* 23:499–518.

Macy, Michael W., and Andreas Flache. 1995. "Beyond Rationality in Models of Choice." *Annual Review of Sociology* 21:73–91.

Martinez-Torres, Maria Elena. 2001. "Civil Society, the Internet, and the Zapatistas." *Peace Review* 13:347–355.

Marullo, Sam. 1988. "Leadership and Membership in the Nuclear Freeze Movement: A Specification of Resource Mobilization Theory." *Sociological Quarterly* 29: 407–427.

McAdam, Doug. 1982. *Political Process and the Development of Black Insurgency, 1930–1970*. Chicago: University of Chicago Press.

McAdam, Doug. 1986. "Recruitment to High Risk Activism: The Case of Freedom Summer." *American Journal of Sociology* 92:64–90.

McAdam, Doug. 1988. *Freedom Summer*. New York: Oxford University Press.

McCarthy, John D., and Clark McPhail. 1998. "The Institutionalization of Protest in the United States." In *The Social Movement Society: Contentious Politics for the New Century*, eds. David S. Meyer and Sidney Tarrow, 83–110. Lanham, MD: Rowman and Littlefield.

McCarthy, John D., and Mayer N. Zald. 1973. *The Trend of Social Movements in America: Professionalization and Resource Mobilization*. Morristown, NJ: General Learning Press.

McCarthy, John D., and Mayer N. Zald. 1977. "Resource Mobilization and Social Movements: A Partial Theory." *American Journal of Sociology* 82:1212–1241.

McCaughey, Martha, and Michael D. Ayers, eds. 2003. *Cyberactivism: Online Activism in Theory and Practice*. New York: Routledge.

McCullough, Michael F. 1991. "Democratic Questions for the Computer Age." In *Computers for Social Change and Community Organizing*, eds. John Downing, Rob Fasano, Patricia A. Friedland, Michael F. McCullough, Terry Mizrahi, and Jeremy J. Shapiro, 9–18. New York: Haworth Press.

McGrenere, Joanna, and Wayne Ho. 2000. "Affordances: Clarifying and Evolving a Concept." *Proceedings of Graphics Interface*, 1–8.

McNair Barnett, Bernice. 1993. "Invisible Southern Black Women Leaders in the Civil Rights Movement: The Triple Constraints of Gender, Race, and Class. *Gender and Society* 7:162–182.

McPhail, Clark. 1994. "The Dark Side of Purpose: Individual and Collective Violence in Riots." *Sociological Quarterly* 35:1–32.

McPhail, Clark, and David Miller. 1973. "The Assembling Process: A Theoretical and Empirical Examination." *American Sociological Review* 38:721–735.

Melucci, Alberto. 1980. The New Social Movements: A Theoretical Approach. *Social Sciences Information. Information Sur les Sciences Sociales* 19:199–226.

Melucci, Alberto. 1985. The Symbolic Challenge of Contemporary Movements. *Social Research* 52:790–816.

244   References

Melucci, Alberto. 1989. *Nomads of the Present: Social Movements and Individual Needs in Contemporary Society*. London: Hutchinson Radius.

Melucci, Alberto. 1994. "A Strange Kind of Newness: What's 'New' in New Social Movements." In *New Social Movements: From Ideology to Identity*, ed. E. Laraña, H. Johnston, and J. R. Gusfield, 101–130. Philadelphia: Temple University Press.

Meyer, David S., and Sidney Tarrow. 1998a. "A Movement Society: Contentious Politics for the New Century." In *The Social Movement Society: Contentious Politics for the New Century*, eds. David S. Meyer and Sidney Tarrow, 1–28. Lanham, MD: Rowman and Littlefield.

Meyer, David, and Sydney Tarrow, eds. 1998b. *The Social Movement Society: Contentious Politics for a New Century*. Lanham, MD: Rowman and Littlefield.

Miller, James A., Susan D. Pennybacker, and Eve Rosenhaft. 2001. "Mother Ada Wright and the International Campaign to Free the Scottsboro Boys, 1931–1934." *American Historical Review* 106:387–430.

Minkoff, Debra C. 1999. "Bending with the Wind: Strategic Change and Adaptation by Women's and Racial Minority Organizations." *American Journal of Sociology* 104:1666–1703.

Minkoff, Debra C. 2002. "Macro-organizational Analysis." In *Methods of Social Movement Research*, eds. Bert Klandermans and Suzanne Staggenborg, 260–285. Minneapolis: University of Minnesota Press.

Minkoff, Debra C., Silke Aisenbrey, and Jon Agnone. 2008. "Organizational Diversity in the U.S. Advocacy Sector." *Social Problems* 55:525–548.

Morris, Aldon D. 1981. "Black Southern Student Sit-in Movement: An Analysis of Internal Organization." *American Sociological Review* 46:744–767.

Morris, Aldon D. 1984. *The Origins of the Civil Rights Movement: Black Communities Organizing for Change*. New York: Free Press.

Mueller, Carol M. 1994. "Conflict Networks and the Origins of Women's Liberation." In *New Social Movements: From Ideology to Identity*, eds. Enrique Larana, Hank Johnston, and Joseph R. Gusfield, 234–263. Philadelphia: Temple University Press.

Mushaben, Joyce. 1989. "The Struggle Within: Conflict, Consensus, and Decision Making among National Coordinators and Grass-roots Organizers in the West German Peace Movement." *International Social Movement Research* 2:267–298.

Myers, Daniel J. 1994. "Communication Technology and Social Movements: Contributions of Computer Networks to Activism." *Social Science Computer Review* 12:251–260.

Nie, Norman H., and Lutz Erbring. 2000. *Internet and Society: A Preliminary Report*. Stanford, CA: Stanford Institute for the Quantitative Study of Society.

Nip, Joyce Y. M. 2004. "The Queer Sisters and Its Electronic Bulletin Board: A Study of the Internet for Social Movement Mobilization." *Information, Communication and Society* 7:23–49.

Norman, Donald A. 1988. *The Psychology of Everyday Things.* New York: Basic Books.

Norris, Pippa. 2002. *Democratic Phoenix: Reinventing Political Activism.* Cambridge: Cambridge University Press.

Oberschall, Anthony. 1973. *Social Conflict and Social Movements.* Englewood Cliffs, NJ: Prentice-Hall.

Oberschall, Anthony. 1993. *Social Movements: Ideologies, Interests, and Identities.* New Brunswick: Transaction.

Oliver, Pamela E. 1993. "Formal Models of Collective Action." *Annual Review of Sociology* 19:271–300.

Olson, Mancur. [1965] 1998. *The Logic of Collective Action: Public Good and the Theory of Groups.* Cambridge, MA: Harvard University Press.

O'Mahony, Siobhán, and Beth A. Bechky. 2008. "Boundary Organizations: Enabling Collaboration among Unexpected Allies." *Administrative Science Quarterly* 58 (3):422–459.

Opp, Karl-Dieter. 1988. "Grievances and Participation in Social Movements." *American Sociological Review* 53:853–864.

Peckham, Michael H. 1998. New Dimensions of Social Movement/Countermovement Interaction: The Case of Scientology and Its Internet Critics. *Canadian Journal of Sociology* 23:317–347.

Pinch, Trevor J., and Wiebe E. Bijker. 1984. "Opening Black Boxes: Science, Technology, and Society." *Social Studies of Science* 14:339–441.

Pinch, Trevor J., and Wiebe E. Bijker. 1987. "The Social Construction of Facts and Artifacts: Or How the Sociology of Science and the Sociology of Technology Might Benefit Each Other." In *The Social Construction of Technological Systems*, eds. Wiebe E. Bijker, Trevor J. Pinch, and Thomas P. Hughes, 17–50. Cambridge, MA: MIT Press.

Pudrovska, Tetyana, and Myra Marx Ferree. 2004. "Global Activism in 'Virtual Space': The European Women's Lobby in the Network of Transnational Women's NGO's on the Web." *Social Politics: International Studies in Gender, State and Society* 11:117–143.

Quan-Haase, Anabel, Barry Wellman, James C. Witte, and Keith N. Hampton. 2002. "Capitalizing on the Net: Social Contact, Civic Engagement, and Sense of Community." In *The Internet in Everyday Life*, eds. Barry Wellman and Caroline Haythornthwaite, 291–324. Oxford: Blackwell.

Rappert, Brian. 2003. "Technologies, Texts, and Possibilities: A Reply to Hutchby." *Sociology* 37:565–580.

Reger, Jo. 2002. "Organizational Dynamics and Construction of Multiple Feminist Identities in the National Organization for Women." *Gender and Society* 16:710–727.

Rejai, Mostafa, and Kay Phillips. 1988. *Loyalists and Revolutionaries: Political Leaders Compared*. New York: Praeger.

Rheingold, Howard. 1993. *The Virtual Community: Homesteading on the Electronic Frontier*. Reading, MA: Addison-Wesley.

Rice, Ronald E., and James E. Katz. 2004. "The Internet and Political Involvement in 1996 and 2000." In *Society Online: The Internet in Context*, eds. Philip N. Howard and Steve Jones, 103–120. Thousand Oaks, CA: Sage.

Robnett, Belinda. 1997. *How Long? How Long? African-American Women in the Struggle for Civil Rights*. New York: Oxford University Press.

Rohlinger, Deana A., Leslie Bunnage, and Jordan Brown. 2009. "The Role of the Internet in U.S. Progressive Politics." Paper presented at the Annual Meeting of the American Sociological Association, San Francisco.

Rosenkrands, Jacob. 2004. "Politicizing Homo Economicus: Analysis of Anti-Corporate Websites." In *Cyberprotest: New Media, Citizens, and Social Movements*, eds. Wim van de Donk, Brian D. Loader, Paul G. Nixon, and Dieter Rucht, 49–68. New York: Routledge.

Rucht, Dieter. 2004. "Movement Allies, Adversaries, and Third Parties." In *The Blackwell Companion to Social Movements*, eds. David A. Snow, Sarah A. Soule, and Hanspeter Kriesi, 197–216. Oxford: Blackwell Publishing.

Rucht, Dieter, and Friedhelm Neidhardt. 2002. "Towards a 'Movement Society'? On the Possibilities of Institutionalizing Social Movements." *Social Movement Studies* 1:7–30.

Rupp, Leila J., and Verta Taylor. 1987. *Survival in the Doldrums: The American Women's Rights Movement, 1945 to the 1960s*. Columbus: Ohio State University Press.

Salter, Lee. 2003. "Democracy, New Social Movements, and the Internet: A Habermasian Analysis." In *Cyberactivism: Online Activism in Theory and Practice*, eds. Martha McCaughey and Michael D. Ayers, 117–144. New York: Routledge.

Scardaville, Melissa C. 2005. "Accidental Activists: Fan Activism in the Soap Opera Community." *American Behavioral Scientist* 48:881–901.

Schulz, Markus S. 1998. "Collective Action across Borders: Opportunity Structures, Network Capacities, and Communicative Praxis in the Age of Advanced Globalization." *Sociological Perspectives* 41:587–616.

Schussman, Alan, and Jennifer Earl. 2004. "From Barricades to Firewalls? Strategic Voting and Social Movement Leadership in the Internet Age." *Sociological Inquiry* 74:439–463.

Scoble, Harry M., and Laurie S. Wiseberg. 1974. "Human Rights and Amnesty International." *Annals of the American Academy of Political and Social Science* 413:11–26.

Scott, James C. 1990. *Domination and the Arts of Resistance: Hidden Transcripts*. New Haven, CT: Yale University Press.

Shirky, Clay. 2008. *Here Comes Everybody: The Power of Organizing without Organizations*. New York: Penguin Press.

Smelser, Neil. 1963. *Theory of Collective Behavior*. New York: Free Press.

Smith, Aaron, Kay Lehman Scholzman, Sidney Verba, and Henry Brady. 2009. *The Internet and Civic Engagement*. Washington, DC: Pew Internet and American Life Project.

Snow, David A. 2004. "Framing Processes, Ideology, and Discursive Fields." In *The Blackwell Companion to Social Movements*, eds. David A. Snow, Sarah A. Soule, and Hanspeter Kriesi, 380–412. Oxford: Blackwell Publishing.

Snow, David A., Sarah A. Soule, and Hanspeter Kriesi. 2004. "Mapping the Terrain." In *Blackwell Companion on Social Movements*, eds. David A. Snow, Sarah A. Soule, and Hanspeter Kriesi, 3–16. Oxford: Blackwell Publishing.

Soule, Sarah A. 1997. "The Student Divestment Movement in the United States and Tactical Diffusion: The Shantytown Protest." *Social Forces* 75:855–883.

Soule, Sarah A., and Jennifer Earl. 2005. "A Movement Society Evaluated: Collective Protest in the United States, 1960–1986." *Mobilization* 10:345–364.

Staggenborg, Suzanne. 1988. "The Consequences of Professionalization and Formalization in the Pro-Choice Movement." *American Sociological Review* 53:585–606.

Staggenborg, Suzanne. 1991. *The Pro-Choice Movement: Organization and Activism in the Abortion Conflict*. Oxford: Oxford University Press.

Stoecker, Randy. 1990. "Taming the Beast: Maintaining Democracy in Community-Controlled Redevelopment." *Berkeley Journal of Sociology* 35:107–126.

Sullivan, Danny. 2007. "Major Search Engines and Directories." <http://searchenginewatch.com/showPage.html?page=2156221> (accessed July 31, 2008).

Tarrow, Sidney. 1994. *Power in Movement: Social Movements, Collective Action, and Politics*. New York: Cambridge University Press.

Tarrow, Sidney. 1998. "Fishnets, Internets, and Catnets: Globalization and Transnational Collective Action." In *Challenging Authority: The Historical Study of Contentious Politics*, edited by Michael P. Hanaganm, Leslie Page Moch, and Wayne te Brake, 228–244. Minneapolis: University of Minnesota Press.

Taylor, Verta. 1989. "Social Movement Continuity: The Women's Movement in Abeyance." *American Sociological Review* 54:761–775.

Taylor, Verta, and Nella Van Dyke. 2004. "'Get up, Stand Up': Tactical Repertoires of Social Movements." In *The Blackwell Companion to Social Movements*, eds. David A. Snow, Sarah A. Soule, and Hanspeter Kriesi, 262–293. Oxford: Blackwell Publishing.

Taylor, Verta, and Nancy E. Whittier. 1992. "Collective Identity in Social Movement Communities: Lesbian Feminist Mobilization." In *Frontiers of Social Movement Theory*, eds. Aldon D. Morris and Carol McClurg Mueller, 104–129. New Haven, CT: Yale University Press.

Tilly, Charles. 1977. "Getting It Together in Burgandy." *Theory and Society* 4:479–504.

Tilly, Charles. 1978. *From Mobilization to Revolution*. Reading, MA: Addison-Wesley Publishing Company.

Tilly, Charles. 1979. "Repertoires of Contention in America and Britain, 1750–1830." In *The Dynamics of Social Movements: Resource Mobilization, Social Control, and Tactics*, eds. Mayer N. Zald and John D. McCarthy, 126–155. Cambridge, MA: Winthrop Publishers.

Tilly, Charles. 1995. "Contentious Repertoires in Great Britain." In *Repertoires and Cycles of Collective Action*, ed. Mark Traugott, 15–42. Durham, NC: Duke University Press.

Tilly, Charles. 1998. "Social Movements and (All Sorts of) Other Political Interactions—Local, National, and International—Including Identities." *Theory and Society* 27:453–480.

United for Peace and Justice. 2007. "Speakers for Massive Jan. 27 Anti-War Rally Announced." <http://www.unitedforpeace.org/article.php?id=3505> (accessed October 30, 2007).

Urbina, Ian. 2007. "Protest Focuses on Iraq Troop Increase." *New York Times*. <http://www.nytimes.com/2007/01/28/washington/28protest.html> (accessed October 29, 2007).

Van Aelst, Peter, and Stefaan Walgrave. 2002. "New Media, New Movements? The Role of the Internet in Shaping the 'Anti-Globalization' Movement." *Information, Communication and Society* 5:465–493.

Van Aelst, Peter, and Stefaan Walgrave. 2004. "New Media, New Movements? The Role of the Internet in Shaping the 'Anti-Globalization' Movement." In *Cyberprotest: New Media, Citizens, and Social Movements*, eds. Wim van de Donk, Brian D. Loader, Paul G. Nixon, and Dieter Rucht, 87–108. New York: Routledge.

van de Donk, Wim, Brian D. Loader, Paul G. Nixon, and Dieter Rucht, eds. 2004. *Cyberprotest: New Media, Citizens and Social Movements*. New York: Routledge.

Vegh, Sandor. 2003. "Classifying Forms of Online Activism: The Case of Cyber-protests against the World Bank." In *Cyberactivism: Online Activism and Theory and Practice*, eds. Martha McCaughey and Michael D. Ayers, 71–95. New York: Routledge.

Wellman, Barry, and Milena Gulia. 1999. "Net Surfers Don't Ride Alone: Virtual Communities as Communities." In *Networks in the Global Village*, ed. Barry Wellman, 331–361. Boulder, CO: Westview Press.

Wellman, Barry, and Caroline Haythornthwaite, eds. 2002. *The Internet in Everyday Life*. Malden, MA: Blackwell Publishing.

Wellman, Barry, Anabel Quan-Haase, Jeffrey Boase, Wenhong Chen, Keith Hampton, Isabel Isla de Diaz, and Kakuko Miyata. 2003. "The Social Affordances of the Internet for Networked Individualism." *Journal of Computer-Mediated Communication* 8 (3).

Wiltfang, Gregory L., and Doug McAdam. 1991. "The Costs and Risks of Social Activism: A Study of Sanctuary Movement Activism." *Social Forces* 69:987–1010.

Wong, Loong. 2001. "The Internet and Social Change in Asia." *Peace Review* 13:381–387.

Wray, Stefan. 1998. "Electronic Civil Disobedience and the World Wide Web of Hacktivism: A Mapping of Extraparliamentarian Direction Action Net Politics." Paper presented at the World Wide Web and Contemporary Cultural Theory conference, Drake University, Des Moines.

Wray, Stefan. 1999. "On Electronic Civil Disobedience." *Peace Review* 11:107–112.

Yardley, William. 2009. "Privacy Looms over Gay Rights Vote." *New York Times*, November 1. <http://www.nytimes.com/2009/11/01/us/01petition.html> (accessed October 31, 2009).

Yang, Guobin. 2007. "How Do Chinese Civil Associations Respond to the Internet? Findings from a Survey." *China Quarterly* 189:122–143.

Zaeske, Susan. 2003. *Signatures of Citizenship*. Chapel Hill: University of North Carolina Press.

Zald, Mayer N. 1970. *Organizational Change: The Political Economy of the YMCA.* Chicago: University of Chicago Press.

Zald, Mayer N., and Roberta Ash [Garner]. 1966. "Social Movement Organizations: Growth, Decay and Change." *Social Forces* 44:327–341.

Zaret, David. 1996. "Petitions and the 'Invention' of Public Opinion in the English Revolution." *American Journal of Sociology* 101:1497–1555.

Zaret, David. 1999. *Origins of Democratic Culture: Printing, Petitions, and the Public Sphere in Early-Modern England.* Princeton, NJ: Princeton University Press.

Index